by

MARION M. LAMB

Professor of Business Administration,
Sacramento State College,
Sacramento, California

Published by

SOUTH-WESTERN PUBLISHING COMPANY

Cincinnati 27   Chicago 44   Burlingame, Calif.   Dallas 2   New Rochelle, N. Y.

E58

WORD STUDIES

ABCDEFGHIJKLMNOPQRSTUVWXYZ

ABCDEFGHIJKLMNOPQRSTUVWXYZ

FIFTH EDITION

PREFACE

In this book we shall approach the study of words through the improvement of spelling. This will lead us to a consideration of the structure of words, their pronunciation, and spelling rules that are usually helpful. Words deserving special attention—such as "spelling demons" and words frequently misused—are covered in detail; and vocabulary-building exercises conclude the book. Supplementary exercises in the workbook planned for use with this textbook are helpful in developing an understanding of words and how they should be used.

For best results, you should get a pocket-size notebook, divide it into alphabetical sections, and record in the appropriate sections all the words that you misspell. To do this, you should have the book with you daily; it will become your personal speller.

Most important is your realization of the value of language to you. Development of word awareness and word mastery is likely to be a slow growth dependent upon sustained interest. Therefore, do not rush at these lessons in an impatient, do-or-die spirit; instead, be leisurely and observant in your approach, remembering that your usage of words tells a great deal about you, and therefore word study is worth your most careful attention. The study of words is rewarding to those who recognize its importance. Failure to recognize its importance is almost certain to be expensive, since we communicate with others through words and we are consequently judged to some extent by the words we use and the way we use them.

The old saying that "Sticks and stones can break my bones, but little words can't hurt me" probably never was true, and certainly it is far from the truth today. Words long and short can hurt you— or help you, depending upon your regard for them. The writer believes that you will be more interested in words after you have read this book and completed the exercises in it. Words can be interesting, but they are like people—you have to know them to be interested in them.

Webster's Third New International Dictionary, unabridged, and *Webster's New Collegiate Dictionary,* 1961 edition, have been used as the references for spelling, syllabication, pronunciation, and definitions in this book.

Marion M. Lamb
Sacramento, California

CONTENTS

PART 1—INFORMATION ABOUT WORDS

PART 2—WORD STRUCTURE

PART 5—WORDS RELATED TO BUSINESS AND ECONOMICS

PART 6—WORDS RELATED TO OCCUPATIONS
AND HUMAN INTERESTS

why GREEK and LATIN? I like INDIAN SIGN LANGUAGE!

DICTIONARY

Background

The earliest writing was picture-writing. "Writers" scratched pictures of objects, persons, and events on the bark of trees and on papyrus, a writing material made from the pith of a plant and used by the ancient Egyptians, Greeks, and Romans as we use paper today. It is believed that the earliest alphabet in which symbols (letters to us) stood for sounds rather than for objects first appeared near Mount Sinai fifteen hundred years before the birth of Christ. These symbols were adopted by the Greeks and called the *alphabet*, a name coined from the names of the first two letters, *alpha* and *beta*. The Romans adopted and simplified the Greek alphabet.

English is made up of words from many countries and tribes involved in England's history. As you read the following account, consider the influences that will probably be brought to bear upon the language in the next two hundred years.

From 55 B. C., Caesar's troops occupied Britain for 400 years. During these centuries, the language of the Romans made little impression upon the language of the Britons because the soldiers did not intermarry with the Britons. After 400 years of British occupation, Rome recalled her troops from Britain to defend Rome. Britain, long protected from invasion, was exposed to marauders who had not shared the Roman civilization. Savage tribes of Picts and Scots from Ireland and Scotland, of Norsemen and Danes from the land of the Vikings, and of the Germanic Angles, Saxons, and Jutes from across the North Sea crossed into Britain in great numbers. Since there were more German invaders than Britons, Britain became Angle-land, or England. Many of the descendants of the Britons (a Celtic people also) fled to the hills of Scotland and Wales when the Anglo-Saxons took over their country in the fifth and sixth centuries, A. D.

If you remember your history, you will recall that these were tremendously eventful years in the history of Europe. The advent of Christ and the establishment of the Christian Church in Rome against great political pressure, the fall of the great Roman Empire in 476 A. D., and the beginning of the "Dark Ages" of Europe took place during these first 500 years after the birth of Christ. The Dark Ages (or Medieval Period) extended from approximately 500 A. D. to approximately 1400 A. D., enlightened by the efforts of the Christian missionaries and concluded by the Renaissance, or "reawakening" during the 14th-16th centuries.

At the end of the sixth century (597 A. D.), St. Augustine landed in Britain as a Christian missionary from Rome. Christianity brought with it a revival of learning and a flourishing civilization. The Christian missionaries recorded the speech of the natives, and since the speech was that of the Angles, this recorded language was called *English* (Anglish). At this time many Latin words were absorbed into the English language, especially those having to do with the church, and also those dealing with everyday life.

In the eighth and ninth centuries, the Danes invaded England, destroying much of the Christian civilization in the name of their own pagan gods. They settled in England, and the mixed language that resulted was chiefly English, with many Danish words added to the language.

In 1066, the Normans invaded England from France (the French province of Normandy). The Normans were "Northmen" or "Norsemen" who had originally come from Scandinavia, but they had lived for 150 years in France and had absorbed the language and the customs of the French. As conquerors of England, they established French as the language of the courts and of the schools, reducing English to the speech of uneducated peasants. For two centuries the two languages were used in England, with French as the literary language and the official language, but with English popular as the spoken language.

In 1204, the fortunes of war separated the English Normans from the French Normans, with the result that the English language and the English customs became important once more, altered considerably by the years of French influence, however. A great many French words became part of the English language, and some "Anglo-French" words represented a combination of the two languages. In 1362 English became the language of the courts and shortly after, it was introduced into the schools as the official language of the country. This English we call Middle English, as contrasted with the Old English of the Anglo-Saxons and the Modern English of the English-speaking world found during the 17th century to the present time.

During the Renaissance, with its emphasis upon classical learning, English scholars added many Greek words to those that had already been introduced into the language by the Romans.

As you can see, English derives from many sources, and this diversity makes it a wonderful language to know—but difficult to learn. Therefore, you should not become discouraged if the language seems inconsistent at times; it is. Moreover, for the average person, reading and writing are relatively recent accomplishments. For many centuries words were used orally for communication, but only the privileged few could read and write—and of course this is true in many parts of the world today. Historians tell us that in Shakespeare's time, just 350 years ago, only half of the population of England could read, and probably few of those who could read could write with any ease.

2

When the opportunity to learn to read and write was extended to the common people of the English-speaking world during the 16th and 17th centuries, there was confusion in the spelling of many words familiar by sound but unfamiliar in written form. Not until the 18th century was a dictionary of English words available. Samuel Johnson's *Dictionary of the English Language*, issued in 1775 after the author had toiled eight years to compile it, was the first attempt at an English dictionary. It was therefore an important book, even though we consider it inadequate today. In 1828 Noah Webster's *American Dictionary of the English Language* was issued. A later edition, *Webster's New International Dictionary*, is still an outstanding, authoritative reference on the English language.

Standardized though our language may be, thanks to the patient scholars who compiled the dictionaries, there are many inconsistencies in spelling that are difficult to accept. *Night, thought, height*— to mention just three—are words that are certainly not spelled according to our pronunciation of them. However, at the time the spelling of these words was established, the *gh* sounds were pronounced. In short, we have altered the pronunciation of many words without changing the spelling. Sometimes sounds are eliminated; sometimes they are changed, as in the words *either* and *neither*; these words were pronounced "ayther" and "nayther" at the time their spelling was determined.

Despite the fact that the pronunciation of words is often at variance with the spelling, it is nevertheless true that students of words look for possible relationship between spelling and pronunciation, as we shall see later. Similarly, they look at word structure in an effort to determine meaning; and when faced with a spelling problem, they consider spelling rules as well as word structure and pronunciation.

...why not SMOKE SIGNALS?

Do you use the dictionary? Do you own a dictionary? If you do not, buy an inexpensive pocket dictionary for daily use. A larger dictionary for home use is a good investment.

What information do you find in the dictionary?

1. The spelling of words
2. The syllabication of words
3. The accenting of words
4. Pronunciation
5. Parts of speech (or function)
6. Derivation of words
7. Meanings
8. The principal parts of verbs
9. The capitalization of proper nouns
10. The use of hyphens in compound words
11. Examples of uses of words (not in all dictionaries)

Some dictionaries have special sections giving the following information:

1. A history of the English language
2. A guide to pronunciation
3. A dictionary of geographical names
4. A dictionary of biographical names
5. A list of signs used in writing and printing
6. A list of abbreviations used in writing and printing
7. A list of the principal rules of spelling
8. A list of the principal rules of punctuation and capitalization
9. A list of commonly used foreign words and phrases
10. Miscellaneous information, such as historical facts, names of the Presidents of the United States of America, names from the Scriptures, names of accredited colleges and universities, etc.

You can see that much of the material that should be mastered by a person who desires to improve his use of language is to be found in the dictionary. In addition, the dictionary is an excellent reference book, containing information pertaining to history, geography, and biography.

How to find a word in the dictionary. All words are arranged alphabetically; therefore, the first step in finding a word is to turn to the section of the dictionary devoted to words beginning with the same letter as the word you desire to find. At the top of each page of the dictionary will be found two guide words; these are the first and last words on the page. The quickest way to find a word is to watch the guide words at the top of the pages.

Spelling of words. In the dictionary a word is printed first in heavy type. This heavy type shows the correct spelling of the word. Occasionally, a word may be spelled in two ways. When this is the case, both spellings are given in the dictionary in heavy type, but the first spelling is the preferred spelling.

Syllabication. The dictionary gives two important facts regarding the syllabication of words. First, it shows into what syllables words are divided; and second, it indicates which syllable or syllables are accented. The first of these facts is important when you write words, as you will learn later; the second is important when you pronounce them.

A syllable is accented when it is stressed or pronounced a little more loudly than the other syllables in the word. Most words have one syllable accented, as the syllable "tend" in "in-tend′." Some words have two syllables accented, as in "su′-per-in-tend′." In this word the greater stress on "tend" is indicated by a heavy accent mark. This syllable is said to have the primary accent. But you will notice that the first syllable is also accented slightly and therefore has a light accent mark. This syllable is said to have the secondary accent.

Dictionary Practice

A. The following words may be spelled in the ways indicated. Copy these words and underscore the preferred spelling.

colour, color	distill, distil
peddler, pedlar, pedler	gypsy, gipsy
good-bye, good-by	practice, practise
advertise, advertize	mediaeval, medieval
grey, gray	esthetic, aesthetic

B. Look up the following words in your dictionary to determine syllabication. Leave a space between syllables, inserting accent marks indicated.

Examples: sep′ a rate
lab′ o ra to′ry

abate	gigantic
accommodate	guessed
calculate	harmonious
eccentric	idol
facilitate	invalidate

C. Write a definition of the word "syllable" that seems to you to express the meaning of the word as we use it in this book.

5

Indication of pronunciation. Immediately following the printing of the word in heavy type in the dictionary will be found the correct pronunciation, which is frequently shown in the respelling of the word. However, it is often possible to show the correct pronunciation without changing the spelling of the word. This is done through the use of diacritical marks.

By using diacritical marks, it is possible to give each of the vowels a number of different sounds. Thus, the vowel "a" can, with the use of diacritical marks, be made to indicate nine different sounds, as follows:

ā as in āte	ă as in căt	a̧ as in wa̧s
á as in cháotic	ä as in ärm	a̱ as in wa̱lnut
â as in câre	ȧ as in ȧsk	ã as in cedãr

The vowel markings are sometimes listed at the top or the bottom of the page in dictionaries, and you can see at a glance the exact sound of any vowel contained in a word on a particular page. Nevertheless, it is well to memorize the common long and short sounds of the vowels in accordance with the following list:

ā as in ate	ī as in ice	o͞o as in food
ă as in cat	ĭ as in sin	o͝o as in foot
ē as in eve	ō as in old	ū as in use
ĕ as in end	ŏ as in not	ŭ as in tub

Just as each vowel has more than one sound, so do several of the consonants have more than one pronunciation. Here are the main examples:

When "s" is pronounced like "z," it may be marked "s̩" as in "wis̩dom."

"C" ordinarily has the sound of "k." Sometimes it has the sound of "s," in which case it may be marked thus: "ç" as in "niçe."

"G" has two sounds: a hard sound heard in "game" and a soft sound heard in "rage." When "g" has a soft sound, it may be marked thus: "ġ" as in "enġine."

"Th" also has two sounds: a soft sound heard in "health" and a heavier sound heard in "smooth." When "th" has a heavy sound, it may be marked thus: t̶h̶ ("th" with a line through it).

The above-mentioned ways of marking the "z" sound of "s," the soft "c," the soft "g," and the heavy "th" are used throughout this book.

Many letters are silent; that is, they are not pronounced. In this book silent consonants are indicated by being printed in italics, as in "right." When two vowels come together with only one sounded,

6

the vowel that is sounded is marked, and the silent vowel is not italicized, as in "brea̅k" and "yie̅ld." Silent "e" at the end of a word is not italicized.

Dictionary Exercise

Give the derivation and the correct pronunciation of the following words:

athletics	diphtheria	Niagara
barbecue	economics	often
bronchial	err	photogenic
carburetor	February	refrigerator
chauffeur	fond	roof
comparable	harass	subsidiary
congratulate	idea	tomato
corps	liaison	toward

 Dictionary practice (Concluded)

Indication of the parts of speech. All words are classified according to their use in the construction of sentences. There are eight classes of words, known as parts of speech. Three of these classes, namely pronouns, conjunctions, and interjections, include words that are so well known that they do not appear in this book—words such as *he, she, it, and, but, oh,* and *ah.*

The part of speech under which a word is classified is indicated in the dictionary by an abbreviation immediately following the pronunciation of the word. The following abbreviations of the parts of speech are used by most dictionaries, and will be used in this textbook:

adjective	*adj.*
adverb	*adv.*
conjunction	*conj.*
noun	*n.*
pronoun	*pron.*
preposition	*prep.*
verb	*v.*

In some cases, the same word may be used as two or even three parts of speech. For example, the word "care" may be used as a verb or a noun, and the word "that" may be used as a pronoun, an adjective, or a conjunction.

In most dictionaries the principal parts of verbs are given, especially if the verbs are irregular in form. These parts are printed immediately after the abbreviation indicating that the word is a verb.

Dictionary Exercise

A. Place an *N.* after each noun, the abbreviation *Adj.* after each adjective, and a *V.* after each verb in the list of compound and hyphenated words at the top of page 8. (The dictionary will help you when you are in doubt.)

bookcase	mother-in-law	understanding
bookkeeping	music-loving	undertake
bridegroom	never-ending	undertone
chalkboard	outlet	outlaw
good-looking	overcoat	uproar
heartbroken	overlook	upstart
homesick	safeguard	waylay
lifelong	typewriter	whitewash
		world-wide

B. Place a *V.* after each verb, the abbreviation *Adv.* after each adverb, and the abbreviation *Conj.* after each conjunction.

accumulate	incidentally	since
affect	really	though
already	referred	transferred
before	rescind	undoubtedly
however	separate	whereas

C. Place the abbreviation *Pron.* after each pronoun, *Prep.* after each preposition, and *Adj.* after each adjective.

all right	hers	theirs
before	immediate	these
berserk	indelible	this
concerning	ours	to
conscientious	probable	until
forcible	rhythmic	which

D. Write the principal parts of each of the following verbs, consulting the dictionary when necessary—**be, have, swim, throw, write.**

E. Write a sentence for each of the verbs in D, using the past tense.

Phonetics is the science of speech sounds considered as elements of language. Knowledge of phonetics makes spelling easier, since the spelling of a word is related to its pronunciation, although the relationship sometimes seems remote.

Of the forty-five sounds in the English language, twenty-six are consonants, with twenty of them in pairs, similar in sound but different in "weight":

> b and p
>> as in *bad* and *pad*
>
> d and t
>> as in *dot* and *tot*
>
> g and k
>> as in *gate* and *Kate*
>
> j and ch
>> an in *Jane* and *chain*
>
> nk and ng
>> as in *rink* and *ring*
>
> th (hard) and th (soft)
>> as in *breathe* and *breath*
>
> v and f
>> as in *vat* and *fat*
>
> w and wh
>> as in *wear* and *where*
>
> z and s
>> as in *zoo* and *Sue*
>
> zh and sh
>> as in *leisure* and *leash*

The other six consonant sounds are expressed by *h*, *l*, *m*, *n*, *r*, and *y*.

Difficulties in reading and writing English words are not caused by consonants. The trouble lies with the five vowels, used to indicate nineteen separate vowel sounds.

The nineteen vowel sounds include the five short vowels, as in *mat*, *met*, *bit*, *not*, *nut*, and the five long vowels, as in *mate*, *mete*, *bite*, *note*, and *mute*. Note that the silent *e* after the consonant following the vowel transforms the short vowel to a long vowel. In some words the long sound of the vowel is expressed by *digraphs* (vowel or consonant combinations); *ai* and *ay*

I'M A MAN OF FEW WORDS, BABE ... FEWER EVERY DAY!

for the long *a*; *ei* and *ea* for the long *e*; *ie*, *y*, and *ye* for the long *i*; *oo*, *oe*, and *ow* for the long *o*; and *ue* and *ew* for the long *u*.

Thus far we have covered only ten of the nineteen vowel sounds: the short sound of each of the vowels and the long sound of these vowels. What about the other nine vowel sounds?

There are three *diphthongs* (combinations of two vowel sounds), each with two different spellings: *au* as in *Paul* and *shawl*; *ou* as in *out* and *now*; and *oi* as in *noise* and *boy*.

Two more vowel sounds are found in the long and the short *oo*, as in *look* and *food*.

The sound of *ah*, as in *Mama*, the two vowel sounds with *r*— *ar*, as in *fair*, and *er*, as in *girl*—and the slurred vowel sound we have in unaccented syllables (as in item, button) complete the vowel sounds stemming from those five overworked letters: *a, e, i, o, u*.

Rudolf Flesch summarizes the importance of phonetics in relation to spelling for the readers of the *Saturday Review* as follows: [1]

> . . . To be a good speller, remember the basic rules of English phonetic spelling—or if you've never learned them, learn them now.
>
> First, consonants: There's only one spelling for almost all consonant sounds—or rather, written consonants are usually sounded in just one regular way. The great exceptions are *c* and *g*, which are sounded hard (as in *call* and *gall*) except before *i* and *e*, when they are sounded soft (as in *cent* and *gent*).
>
> This rule will take care of such spelling demons as *courageous, serviceable*, and *manageable*.
>
> Also, note that the *zh* consonant sound (as in *Zsa Zsa Gabor*) is usually spelled as a single *s*, as in *vision, leisure, enclosure, pleasure, treasure*. Remember that when doubts assail you about words such as *occasion* and *incision*.
>
> Next, vowels: The vowels *a, e, i, o*, and *u* are sounded as short vowels when followed by just one consonant (as in *mat, pet, kit, not, cut*) but sound "like their names" when followed by one consonant plus a vowel (as in *mate, Pete, kite, note, cute*).
>
> This means that if you want to preserve a short vowel sound in a verb form, adjective, etc., you have to double the consonant—as in *gabby, Peggy, filling, topper, nutty*.
>
> The other way around, you can drop the silent *e* that marks the long vowel sound when the word is changed so that you get another vowel after the consonant instead—as in *likable, salable, usable, competing, rosy, unruly.* . . . [2]

---

[1] Material in this lesson adapted from Rudolf Flesch's *Why Johnny Can't Read* (New York: Harper & Brothers, 1955), pp. 24-32.

[2] Rudolf Flesch, "How to be a Perfect Speller," *Saturday Review* (January 14, 1961), pp. 41, 42.

A. What are the short sounds of each of the vowels? Write five one-syllable words illustrating each sound.

B. What are the long sounds of each of the vowels? Write five one-syllable words illustrating each sound.

C. The sound of *f* is expressed by *gh* in some word endings and by *ph* in some word beginnings. Give two examples of each.

D. What is a digraph? Give five one-syllable words containing digraphs.

E. What is a diphthong? List five words containing diphthongs.

F. Explain the spelling of the following words:

tap—tape	grant—giant
bet—beat	center—crater
fed—feed	coat—cent
hug—huge	wrangling—ranging
gate—gist	egg—edge

5   Steps in studying words

Your competence in spelling depends upon several abilities. First of all you must know the exact pronunciation of the word you desire to spell. If you mispronounce a word, you will probably misspell it.

Then, too, your ability to spell a word correctly will depend upon your having a clear mental picture of the word as it looks when spelled correctly. If you should see a word with which you are thoroughly familiar, such as "first" written "frist," you would not need to spell out the individual letters of the word in order to know that it is misspelled. The word would *look* wrong. That is because you have a mental picture of the word as it appears when spelled correctly. (In order to help you to obtain correct mental pictures, most of the words that you are expected to study in this book are printed first in heavy type, without being divided into syllables, and without diacritical marks.)

Finally, your ability to spell some words will depend upon your knowing and using the few spelling rules that are presented in the following pages, and upon your knowledge of the common prefixes and suffixes.

Steps in Spelling Improvement

How should you study words? Suppose you try the following plan which many students have found very helpful:

1. Look carefully at the word so that you will have a mental picture of it.
2. Pronounce the word aloud. Then think what it means. Do this several times.
3. Next spell the word orally, syllable by syllable, several times.

11

4. Give special attention to the vowels. If, for example, you have the word "specimen," notice that it is spelled with "e" (men) not "a"; or, if you have the word "separate," notice that the second vowel is "a" not "e." Also notice any silent letters in the word.

5. Now with eyes closed, pronounce the word. Try to recall how it looks. Spell it slowly.

6. Finally, write the word from memory. Decide whether it "looks right," and then refer to the textbook to see whether you have written it correctly. If you made an error, restudy the word.

Steps in Language Improvement

1. Develop word awareness. Listen critically to the words you hear each day. Listen to your own words. What about your word selection? Pronunciation?

2. Have at hand a good dictionary, easy to handle.

3. Keep at hand a pocket-sized notebook, separated into alphabetic divisions, for recording new or troublesome words.

4. Set aside a period each day for reading good current books or magazines. An hour at the end of the day is excellent. (This daily reading will not only increase your vocabulary and improve your language skills, but it will also make you a more interesting person.)

5. Underscore troublesome words in books, magazines, and papers as you read. Before you discard or lay aside this reading matter, copy the underscored words into your indexed notebook.

6. Look up these words in the dictionary, recording the meaning of each word. Pronounce each word aloud; spell it syllable by syllable.

7. Record words you misspell, recording each one syllable by syllable. Underscore the syllables that have been mispelled.

8. If a word is not spelled as it is pronounced, pronounce the word aloud to yourself as it is spelled; this "wrong pronunciation" will help you to remember the right spelling.

9. Collect spelling tests based on (1) the most frequently used words in the language, and (2) the most frequently misspelled words in the language. Record in your notebook all words that you misspell on such tests.

10. Frequently review the words in your notebook. Write at least one sentence for each word.

11. See if you can trace a pattern in the errors that you make, and then diagnose the reason for the errors. Do you skip syllables? Do you transpose letters? Do you omit silent letters? Do you miss easy words or difficult words? Are most of your errors at the beginning of words, in the middle of words, or in word endings?

In short, be intelligent about your errors!

Dictionary Practice

Indication of the meaning of words. Probably the most important information given in the dictionary regarding a word is its meaning. The meaning is most important because a person seldom has occasion to spell a word or to pronounce it unless he knows its meaning and can use it. In every dictionary, more space is devoted to the meaning of words than to any other type of information.

Dictionary Exercise

A. Give the first meaning for each of the following words:

> adhere
> admonish
> charitable
> compensate
> consensus
> reconcile
> revoke
> solitary
> superficial
> unanimous

B. Use each of the words in A in a sentence.

C. Differentiate the meanings of the following words:

> deny—contradict
> derelict—delinquent
> fluctuate—waver
> income—salary
> infer—imply
> manufacture—construct
> perforate—puncture
> products—merchandise
> salary—wages
> value—price

D. Use each of the words in C in a sentence.

E. List all the information given in your dictionary for the following words:

> bread
> gorilla
> philanthropy

THEY'RE ALL GREEK TO ME!

ANGLO-SAXON
FRENCH GREEK LATIN

Part 2 ◢ WORD STRUCTURE

The purpose of this part is to lead you to an awareness of the structure of words—the way they are built. The thought that there are word families may be new to you, and the idea that we modify word meanings by inflections may also be new to you.

In a more detailed study of words, we would learn the common root words from which derivatives stem so that we would be able to perceive the literal meaning of unfamiliar words. In this book, however, we shall limit our attention to prefixes and suffixes and their meanings. To stress these word beginnings and endings, we have grouped words according to prefixes and suffixes.

A Word about Word Families

Just as human families branch from common ancestors, so do word families branch from common ancestral stems. These stems are parts of words found in other languages, as in Latin, Greek, and French. Combined with the prefixes and suffixes of our language, they give us a great number of our words and they are therefore of importance in studying the history of the English language. However, since we are interested in becoming familiar with words rather than in tracing their development, we shall limit our consideration of word stems and word families to a few words and one or two examples considered in detail.

Consider the stem *vert* (sometimes *vers*), meaning *to turn*. We have derivatives such as *divert, revert, convert, introvert, extrovert, adversary,* and *controversy,* all having the core meaning *to turn*. With a little knowledge of the meaning of prefixes and suffixes, a person could define all these words literally. For example, the verb *convert* means literally *to turn with*; the noun *convert* means *one who has turned with*. Do you see the relationship of these literal meanings to the dictionary meanings?

You will note that a prefix usually determines the meaning of a word, whereas a suffix usually only modifies meaning and indicates the function of the word—that is, its place in the sentence as noun, adjective, verb, adverb, or other part of speech. For example, let us take several words branching from *equ*: *equal* (noun and adjective); *equate* (verb); *equally* (adverb). Notice that the suffixes change the words according to function, but they do not change the basic meaning. However, if we place the prefix *un* before *equal* or *equally*, we change the meaning of these words.

Before we further discuss prefixes and suffixes, however, we shall look again at letter combinations and syllables.

As you know, words are comprised of letters of the alphabet, and these letters are of two kinds: vowels and consonants. The vowels are *a, e, i, o,* and *u,* and sometimes *y.* You will notice that words have at least one vowel, with the letter *y* sometimes used as a vowel with one of the sounds of *i,* as in *my, by, fly, cyst, cypress, crystal,* and *cynical.*

All the vowels and a few of the consonants have more than one pronunciation, usually depending upon spelling—that is, the relative position of letters within the word. For example, with few exceptions, *y, i,* or *e* after *g* or *c* will give these two consonants the soft sound of *j* or *s* (*range, recite, cymbal*), whereas *a, u,* or *o* and all consonants except *h,* placed after *g* or *c,* will give these consonants the hard sound of *gay* or *k* (*goat, gate, case, cut*). Similarly, the letter *d* inserted before *g* softens the *g* to the *j* sound, a rule that explains why an *e* is unnecessary after the *g* in *acknowledgment* and *judgment.* Here we find one of the purposes of spelling—to indicate the correct pronunciation of the word. Conversely, if you know the correct pronunciation of a word, you have a clue to its spelling.

A *diphthong* is a vowel combination blended into a distinctive sound different from the individual vowels in the blend—*oi,* as in *oil;* and *ou,* as in *out.*

A *digraph* is a combination of two letters to produce a single sound; these letters may be consonants or vowels. In consonants, we have digraphs such as *ch, th,* and *ph;* sometimes these are called "consonantal diphthongs." In some words a vowel is given the long sound by the insertion of a second vowel after the chief vowel, as in *fail, boat, lean.*

A. In the following words, underscore the digraphs with one line and mark the diphthongs with a double underscore.

believe	deceive	main
boys	diphthong	south
chain	eight	this
chair	fail	mouth
contain	load	pamphlet

B. Explain the relationship of spelling to the pronunciation of the following words:

bicarbonate	decay	ice
bicycle	decide	race
can't	decoy	rack
cent	gallant	rage
coat	gem	recall
coin	gentleman	recite
cyst	golden	record

C. Write three words representing each of the following vowel combinations: **eu (ū), oi, ou, yä** (as in *yacht*).

7 Syllables

Letters are grouped into *syllables* (or sounds), accented or un-accented according to the pronunciation of the word. What, precisely, is a syllable? The dictionary tells us that a syllable is "an elementary sound, or a combination of such sounds, uttered with a single effort or impulse of the voice, and constituting a word or a part of a word."

Following this definition, we find that the word *raised* has only one syllable because it is uttered with a single impulse of the voice, whereas *acted* has two syllables because two impulses of the voice are required to pronounce the word. In *acted* the first syllable is accented. When there is a question as to which syllable in a word is accented, the dictionary must be the final authority.

Dictionary Exercise

Look up the following words in your dictionary and copy them with the syllables clearly indicated and accented.

Examples: occurred   oc-curred′
           occurring   oc-cur′ ring

necessary
nevertheless
noticeable
occasionally
occurred
occurrence
omission
optimistic
opportunity
outrageous
parallel
parliament
particularly
permissible
perseverance
persistent
practically
preference
preferred
principal
privilege
procedure
professional
prominent
psychology
reprehensible
superintendent

A *prefix* is a combination of letters placed *before* a word or word root to modify the meaning of the original word. Some of the common prefixes are *a, ac, ad, ant, bene, bi, col, con, de, di, dis, ex, for, fore, inter, in, im, mis, ob, over, per, pro, pur, re, sub, sup, super, trans, un, under*—each of which has its own meaning.

A *suffix* is a combination of letters placed *after* a word or word root to clarify the meaning of the word or to indicate person, number, tense, mood, etc. These word endings that clarify meaning are called *inflections*. Some of the common suffixes are *able* or *ible, age, al, ant* or *ent, ar, ance* or *ence, ary, el, en, er, ery, ful, ral, in, rous, ise, ity, ize, le, ness, om, on, or, ory, ous, sion, tion, ual.*

Endings of verbs and nouns. In verbs, the endings usually indicate the time of action and the number of persons or things taking action: John *acts* quickly, but his parents *act* slowly—He *acted* on our suggestion at once, but they *will act* slowly.

Endings of nouns. In nouns, the endings indicate the singular or plural form of the noun (that is, one thing or person, or more than one). Noun endings may also indicate possession.

Examples: The boy*s* in that class are well behaved. (Plural)
We had the boy*'s* books. (One boy)
We had the boys*'* books. (More than one boy)

Notice the placement of the apostrophe in these possessives.

Because of the meanings expressed by these various word endings called *inflections*, we should observe words most carefully to be sure that we understand the form and the exact meaning intended.

A. After reading the following word groups, define each of the five prefixes:

1. disability, disadvantage, disappear, disappoint, disapprove.
2. misbehave, misconduct, misdemeanor, misfire, mishap.
3. subcontract, sublet, submarine, subordinate, subsoil.
4. supercharge, superficial, superfluous, superintend, superior.
5. transact, transcend, transcribe, transfer, transform.

B. Write five words for each of the following prefixes, explaining the meaning of the prefix: **bi, inter, over, pro,** and **un.**

C. After reading the following word groups, define each of the five suffixes:

1. bountiful, helpful, plentiful, restful, useful.
2. conformity, deformity, peculiarity, popularity, prosperity.
3. blessedness, fairness, gentleness, helpfulness, kindness.
4. actor, doctor, factor, motor, sponsor.
5. gradual, ritual, sensual, usual, visual.

D. Write five words for each of the following suffixes, explaining the meaning of the suffix: **able** or **ible, age, er, ise,** and **tion.**

Sometimes it seems that words are as complex as the individuals who use them. As indicated in Lesson 8, prefixes and suffixes are added to "root words" to indicate meaning. The prefixes, placed before the basic words, change meaning or modify meaning; suffixes, placed after the basic words, clarify meaning by showing relationship of words within the sentence—*act* (noun or verb); *active* (adjective); *action* (noun); *activate* (verb—to make active); etc.

Consider, for illustration, just a few of the many English words that stem from the French word *porter*, which in turn is derived from the Latin *portare*, meaning *to carry*.

Porter (one who carries); port*able* (something that can be carried); port*age* (act of carrying); port*al* (place into which something is carried); port*folio* (device for carrying); *re*port (carry back); *re*port*er* (one who carries back); *de*port (carry from); *de*port*ation* (act of carrying away from); *im*port (carry in); *sup*port (under-carry, or uphold).

You need not study foreign languages to become aware of the significance of prefixes and suffixes; close observation of words plus some knowledge of prefixes and suffixes will help in analyzing words.

Dictionary Exercise

A. Copy the following words, underlining the prefixes and explaining the meaning of each prefix in relation to the rest of the word:

adventure	diagram	imperil
automobile	disease	introduce
bicycle	dislike	misspell
circumference	endanger	proceed
comparison	exhibit	return
contradict	extraordinary	superintendent
descend	hemisphere	transpose

B. Copy the following words, underlining the suffixes and explaining the significance of each suffix:

action	congratulatory	postage
adviser	gracious	primary
actor	hearten	selective
amusement	leatherette	servant
appearance	lovable	sickness
cheerful	outrageous	signal
collectible	particular	slavery

C. List as many prefixes as you can, together with their meanings.

D. List as many suffixes as you can, together with their meanings.

E. What do the words *prefix* and *suffix* mean?

A *simple* word is a single word that may or may not have a prefix and/or a suffix. *Note* is a simple word, for example; *connote* is a simple word also, even though it has a prefix; and *connotation* is a simple word even though it has both a prefix and a suffix.

Noteworthy is a compound word, however, for it is made up of two single words combined into a new meaning. A *compound* word is a word coined from two or more other words. A compound word may be written as one word, as two words, or as a hyphenated word: *bookkeeping, businessman, setup, attorney general, judge advocate, court-martial, by-product,* etc.

A hyphenated word that comes into everyday usage is likely to become a compound word if it can be conveniently written as a compound word. However, a hyphen is always used:

1. When compound numbers below one hundred are written as words, as in "thirty-one."
2. When, used as an adjective, a word expressing number precedes "class" or "rate," as in "first-class" and "third-rate."
3. When "ex" precedes titles, as in "ex-president."
4. When two or more words are used together as a single word, especially as an adjective, as in "ten-gallon hats."

able-bodied	*adj.* Having a strong body.
bad-tempered	*adj.* Having a bad temper.
brother-in-law	*n.* The brother of one's husband or wife.
ex-president	*n.* A former president.
far-reaching	*adj.* Having a wide influence.
first-rate	*adj.* Very good.
good-natured	*adj.* Possessing a desire to please.
ill-mannered	*adj.* Rude.
long-lived	*adj.* Having a long life.
made-to-order	*adj.* Specially made.
old-fashioned	*adj.* Adhering to old ideas.
second-class	*adj.* Inferior; second-rate.
self-possessed	*adj.* Composed in manner; calm.
sight-seeing	*adj.* Engaged in seeing sights.
so-called	*adj.* Commonly named but doubtful.
thirty-five	*adj.* A cardinal numeral.
up-to-date	*adj.* New; modern; extending to the present time.
well-bred	*adj.* Refined in manners.
write-up	*n.* A written description.

A. Write a sentence for each of the following compound words:
breakdown   namesake   textbook   classroom   blackout

B. Would you say that **aerospace, telecast,** and **jetliner** are compound words? Defend your answers.

C. Consult your dictionary for the pronunciation and meaning of the following words:

profit-sharing (*adj.*) **secretary-elect** **self-confidence** **trade-union** (*adj.*)

As stated on page 17, a prefix is a syllable or a combination of syllables placed at the beginning of a word to change its meaning. Consider the change in meaning in the following words achieved by using the appropriate negative prefix:

> polite—impolite; necessary—unnecessary; regard—disregard; responsible—irresponsible; effective—ineffective

Similarly, a suffix is a syllable or a combination of syllables added to a word to modify its meaning. Consider the changes made by suffixes in the following words:

> change—changeable; changing—changeless; help—helpless; helpful—helpfulness; friend—friendship; friendly—friendless

Most words in the English language are derivatives; that is, they are derived from other words. A derivative always consists of a stem, or main syllable, and one or more prefixes and/or suffixes. Thus, the word "container" is a derivative in which "tain" is the stem, "con" is a prefix, and "er" is a suffix. Sometimes a word will have more than one prefix and/or more than one suffix. Thus, the word "receivership" is made up of the stem "ceiv," with the prefix "re" preceding it, and the two suffixes "er" and "ship" following it. "Reconstruction" is made up of the stem "struc," with the two prefixes "re" and "con" preceding it, and one suffix "tion" following it.

It is easier to spell a derivative if you perceive the stem in the derivative and then attach the prefixes and/or suffixes. The adverb "really," for example, which is often misspelled, would cause little trouble if it were remembered that it is the word "real" plus the suffix "ly." Similarly, there would be no question about the number of *s's* in words such as "disappoint" and "misspell" if the writer would look first for the basic word, for he would then recognize the prefix and determine the spelling accordingly.

A. Define each of the following prefixes, following the definition with three well-known words illustrating the prefix:

circum	mis	peri	in	super
pre	extra	auto	inter	ultra
tri	mono	con	counter	anti
bi	pro	ante	de	dis

B. Define each of the following suffixes, following the definition with three well-known words illustrating the suffix:

ee	like	er	ary (*adj.*)	ant
ful	hood	ic	ary, arium (*n.*)	wise
ous, ious	ment	ist	cle	al
less	tion, sion	age	let	ence

C. Give the literal meaning of the names of the days of the week: **Monday, Tuesday, Wednesday, Thursday, Friday, Saturday,** and **Sunday.**

The prefixes "com," "con," and "co" signify "with" or "together."
In what way does this meaning apply to the following words?

combine	(cŏm bīne')	v.	To unite; to join.
committee	(cŏm mĭt' tĕe)	n.	An appointed group.
communicate	(cŏm mū' nĭ cāte)	v.	To make known.
companion	(cŏm păn' ion)	n.	An associate.
comparison	(cŏm păr' ĭ sòn)	n.	Act of comparing.
compile	(cŏm pīle')	v.	To collect.
complicate	(cŏm' plĭ cāte)	v.	To make difficult.
compose	(cŏm pōşe')	v.	To put together.
comprehensive	(cŏm'prḗ hĕn' sĭve)	adj.	Inclusive.
comrade	(cŏm' răde)	n.	A companion.
conciliate	(cŏn çĭl' ĭ āte)	v.	To reconcile.
condense	(cŏn dĕnse')	v.	To make more compact.
condolence	(cŏn dō' lĕnçe)	n.	An expression of sympathy.
confer	(cŏn fēr')	v.	To hold conversation.
conform	(cŏn fôrm')	v.	To adapt to.
congratulate	(cŏn grăt' ủ lāte)	v.	To wish joy to.
connect	(cŏn nĕct')	v.	To join.
consensus	(cŏn sĕn' sŭs)	n.	Agreement.
consign	(cŏn sī gn')	v.	To entrust with.
consolidate	(cŏn sŏl' ĭ dāte)	v.	To unite; to combine.
construction	(cŏn strŭc' tion)	n.	A putting together.
coherent	(cō hēr' ĕnt)	adj.	"Sticking" together.
coincidence	(cō ĭn' cĭ dĕnçe)	n.	Unplanned concurrence of events.
cooperate	(cō ŏp' ēr āte)	v.	To act with others.
coordinate	(cō ôr' dĭ nắte)	adj.	Of the same rank.
co-workers	(cō-wŏr' kērs)	n.	Those working together.

A. Write a sentence for each of the following words:

compile   comprehensive   conciliate   conform   consign

B. Form a noun from each of the following words:

combine   compose   confer   connect   consign

C. For each of the following expressions there is a word beginning with the prefix *com* or *con*. Copy the expression, then write the word; use the dictionary if necessary.

com	con
1. To direct authoritatively	1. To close
2. To start	2. Agreement
3. A promise to do something	3. To admit
4. Agitation	4. To seize
5. Merciful	5. A battle

The prefix "de" signifies "down" or "away." What is the meaning of "de" in each of the following words?

decrepit	(dĕ crĕp′ ĭt)	*adj.* Broken down with age.
deduction	(dĕ dŭc′ tion)	*n.* That which is taken away.
degrade	(dĕ grāde′)	*v.* To reduce in rank.
departure	(dĕ pär′ tŭre)	*n.* A going away.
depreciation	(dĕ prē′ ci ā′ tion)	*n.* A lessening in value.
	shĭ	
descend	(dĕ scĕnd′)	*v.* To go down.
despise	(dĕ spīṣe′)	*v.* To look down upon.
detach	(dĕ tăch′)	*v.* To part; to separate.
deteriorate	(dĕ tēr′ ĭ ŏ rāte′)	*v.* To grow worse.
deviate	(dē′ vĭ āte)	*v.* To turn aside from.

The prefix "ex" signifies "out of," "away from," or "beyond." What is the meaning of "ex" in the following words?

exaggeration	(ex ag′ gēr ā ′ tion)	*n.* An overstatement.
	ĕg zăj′	
excel	(ĕx çĕl′)	*v.* To go beyond; to surpass.
exceptional	(ĕx çĕp′ tion ăl)	*adj.* Rare; out of the ordinary.
excessive	(ĕx çĕs′ sĭve)	*adj.* Beyond a just amount.
exhale	(ĕx hāle′)	*v.* To breathe out.
exile	(ex′ ile)	*n.* One driven from his coun-
	ĕg′ zīl	try. *v.* To banish.
exorbitant	(ex or′ bĭ tănt)	*adj.* More than a just price.
	ĕg zŏr′	
explode	(ĕx plōde′)	*v.* To burst noisily.
export	(ĕx pōrt′)	*v.* To send abroad.
expulsion	(ĕx pŭl′ sion)	*n.* A driving or forcing out.

A. Consult your dictionary as to the pronunciation and the meaning of the following words:

deflate   dejection   depression   exempt   exonerate

B. Complete each of the following sentences by filling in a word from this lesson.

1. Does the United States (   ) cotton?
2. He had the appearance of a (   ) old man.
3. Mary seems to (   ) in a number of sports.
4. What is the time of (   ) of the jetliner?
5. She proved to be an (   ) student.
6. The usher will (   ) the stub of the ticket.
7. We will make a (   ) for payment in cash.
8. The newspaper report was an (   ) of the facts.
9. He is an (   ) from Russia.
10. Mrs. Hill started to (   ) the stairs.

The prefixes "im" and "in" signify "not" or "in." What is the meaning of "im" or "in" in each of the following words?

immaterial	(ĭm′ mȧ tē′ rĭ ăl)	*adj.*	Of no consequence; unimportant.
immortal	(ĭm môr′ tăl)	*adj.*	Not mortal; undying.
impartial	(ĭm pär′ tial) shăl	*adj.*	Not partial; just.
impassable	(ĭm pȧss′ ȧ ble)	*adj.*	Cannot be passed or traveled.
imperfect	(ĭm pẽr′ fĕct)	*adj.*	Not perfect; defective.
impersonal	(ĭm pẽr′ sȯn ăl)	*adj.*	Not personal.
impossible	(ĭm pǒs′ sĭ ble)	*adj.*	Not possible.
improbable	(ĭm prǒb′ ȧ ble)	*adj.*	Unlikely to be true.
inadequate	(ĭn ăd′ ē quate) kwĭt	*adj.*	Not adequate; insufficient.
incapable	(ĭn cā′ pȧ ble)	*adj.*	Not capable; unable.
incapacitate	(ĭn′ cȧ păç′ ĭ tāte)	*v.*	To disable.
incomplete	(ĭn′ cǒm plēte′)	*adj.*	Not complete; not finished.
inconvenient	(ĭn′ cǒn vēn′ ient) yĕnt	*adj.*	Not convenient.
incorrect	(ĭn′ cǒr rĕct′)	*adj.*	Not correct; faulty.
independent	(ĭn′ dē pĕnd′ ĕnt)	*adj.*	Not dependent.
indirectly	(ĭn′ dĭ rĕct′ lў)	*adv.*	Not directly.
indiscreet	(ĭn′ dĭs crēēt′)	*adj.*	Not discreet; rash.
inevitably	(ĭn ĕv′ ĭ tȧ blў)	*adv.*	Unavoidably.
informal	(ĭn fôr′ măl)	*adj.*	Without ceremony.
inject	(ĭn jĕct′)	*v.*	To force in.
insanity	(ĭn săn′ ĭ tў)	*n.*	Lack of sanity; madness.
insensible	(ĭn sĕn′ sĭ ble)	*adj.*	Without feeling.
insignificant	(ĭn′ sĭg nĭf′ ĭ cănt)	*adj.*	Unimportant.
intolerant	(ĭn tŏl′ ẽr ănt)	*adj.*	Not tolerant.
invasion	(ĭn vā′ sion) zhŭn	*n.*	Act of entering for attack.

A. Consult your dictionary for the pronunciation and meaning of the following words:

inaudible   incomparable   indispensable   insolence   install

B. Find a word beginning with *in* for each of the following definitions:

1. To make bigger
2. Uninterested
3. To ask as a guest ~~of~~ invite
4. To teach instruct
5. To offend insult
6. Uncertain
7. Not finished incomplete
8. Hard to believe
9. Discomfort
10. Untrue

The prefix "inter" signifies "between," or "among." What is the meaning of "inter" in each of the following words?

intercede	(ĭn' tẽr çēde')	v.	To act between parties.
intercept	(ĭn' tẽr çĕpt')	v.	To stop or seize.
intercollegiate	(ĭn' tẽr cŏl lē' gĭ ate) ĭt	adj.	Carried on between colleges.
interfere	(ĭn' tẽr fēre')	v.	To clash.
intermediate	(ĭn' tẽr mē' dĭ áte)	adj.	Between extremes.
intermingle	(ĭn' tẽr min' gle) mĭng'	v.	To mingle together.
international	(ĭn' tẽr nǎ' tion ăl)	adj.	Between nations.
interrupt	(ĭn' tẽr rŭpt')	v.	To break into.
interval	(ĭn' tẽr vǎl)	n.	Space of time.
intervene	(ĭn' tẽr vēne')	v.	To come between.

The prefix "re" signifies "back to" or "again." What is the meaning of "re" in each of the following words?

reconcile	(rĕc' ŏn çīle)	v.	To make friendly again.
recover	(ré cŏv' ẽr)	v.	To take again; to regain.
redeem	(ré dēēm')	v.	To buy back.
reelect	(rē' é lĕct')	v.	To elect again.
reform	(ré fôrm')	v.	To restore to good state.
reinstate	(rē' ĭn stãte')	v.	To place in possession again.
remind	(ré mīnd')	v.	To cause one to remember.
replacement	(ré plāçe' mĕnt)	n.	Restoration.
reproduce	(rē' pró dūçe')	v.	To produce again; to repeat.
reunion	(ré ūn' ion) yŭn	n.	A reuniting of persons.

A. Consult your dictionary for the pronunciation and meaning of the following words:

intermittent   interwoven   refute   renominate   restoration

B. Form a noun from each of the following words:

interfere	intervene	recover	reform	remind
interrupt	reconcile	reelect	reinstate	reproduce

C. Each of the following definitions can be covered by a word beginning with *inter*. How many of them do you know?

1. Entreaty in behalf of others
2. To seize before arrival at destination
3. Mutually dependent
4. To meddle
5. Inside; inner
6. Without termination; endless
7. Alternating; recurrent
8. Affecting two or more nations
9. To explain; translate
10. To question

The prefix "mis" signifies "wrong," "amiss," or "ill."

misapplication	(mĭs′ ăp plĭ cā′ tion)	n. A wrong application.
misapply	(mĭs′ ăp plȳ′)	v. To apply wrongly.
misbehave	(mĭs′ bĕ hāve′)	v. To behave in defiance of rules.
misdeed	(mĭs dēēd′)	n. An evil deed.
misfit	(mĭs fĭt′)	n. Poor fit.
misfortune	(mĭs fôr′ tŭne)	n. Bad luck.
misgiving	(mĭs gĭv′ ĭng)	n. Sense of distrust.
mishandle	(mĭs hăn′ dle)	v. To handle wrongly.
misleading	(mĭs lēad′ ĭng)	adj. Leading astray.
mispronounce	(mĭs′ prṓ nounçe′)	v. To pronounce incorrectly.

The prefix "dis" means "apart" or "away." How does this meaning apply in the following words?

disability	(dĭs′ à bĭl′ ĭ tȳ)	n. Weakness.
disconnect	(dĭs′ cŏn nĕct′)	v. To disunite.
discourage	(dĭs coûr′ age) ij	v. To depress.
discover	(dĭs cŏv′ ẽr)	v. To find, reveal.
discrepancy	(dĭs crĕp′ ăn cȳ)	n. Difference.
discriminate	(dĭs crĭm′ ĭ nāte′)	v. To mark as different.
discuss	(dĭs cŭss′)	v. To argue, debate.
dispose	(dĭs pōṣe′)	v. To distribute; to incline.
dispute	(dĭs pūte′)	v. To quarrel.
distract	(dĭs trăct′)	v. To divert, agitate.

A. Indicate the pronunciation and the meaning of the following words:

misjudge   mismanage   misplay   misspell   misspend

B. Write a sentence for each of the following words:

misbehave   misgovern   misleading   misquote   misunderstand
misfortune   mislay   misname   misrule   misuse

C. Use each of the following words in a sentence:

disability   discourage   discrepancy   discriminate   distract

D. For each of the following words and expressions there is a word beginning with the prefix *dis*. How many can you get?

1. To weaken
2. To differ with
3. To vanish
4. To deprive of weapons
5. A calamity
6. To reject
7. To detect
8. To bother
9. Not content
10. Contempt

The prefix "sub" signifies "under," "below," or "inferior." What is the meaning of "sub" in each of the following words?

subcommittee	(sŭb′ cŏm mĭt′ tĕe)	*n.* An under committee.
subdued	(sŭb dūed′)	*adj.* Brought under; conquered.
subjugate	(sŭb′ jụ gāte)	*v.* To bring under control of.
submarine	(sŭb′ mȧ rine′) rēn′	*adj.* Under water in the sea.
submerge	(sŭb mēr′ġe′)	*v.* To put under water.
submit	(sŭb mĭt′)	*v.* To yield; to surrender.
subordinate	(sŭb ôr′ dĭ nȧte)	*adj.* Holding an inferior rank.
subscribe	(sŭb scrībe′)	*v.* To sign one's name.
subsoil	(sŭb′ soil′)	*n.* Soil under the surface soil.
subway	(sŭb′ wāy′)	*n.* An underground way.

The prefix "un" signifies "not."

unaffected	(ŭn′ ăf fĕct′ ĕd)	*adj.* Not affected; plain; simple.
unavoidable	(ŭn′ ȧ void′ ȧ ble)	*adj.* Not avoidable; inevitable.
uncertain	(ŭn çēr′ taĭn)	*adj.* Not certain; not sure.
unclaimed	(ŭn clāimed′)	*adj.* Not claimed.
unconscious	(ŭn cŏn′ scious) shŭs	*adj.* Not conscious; not aware.
undivided	(ŭn′ dĭ vīd′ ĕd)	*adj.* Not divided; unbroken.
uneventful	(ŭn′ ė vĕnt′ fụl)	*adj.* Not eventful; monotonous.
unfavorable	(ŭn fā′ vŏr ȧ ble)	*adj.* Not favorable; adverse.
unlike	(ŭn līke′)	*adj.* Not similar.
unnecessary	(ŭn nĕç′ ĕs sa rў) sĕr′	*adj.* Not necessary; useless.

A. Consult your dictionary for the pronunciation and meaning of the following words:

subcontract   subsidiary   subterranean   unbiased   uncouth

B. Complete each of the following sentences by filling in a word from this lesson.

1. Surely they will never (   ) to such injustice.
2. There were many (   ) letters in the post office.
3. He held a (   ) position in the company.
4. The (   ) was very black and rich.
5. The weather is (   ) for a picnic.
6. How (   ) him to be so petty.
7. The colonists attempted to (   ) the natives.
8. Will you (   ) to this petition?
9. Please give me your (   ) attention.
10. The chairman appointed a (   ).

C. Find a word beginning with *sub* for each of the following:

1. To divide again
2. To conquer
3. Elevated, lofty
4. To plunge into water
5. Following, later
6. Financial aid

The prefix "bi" signifies "two."

bicycle	(bī′ çў cle)	n. Vehicle with two wheels.
biennial	(bī ĕn′ nĭ ăl)	adj. Every two years.
biped	(bī′ pĕd)	n. A two-footed animal.
bisect	(bī sĕct′)	v. To divide into two parts.
biweekly	(bī wēek′ lў)	adj. Every two weeks.

The prefix "tri" signifies "three."

triangle	(trī′ an′ gle) ăng′	n. Figure with three angles.
triennial	(trī ĕn′ nĭ ăl)	adj. Every three years.
triple	(trī′ ple)	adj. Threefold.
tripod	(trī′ pŏd)	n. A three-legged stand.
trisect	(trī sĕct′)	v. To divide into three parts.

The prefix "quad" signifies "four."

quadrennial	(quad rĕn′ nĭ ăl)	adj. Every four years.
quadrille	(quå drille′)	n. A square dance.
quadroon	(quạd rōōn′)	n. A person of one-fourth Negro ancestry.
quadruped	(quạd′ rụ pĕd)	n. A four-footed animal.
quadruple	(quạd′ rụ ple)	adj. Fourfold.

The prefix "semi" signifies "half" or "partly."

semiannual	(sĕm′ ĭ ăn′ nŭ ăl)	adj. Twice a year.
semicircle	(sĕm′ ĭ çir′ cle)	n. A half circle.
semicivilized	(sĕm′ ĭ çĭv′ ĭ līzed)	adj. Partly civilized.
semimonthly	(sĕm′ ĭ mónth′ lў)	adj. Twice a month.
semiprecious	(sĕm′ ĭ prĕ′ cious) shŭs	adj. Partly precious.

A. Consult your dictionary for the pronunciation and meaning of the following words:

bicentennial   bicuspid   semidetached   trio   triplicate

B. Complete each of the following sentences by filling in a word from this lesson.

1. The camera rested upon a (   ).
2. Some American Indians were (   ).
3. Man is a (   ).
4. A (   ) has three sides.
5. The amethyst is a (   ) stone.
6. He rode to work on his (   ).
7. The horse is a domesticated (   ).
8. Our presidential election is a (   ) affair.
9. Have you ever danced a (   )?
10. The sun seems to move in a (   ).

This list contains the most frequently misspelled words in Lessons 12 to 18 inclusive. Review the meanings of the prefixes used in these lessons.

Words beginning with "com," "con," or "co"

committee	conciliate	congratulate
comparison	condense	cooperate
comprehensive	condolence	coordinate

Words beginning with "de" or "ex"

decrepit	descend	exhale
depreciation	deteriorate	exonerate
depression	exceptional	exorbitant

Words beginning with "im" or "in"

impartial	incapacitate	indiscreet
impersonal	inconvenient	inevitably
inadequate	incorrect	insensible

Words beginning with "inter" or "re"

intercede	intermingle	reelect
intercept	interrupt	reinstate
intermediate	reconcile	reproduce

Words beginning with "mis" or "dis"

misbehave	misleading	discourage
misfit	mispronounce	discrepancy
misfortune	disability	distract

Words beginning with "sub" or "un"

subdued	subordinate	unbiased
submerge	unaffected	unconscious
submit	unavoidable	unnecessary

Prefixes signifying numbers

biennial	quadruple	semiannual
biweekly	triangle	semimonthly

The suffixes "able" and "ible" both signify "able to," "fit to be," or "worthy to be," but no definite rule can be given as to when "able" is to be used and when "ible" is to be used. However, it is helpful to remember that "able" is more frequently used.

abominable	(à bŏm′ ĭ nà ble)	adj.	Detestable; hateful.
acceptable	(ăc çĕpt′ à ble)	adj.	Worthy of being accepted.
amenable	(à mē′ nà ble)	adj.	Willing to yield.
available	(à vāil′ à ble)	adj.	Able to be used; attainable.
charitable	(chăr′ ĭ tà ble)	adj.	Kind; benevolent; liberal.
dependable	(dĕ pĕnd′ à ble)	adj.	Able to be depended upon.
durable	(dū′ rà ble)	adj.	Able to endure; lasting.
immovable	(ĭm mọv′ à ble)	adj.	Stationary.
innumerable	(ĭn nū′ mēr à ble)	adj.	Not able to be numbered.
intolerable	(ĭn tŏl′ ẽr à ble)	adj.	Not able to be endured.
laudable	(laud′ à ble)	adj.	Worthy of being commended.
miserable	(mĭṣ′ ẽr à ble)	adj.	In a state of misery.
notable	(nō′ tà ble)	adj.	Worthy of note; remarkable.
objectionable	(ŏb jĕc′tion à ble)	adj.	Likely to be objected to.
passable	(pàss′ à ble)	adj.	Able to be passed; mediocre.
probable	(prŏb′ à ble)	adj.	Able to be believed; likely.
profitable	(prŏf′ ĭt à ble)	adj.	Able to make a profit; useful.
questionable	(ques′ tion à ble) kwĕs′ chŭn	adj.	Inviting inquiry.
reasonable	(rēa′ ṣon à ble)	adj.	Within the bounds of reason.
remarkable	(rĕ mãrk′ à ble)	adj.	Worthy of being noticed.
respectable	(rĕ spĕct′ à ble)	adj.	Worthy of respect.
teachable	(tēach′ à ble)	adj.	Capable of being taught.
unspeakable	(ŭn spēak′ à ble)	adj.	Not fit to be spoken.
valuable	(văl′ û à ble)	adj.	Worth a relatively high price.
venerable	(vĕn′ ẽr à ble)	adj.	Worthy of honor.

A. Consult your dictionary for the pronunciation and meaning of the following words:

adaptable adjustable advisable commendable hospitable

B. From what verbs are the following adjectives derived?

acceptable dependable laudable passable teachable

C. Notice that the prefixes "im" in "immovable"; "in" in "innumerable"; and "un" in "unspeakable" signify "not" and make the words negative in meaning. Attach a negative prefix to each of the following words:

acceptable available charitable probable profitable

D. Write a sentence for each of the words in C.

Remember that the suffix "ible" has the same meanings as "able." The suffix "ible" is usually used after words ending in "s" or the "s" sound.

accessible	(ăc çĕs'sĭ ble)	adj.	Easy of access.
admissible	(ăd mĭs' sĭ ble)	adj.	Worthy of being admitted.
audible	(au' dĭ ble)	adj.	Able to be heard.
contemptible	(cŏn tĕmpt' ĭ ble)	adj.	Deserving of contempt.
convertible	(cŏn vērt' ĭ ble)	adj.	Able to be converted.
credible	(crĕd' ĭ ble)	adj.	Worthy of being believed.
digestible	(dĭ ġĕst' ĭ ble)	adj.	Capable of being digested.
divisible	(dĭ vĭs̡' ĭ ble)	adj.	Capable of being divided.
edible	(ĕd' ĭ ble)	adj.	Fit to be eaten.
expressible	(ĕx prĕss' ĭ ble)	adj.	Able to be expressed.
feasible	(fēa' s̡ĭ ble)	adj.	Able to be done.
flexible	(flĕx' ĭ ble)	adj.	Capable of being bent.
incorrigible	(ĭn cŏr' rĭ ġĭ ble)	adj.	Not able to be corrected.
indefensible	(ĭn' dĕ fĕn' sĭ ble)	adj.	Not able to be defended.
indestructible	(ĭn' dĕ strŭct' ĭ ble)	adj.	Cannot be destroyed.
inexhaustible	(ĭn' ex haust' ĭ ble) ĕgz	adj.	Cannot be exhausted.
infallible	(ĭn făl'lĭ ble)	adj.	Unfailing; unerring.
invisible	(ĭn vĭs̡' ĭ ble)	adj.	Incapable of being seen.
irresistible	(ĭr' rĕ s̡ĭst' ĭ ble)	adj.	Overpowering.
legible	(lĕġ' ĭ ble)	adj.	Able to be read; plain.
perceptible	(pēr çĕp' tĭ ble)	adj.	Able to be noticed.
possible	(pŏs' sĭ ble)	adj.	Capable of being; thinkable.
responsible	(rĕ spŏn' sĭ ble)	adj.	Able to answer for one's conduct; accountable.
susceptible	(sŭs çĕp' tĭ ble)	adj.	Easily affected.
tangible	(tăn' ġĭ ble)	adj.	Able to be touched; real.

A. Consult your dictionary for the pronunciation and meaning of the following words:

combustible   indelible   intangible   irrepressible   permissible

B. From what verbs are the following adjectives derived?

admissible   convertible   digestible   expressible   flexible

C. Notice that the prefix "in" in "indefensible" and "indestructible" signifies "not" and makes the words negative in meaning. Attach a negative prefix to each of the following words:

accessible   audible   credible   divisible   tangible

D. Write a sentence for each of the words in C.

The suffixes "ance" and "ence" mean "act of" or "state of."

abeyance	(a bey′ ănçe) bā′	n. Temporary suspension.
acceptance	(ăc çĕpt′ ănçe)	n. Act of accepting.
alliance	(ăl lī′ ănçe)	n. State of being allied; a union.
assurance	(ăs sur′ ănçe) shoͦoͫr′	n. Act of assuring; confidence.
endurance	(ĕn dūr′ ănçe)	n. Act of enduring.
fragrance	(frā′ grănçe)	n. A pleasing odor.
insurance	(ĭn sur′ ănçe) shoͦoͫr′	n. Act of insuring.
observance	(ŏb ẓĕrv′ ănçe)	n. Act of observing a custom; a ceremony.
performance	(pẽr fôrm′ ănçe)	n. Act of performing.
temperance	(tĕm′ pẽr ănçe)	n. State of moderation.

absence	(ăb′ sĕnçe)	n. State of being absent.
benevolence	(bĕ nĕv′ ó lĕnçe)	n. An act of kindness.
conference	(cŏn′ fẽr ĕnçe)	n. Act of conferring; formal consultation.
confidence	(cŏn′ fĭ dĕnçe)	n. Act of confiding; trust.
correspondence	(cŏr′ rĕ spŏn′ dĕnçe)	n. Act of corresponding.
experience	(ĕx pē′ rĭ ĕnçe)	n. Living through an event.
independence	(ĭn′ dĕ pĕnd′ ĕnçe)	n. State of being independent.
innocence	(ĭn′ nó çĕnçe)	n. State of being innocent.
residence	(rĕṣ′ ĭ dĕnçe)	n. Act of residing.
reverence	(rĕv′ ẽr ĕnçe)	n. State of being respected.
silence	(sī′ lĕnçe)	n. State of being silent.

A. Consult your dictionary for the pronunciation and meaning of the following words:

contrivance   eloquence   guidance   inheritance   negligence

B. Write a sentence for each of the five words in A.

C. Complete each of the following sentences by filling in a word from this lesson.

1. Have you sent your (   ) of the invitation?
2. The United States declared its (   ) on July 4.
3. He gave his (   ) that he would be present.
4. Have you had any (   ) in office work?
5. (   ) from class will not be excused.
6. Do you carry (   ) on your car?
7. There was an (   ) between the two countries.
8. The voter claimed (   ) in this state.
9. We enjoyed the theatrical (   ).
10. He declared his (   ) of the crime.

The suffixes "ant" and "ent" are used to form both adjectives and nouns. When used with nouns, either suffix signifies "one who."

abundant	(à bŭn′ dănt)	*adj.* Abounding; plentiful.
applicant	(ăp′ plĭ cănt)	*n.* One who applies.
assistant	(ăs sĭst′ ănt)	*n.* One who assists.
attendant	(ăt tĕnd′ănt)	*n.* One who attends.
brilliant	(brĭl′ liant) yănt	*adj.* Sparkling; very bright.
ignorant	(ĭg′ nŏ rănt)	*adj.* Lacking knowledge.
inhabitant	(ĭn hăb′ ĭ tănt)	*n.* One who inhabits.
occupant	(ŏc′ cŭ pănt)	*n.* One who occupies.
pleasant	(plĕas̠′ ănt)	*adj.* Pleasing.
reluctant	(rĕ lŭc′ tănt)	*adj.* Unwilling; disinclined.
apparent	(ăp păr′ĕnt)	*adj.* Appearing; visible.
component	(cŏm pō′ nĕnt)	*adj.* Comprising. *n.* A part.
convenient	(cŏn vēn′ ient) yĕnt	*adj.* Affording ease.
correspondent	(cŏr′ rĕ spŏnd′ ĕnt)	*n.* One who corresponds.
diligent	(dĭl′ ĭ ġĕnt)	*adj.* Perseveringly attentive; industrious.
obedient	(ŏ bē′ dĭ ĕnt)	*adj.* Willing to obey.
opponent	(ŏp pō′ nĕnt)	*n.* One who opposes.
permanent	(pĕr′ mȧ nĕnt)	*adj.* Lasting; abiding.
persistent	(pĕr sĭst′ ĕnt)	*adj.* Enduring.
resident	(rĕs̠′ ĭ dĕnt)	*n.* One who resides.

A. Consult your dictionary for the pronunciation and meaning of the following words:

despondent   equivalent   insolvent   prudent   urgent

B. Use each of the five words in A in a sentence.

C. Complete each of the following sentences by filling in a word from this lesson.

    1. Ernie Pyle achieved fame as a war (   ).
    2. New York is the (   ) home of the United Nations.
    3. The company became (   ) and went out of business.
    4. You seem (   ) to go with us.
    5. He was employed as an (   ) to the manager.
    6. Who was the (   ) of the car?
    7. The senator was a formidable (   ) in debate.
    8. The chairman was (   ) of parliamentary law.
    9. The team was (   ) over its defeat.
  10. A good citizen is (   ) to the law.

This list contains the most frequently misspelled words in Lessons 20 to 23 inclusive. Review the meanings of the suffixes used in these lessons.

Words ending in "able"

abominable	intolerable
adjustable	laudable
amenable	miserable
charitable	passable
durable	questionable
hospitable	respectable
immovable	venerable

Words ending in "ible"

accessible	incorrigible
admissible	indefensible
audible	indelible
credible	infallible
edible	irresistible
feasible	perceptible
flexible	susceptible

Words ending in "ance" or "ence"

abeyance	benevolence
assurance	conference
fragrance	experience
observance	independence
temperance	negligence

Words ending in "ant" or "ent"

abundant	apparent
attendant	convenient
brilliant	correspondent
ignorant	diligent
inhabitant	persistent

Words ending in "er"

The suffix "er" is used to signify "one who" or "that which." It also shows the comparative degree of adjectives, as in *sweeter, nicer,* and *fairer.*

Nouns

admirer	(ăd mīr′ ẽr)	*n.*	One who admires.
adviser	(ăd vīṣ′ ẽr)	*n.*	One who gives advice.
consumer	(cŏn sũm′ ẽr)	*n.*	One who consumes.
customer	(cŭs′ tóm ẽr)	*n.*	One who repeatedly buys.
designer	(dḗ ṣīgn′ ẽr)	*n.*	One who designs.
founder	(found′ ẽr)	*n.*	One who establishes.
laborer	(lā′ bŏr ẽr)	*n.*	One who does physical labor.
philosopher	(phĭ lŏs′ ŏ phẽr)	*n.*	One versed in philosophy.
photographer	(phṓ tŏg′ rȧ phẽr)	*n.*	A maker of photographs.
prisoner	(prĭṣ′ on ẽr)	*n.*	One held under restraint.
purchaser	(pûr′ chȧs ẽr)	*n.*	One who buys.
remainder	(rḗ māin′ dẽr)	*n.*	That which is left.
reminder	(rḗ mīnd′ ẽr)	*n.*	That which reminds one.

Adjectives

earlier	(ẽar′ lĭ ẽr)	*adj.*	Comparative of "early."
friendlier	(friĕnd′ lĭ ẽr)	*adj.*	Comparative of "friendly."
happier	(hăp′ p̆ĭ ẽr)	*adj.*	Comparative of "happy."
prettier	(pret′ t̆ĭ ẽr) prĭt′	*adj.*	Comparative of "pretty."
simpler	(sĭm′ plẽr)	*adj.*	Comparative of "simple."
smoother	(smōōth′ ẽr)	*adj.*	Comparative of "smooth."

A. Consult your dictionary for the pronunciation and meaning of the following words:

charter   promoter   slander   voucher   waiver

B. Use each of the five words in A in a sentence.

C. Complete each of the following sentences by filling in a word from this lesson.

   1. A good salesman tries to be of service to his (   ).
   2. The corporation applied for its (   ) in Ohio.
   3. I have always been an (   ) of his skill.
   4. Clara Barton was the (   ) of the Red Cross.
   5. He relinquished claim to the goods when he gave me his (   ).
   6. She hoped to earn her living as a (   ) of gowns.
   7. I will send you a note as a (   ) of the meeting.
   8. The teacher acted as (   ) to his students.
   9. The meeting is at an (   ) hour than we planned.
 10. The local (   ) specializes in pictures of children's pets.

The suffix "or" means "one who" or "that which." It may also mean "act of" or "state of." Notice that "or" rather than "er" is generally used after the letter "t."

actor	(ăc′ tŏr)	n. One who acts; a stage player.
administrator	(ăd mĭn′ ĭs trā′ tŏr)	n. One who administers or manages.
bachelor	(băch′ ĕ lŏr)	n. An unmarried man.
candor	(căn′ dŏr)	n. State of being frank.
collector	(cŏl lĕc′ tŏr)	n. One who collects.
conductor	(cŏn dŭc′ tŏr)	n. A director.
contractor	(cŏn trăc′ tŏr)	n. One who contracts.
distributor	(dĭs trĭb′ ŭ tŏr)	n. One who distributes.
doctor	(dŏc′ tŏr)	n. A physician.
editor	(ĕd′ ĭ tŏr)	n. One who edits.
elevator	(ĕl′ ĕ vā′ tŏr)	n. A hoisting machine or lift.
error	(ĕr′ rŏr)	n. Mistake.
inspector	(ĭn spĕc′ tŏr)	n. One who inspects.
inventor	(ĭn vĕn′ tŏr)	n. One who invents.
odor	(ō′ dŏr)	n. Scent.
originator	(ŏ rĭg′ ĭ nā′ tŏr)	n. One who originates.
possessor	(pōs sĕss′ ŏr)	n. One who possesses.
proprietor	(prŏ prī′ ĕ tŏr)	n. One who owns.
protector	(prō tĕc′ tŏr)	n. One who protects.
radiator	(rā′ dĭ ā′ tŏr)	n. That which radiates.
selector	(sĕ lĕc′ tŏr)	n. One who, or that which, selects.
senator	(sĕn′ à tŏr)	n. Member of the Senate.
separator	(sĕp′ à rā′ tŏr)	n. A mechanical device for separating.
visitor	(vĭs′ ĭ tŏr)	n. One who visits.

A. Consult your dictionary for the pronunciation and meaning of the following words:

dictator   donor   educator   factor   predecessor

B. From what verbs are the following nouns derived?

collector   distributor   inspector   separator   visitor

C. Form sentences containing the following words:

administrator   distributor   proprietor   radiator

Words ending in "ar"

The suffix "ar," when added to nouns, means "one who" or "that which." When added to adjectives, it means "of the nature of." How do these meanings apply in the following words?

angular	(ăn' gŭ lär)	*adj.*	Sharp-cornered.
beggar	(bĕg' gär)	*n.*	One who begs.
circular	(cir' cŭ lär) sûr'	*adj.*	Round.
columnar	(cŏ lŭm' när)	*adj.*	Formed in columns.
familiar	(fȧ mĭl' iar) yẽr	*adj.*	Well-known.
globular	(glŏb' ŭ lär)	*adj.*	Globe-shaped.
insular	(ĭn' sŭ lär)	*adj.*	Pertaining to an island.
irregular	(ĭr rĕg' ŭ lär)	*adj.*	Not in line with rules.
linear	(lĭn' ē är)	*adj.*	Consisting of lines.
molecular	(mȯ lĕc' ŭ lär)	*adj.*	Consisting of molecules.
particular	(pär tĭc' ŭ lär)	*adj.*	Attentive to details.
peculiar	(pȇ cūl' iar) yẽr	*adj.*	Queer; strange.
polar	(pō' lär)	*adj.*	Pertaining to a pole.
popular	(pŏp' ŭ lär)	*adj.*	Approved by people.
registrar	(rĕg' ĭs trär)	*n.*	One who keeps records.
secular	(sĕc' ŭ lär)	*adj.*	Pertaining to things not religious.
seminar	(sĕm' ĭ när)	*n.*	Class in original research.
similar	(sĭm' ĭ lär)	*adj.*	Having a general likeness.
singular	(sin' gŭ lär) sĭng'	*adj.*	Unusual.

A. Use the following words in sentences:

circular   columnar   registrar   secular   seminar

B. Complete each of the following sentences by filling in a word from this lesson.

1. The bookkeeper made the entry in a (   ) journal.
2. Puerto Rico is an (   ) territory of the United States.
3. The (   ) kept a record of the students' grades.
4. The minister had little interest in (   ) affairs.
5. The program is very (   ) to that of last year.
6. This book is (   ) in content to the one used by our class.
7. The same (   ) has stood on this corner for five years.
8. They are both very (   ) with their classmates.
9. John's conduct is (   ).
10. His suggestions in the science (   ) are brilliant.

C. From what nouns are the following adjectives derived?

circular	globular	molecular	polar
familiar	linear	particular	singular

This list contains the most frequently misspelled words in Lessons 25 to 27 inclusive. Review the meanings of the suffixes used in these lessons.

Words ending in "er"

adviser
consumer
customer
designer
earlier
friendlier
philosopher
photographer
prettier
purchaser
simpler
smoother

Words ending in "or"

administrator
candor
contractor
distributor
educator
elevator
originator
possessor
predecessor
proprietor
radiator
separator

Words ending in "ar"

angular
circular
columnar
familiar
insular
irregular
linear
molecular
particular
polar
popular
registrar

I Can't spell, "TEACH"— but my friends get the MESSAGE!

The suffixes "ize," "ise," and "yze" mean "to make" or "to do." Of these endings, "ize" is the most common. Usually when the first part of the word is a word in itself, use "ize," as in *itemize*. When the first part of the word is not a word in itself, use "ise," as in *merchandise*. A few words derived from the Greek language use "yze" or "yse."

apologize	(à pŏl′ ô ġīze)	v. To make an apology.
authorize	(au′ thôr īze)	v. To clothe with authority.
characterize	(chăr′ ăc tēr īze′)	v. To indicate the character of.
emphasize	(ĕm′ phà sīze)	v. To make emphatic.
fertilize	(fĕr′ tĭ līze)	v. To make fertile.
localize	(lō′ căl īze)	v. To make local.
materialize	(mà tē′ rĭ ăl īze′)	v. To become a realized fact.
modernize	(mŏd′ ērn īze)	v. To make modern.
specialize	(spĕ′ cial īze) shăl	v. To focus on a special area.
standardize	(stănd′ ārd īze)	v. To render standard.

chastise	(chăs tīṣe′)	v. To punish.
despise	(dĕ spīṣe′)	v. To look upon with contempt.
devise	(dĕ vīṣe′)	v. To invent; to give by will.
exercise	(ĕx′ ēr çīṣe)	v. To practice.
merchandise	(mēr′ chăn dīṣe)	v. To trade. n. Goods to be sold.
revise	(rĕ vīṣe′)	v. To correct.
supervise	(sū′ pēr vīṣe)	v. To superintend.
surmise	(sûr mīṣe′)	v. To imagine. n. A suspicion or a guess.
surprise	(sûr prīṣe′)	v. To take unawares. n. The act of taking unawares.

analyze	(ăn′ à lӯze)	v. To make an analysis.
paralyze	(păr′ à lӯze)	v. To strike with paralysis.

A. Consult your dictionary for the pronunciation and meaning of the following words:

compromise   itemize   monopolize   sympathize   visualize

B. Give a noun and an adjective that are related to each of the following verbs. Example: apologize (noun, *apology*; adjective, *apologetic*).

analyze	characterize	fertilize	paralyze	specialize
authorize	emphasize	localize	revise	supervise

C. Use each of the words in A and B in a sentence.

Words ending in "ment"

The suffix "ment" is used to form nouns, mostly from verbs, and signifies "act of," "state of," or "that which is."

accomplishment	(ăc cŏm′ plĭsh mĕnt)	n.	That which is accomplished.
adjournment	(ăd joûrn′ mĕnt)	n.	Act of adjourning.
adjustment	(ăd jŭst′ mĕnt)	n.	Act of adjusting.
agreement	(à grēē′ mĕnt)	n.	State of agreeing.
amusement	(à mūṣe′ mĕnt)	n.	State of being amused.
assignment	(ăs sīgn′ mĕnt)	n.	That which is assigned.
confinement	(cŏn fīne′ mĕnt)	n.	State of being confined.
contentment	(cŏn tĕnt′ mĕnt)	n.	State of being contented.
development	(dé vĕl′ ȯp mĕnt)	n.	State of developing.
disappointment	(dĭs′ ăp point′ mĕnt)	n.	State of being disappointed.
discernment	(dĭs cern′ mĕnt) zĕrn′	n.	Act of discerning.
encouragement	(ĕn coûr′ age mĕnt) ij	n.	That which encourages.
enjoyment	(ĕn joy′ mĕnt)	n.	Act or state of enjoying.
enlargement	(ĕn lärġe′ mĕnt)	n.	State of being enlarged.
environment	(ĕn vī′ rȯn mĕnt)	n.	Surroundings.
establishment	(ĕs tăb′ lĭsh mĕnt)	n.	That which is established.
fulfillment	(fụl fĭll′ mĕnt)	n.	Act of fulfilling.
government	(gȯv′ ẽrn mĕnt)	n.	That which governs.
improvement	(ĭm prọve′ mĕnt)	n.	State of being improved.
measurement	(meas′ ure mĕnt) mĕzh′ ẽr	n.	Act or result of measuring.
pavement	(pāve′ mĕnt)	n.	That which is paved.
punishment	(pŭn′ ĭsh mĕnt)	n.	Act of punishing.
refinement	(ré fīne′ mĕnt)	n.	Act or result of refining.
sentiment	(sĕn′ tĭ mĕnt)	n.	Feeling; an opinion.
treatment	(trēat′ mĕnt)	n.	Manner of treating.

A. Consult your dictionary for the pronunciation and meaning of the following words:

appointment   astonishment   embarrassment
ornament   resentment

B. Use each of the words in A in a sentence.

C. Form sentences containing the following words:

adjournment assignment discernment fulfillment sentiment
adjustment contentment environment refinement treatment

The suffix "tion" is generally pronounced "shun" and usually follows a vowel or the consonant "c." It means "state of" or "act of."

agitation	(ăġ′ ĭ tā′ tion)	n. Act of agitating.
alteration	(al′ tĕr ā′ tion)	n. Act of altering; change.
approbation	(äp′ prŏ bā′ tion)	n. Act of approving.
commendation	(cŏm′ mĕn dā′ tion)	n. Act of commending.
consultation	(cŏn′ sŭl tā′ tion)	n. Act of consulting.
demonstration	(dĕm′ ȯn strā′ tion)	n. Act of demonstrating; a proof.
desolation	(dĕs′ ȯ lā′ tion)	n. State of being desolated.
exhibition	(ĕx′ hĭ bĭ′ tion)	n. Act of exhibiting; display.
indication	(ĭn′ dĭ cā′ tion)	n. Act of indicating.
intimation	(ĭn′ tĭ mā′ tion)	n. Act of intimating; a hint.
nomination	(nŏm′ ĭ nā′ tion)	n. Act of naming for office.
notification	(nō′ tĭ fĭ cā′ tion)	n. Act of notifying; a notice.
preservation	(prĕṣ′ ĕr vā′ tion)	n. State of being preserved.
recollection	(rĕc′ ȯl lĕc′ tion)	n. Act of calling to mind.
reduction	(rĕ dŭc′ tion)	n. State of being reduced.
repetition	(rĕp′ ḗ tĭ′ tion)	n. Act of repeating.
resignation	(rĕṣ′ ĭg nā′ tion)	n. Act of resigning.
restoration	(rĕs′ tȯ rā′ tion)	n. Act of restoring.
restriction	(rĕ strĭc′ tion)	n. Act of restricting.
revolution	(rĕv′ ȯ lū′ tion)	n. Act of turning around.
selection	(sĕ lĕc′ tion)	n. Act of selecting; the thing selected.
supposition	(sŭp′ pȯ ẓĭ′ tion)	n. Act of supposing; an opinion.
taxation	(tăx ā′ tion)	n. Act of taxing.
translation	(trăns lā′ tion)	n. Act of translating.
vexation	(vĕx ā′ tion)	n. State of being displeased.

A. Consult your dictionary for the pronunciation and meaning of the following words:

assumption   conservation   duration   insertion   toleration

B. Give a verb and an adjective that are related to each of the following nouns. Example: agitation (verb, *agitate*; adjective, *agitated*).

alteration   consultation   desolation   preservation   restriction
commendation   demonstration   exhibition   repetition   taxation

C. Use each of the words in A and B in a sentence.

The suffix "sion" is equivalent in meaning to "tion." The ending "sion" has two pronunciations. After a consonant, "sion" is pronounced "shun"; as in the words *mission* and *extension*. After a vowel, however, "sion" is pronounced "zhun," as in *confusion, explosion,* and *revision.*

admission	(ăd mĭs′ sion)	*n.*	Act of admitting; entrance fee.
allusion	(ăl lū′ sion) zhŭn	*n.*	Act of alluding; a hint.
collision	(cŏl lĭ′ sion) zhŭn	*n.*	Act of colliding; a clash.
concession	(cŏn çĕs′ sion)	*n.*	Act of conceding; a grant.
confusion	(cŏn fū′ sion) zhŭn	*n.*	State of disorder.
discussion	(dĭs cŭs′ sion)	*n.*	Act of discussing; a debate.
explosion	(ĕx plō′ sion) zhŭn	*n.*	Act of exploding.
extension	(ĕx tĕn′ sion)	*n.*	Act of extending.
impression	(ĭm prĕs′ sion)	*n.*	Act of impressing; an opinion.
mission	(mĭs′ sion)	*n.*	A sending on some service.
occasion	(ŏc cā′ sion) zhŭn	*n.*	An occurrence.
omission	(ṍ mĭs′ sion)	*n.*	Something left undone.
oppression	(ŏp prĕs′ sion)	*n.*	Act of oppressing; tyranny.
permission	(pēr mĭs′ sion)	*n.*	Act of permitting; consent.
possession	(pŏs ṣĕs′ sion)	*n.*	Act of possessing; property.
revision	(rḗ vĭ′ sion) zhŭn	*n.*	Act of revising; a review.
supervision	(sū′ pēr vĭ′ sion)	*n.*	Act of overseeing.

The suffix "cian" indicates "one skilled in," and is pronounced "shun."

magician	(mȧ ġĭ′ cian)	*n.*	One skilled in magic.
musician	(mṹ ṣĭ′ cian)	*n.*	One skilled in music.
physician	(phў ṣĭ′ cian)	*n.*	One skilled in medicine.
politician	(pŏl′ ĭ tĭ′ cian)	*n.*	One skilled in politics.
technician	(tĕch nĭ′ cian)	*n.*	One skilled in technical details of a subject.

A. Consult your dictionary for the pronunciation and meaning of the following words:

comprehension   dimension   provision   succession   suspension

B. Use each of the words in A in a sentence.

C. Complete each of the following sentences by filling in a word from this lesson.

1. The commanding officer was sent on a ( ) to China.
2. Unless we adhere to the rule, we will have great ( ).
3. We were mystified by the performance of the ( ).
4. ( ) is nine points of the law.
5. The ( ) of the two automobiles occurred yesterday.
6. I listened to the ( ) about the coming election.
7. Did you receive ( ) to leave the room?
8. The bank allowed an ( ) of time for payment.
9. Mr. Payne made no ( ) to the unfortunate incident.
10. The ( ) destroyed the chemical plant.

A. Copy the following sentences, substituting the appropriate words from Lessons 31 and 32 for the blanks.

1. He gave a (   ) of the superiority of his product over competing products.
2. Have you received a (   ) of his change of address?
3. She submitted her (   ) immediately after her marriage.
4. Fortunately, no one was hurt in the three-car (   ).
5. He has received (   ) to go to Boston for a week.

B. Give the rule that applies to the spelling of the suffix in each of the following words. Remember that the "zhun" sound is expressed by *sion* following a vowel.

admission	consultation	nomination
agitation	demonstration	notification
alteration	explosion	recollection
commendation	extension	resignation
concession	impression	session
confession	mission	supervision

C. Form words by adding an appropriate ending (*tion, sion, cian*) to the parts given. Use your dictionary when in doubt.

approba_____	peti_____
commenda_____	posi_____
depres_____	selec_____
electri_____	solu_____
exclu_____	statisti_____
intima_____	succes_____
inven_____	taxa_____
musi_____	transla_____
nomina_____	vexa_____
occa_____	vi_____

This list contains the most frequently misspelled words in Lessons 29 to 33 inclusive. Review the meanings of the suffixes used in these lessons.

Words ending in "ize," "ise," or "yze"

analyze
apologize
authorize
chastise
compromise
fertilize

materialize
merchandise
monopolize
paralyze
specialize
supervise

Words ending in "ment"

accomplishment
adjournment
assignment
disappointment

discernment
embarrassment
environment
government

Words ending in "tion"

agitation
approbation
assumption
exhibition

recollection
supposition
toleration
vexation

Words ending in "sion" or "cian"

collision
comprehension
impression
magician
musician

occasion
oppression
permission
physician
politician

Rule 1. If a word ends in "e," *generally* retain the "e" when adding a suffix beginning with a consonant to keep the pronunciation of the original word intact.

advance	advancement	induce	inducement
arrange	arrangement	loose	loosely
complete	completely	manage	management
disgrace	disgraceful	nine	ninety
enforce	enforcement	positive	positively
excite	excitement	rare	rarely
extreme	extremely	resource	resourceful
false	falsehood	sincere	sincerely
house	household	taste	tasteless
immediate	immediately	whole	wholesome

Rule 2. In a word ending in "ge," the final "e" may be dropped before a suffix if the letter "d" precedes the "g," for the letter "d" in this position "softens" the "g."

abridge	abridging	abridgment
acknowledge	acknowledging	acknowledgment
judge	judging	judgment

Rule 3. In words ending in "ue," the final "e" may be dropped before a suffix.

argue	arguing	argument	
continue	continuing	continuous	continual
due	duly	duty	dutiful
pursue	pursuing	pursuant	
true	truly		

A. Consult your dictionary for the pronunciation and meaning of the following words:

apprenticeship   disbursement   reimbursement
     vagueness   venturesome

B. In accordance with Rule 1, add "ment" to each of the following words:

announce   commence   engage   improve   state

C. Add "less" to the following words:

change   home   hope   sense   spine

D. Add "ful" to the following words:

grace   grate   peace   revenge   spite

E. Select ten of the words in A-D and write a sentence containing each word.

Rule 4. If a word ends in "e," *generally* drop the "e" when adding a suffix beginning with a vowel.

advise	advising	force	forcibly
amaze	amazing	investigate	investigating
announce	announcing	oblige	obliging
appraise	appraisal	obscure	obscurity
describe	describing	organize	organizing
desire	desirable	release	releasing
dine	dining	surprise	surprising
eliminate	eliminating	trouble	troubling
enclose	enclosure	write	writing

The word "dining" is frequently misspelled. Be sure that you spell it with one "n."

Rule 5. In the following words, the final "e" is retained before the suffix to keep the "c" and "g" sounds "soft":

change	changeable	enforce	enforceable
charge	chargeable	notice	noticeable
		service	serviceable

A. Consult your dictionary for the pronunciation and meaning of the following words:

advisory   competing   fascinating   imaginable   involving

B. In accordance with Rule 4, add "able" to each of the following words:

forgive   imagine   love   move   use

C. Add "ed" to the following words:

amuse   associate   continue   exercise   revere

D. Add "ing" to the following words:

come   force   hope   issue   owe

E. Select ten of the words in A-D and write a sentence containing each word.

Rule 1. When a suffix beginning with a vowel is added to a word of one syllable that ends in a single consonant preceded by a single vowel, *usually* double the final consonant. The consonant is doubled to preserve the short sound of the vowel in the original word.

bag	baggage	sad	saddest
bid	bidding	set	setting
drag	dragged	slip	slippery
get	getting	step	stepping
hot	hotter	stir	stirring
knit	knitted	swim	swimmer
put	putting	trim	trimmer
rag	ragged	whip	whipped

Rule 2. When a suffix beginning with a vowel is added to a word of more than one syllable that is accented on the last syllable, and that ends in a single consonant preceded by a single vowel, *usually* double the final consonant.

acquit	acquittal	excel	excelled
admit	admittance	forbid	forbidden
allot	allotted	forget	forgetting
commit	committee	omit	omitted
compel	compelled	permit	permitted
control	controllable	prefer	preferred
equip	equipped	refer	referring

A. Consult your dictionary for the pronunciation and meaning of the following words:

clipping   conferred   deferred   incurred   remittance

B. The noun "runner" is formed from the verb "run" and follows Rule 1. Form nouns from each of the following verbs. Do they follow Rule 1 or Rule 2?

abet   begin   chop   occur   rebel   wrap

C. Use each of the words in A and B in a sentence.

Rule 3. We have seen in Rule 2, Lesson 37, that in a word of more than one syllable ending in a single consonant preceded by a single vowel, the final consonant is *usually* doubled provided the last syllable is accented. It may be concluded, therefore, that the final consonant is *not* doubled if the accent is *not* on the last syllable.

marvel	marvelous	poison	poisoning
merit	merited	travel	traveling
		tunnel	tunneling

Rule 4. When a suffix beginning with a vowel is added to a word of more than one syllable, the final consonant is *not* doubled if the new word does *not* retain the same accent as the root.

defer	(dḗ fẽr′)	deference	(dĕf′ ẽr ĕnçe)
habit	(hăb′ ĭt)	habitual	(hȧ bĭt′ ủ ăl)
infer	(ĭn fẽr′)	inference	(ĭn′ fẽr ĕnçe)
prefer	(prḗ fẽr′)	preference	(prĕf′ ẽr ĕnçe)
refer	(rḗ fẽr′)	reference	(rĕf′ ẽr ĕnçe)

Rule 5. Since, according to Rules 1 and 2, Lesson 37, the final consonant is *usually* doubled only when it is preceded by a vowel, it is evident that the final consonant is *not* doubled when it is preceded by another consonant.

bring	bringing	suggest	suggestive
burn	burner	warn	warned
climb	climbing	wound	wounded

A. Consult your dictionary for the pronunciation and meaning of the following words:

absorbing   continental   formality   protested   reflecting

B. Form the past tense and the present participle of each of the following verbs in accordance with Rule 3:

benefit   inhabit   limit   profit   rival

C. Form the past tense and the present participle of each of the following verbs in accordance with Rule 5:

adopt   attend   concern   exist   pack

D. Select ten of the words in A-C and write a sentence containing each word.

Rule 1. If a word ends in "y" preceded by a consonant, *generally* change the "y" to "i" when adding any suffix except one beginning with "i."

accompany	accompanied	necessity	necessities
busy	business	ordinary	ordinarily
carry	carriage	satisfy	satisfied
courtesy	courtesies	signify	significant
glory	glorious	steady	steadily
hurry	hurried	supply	supplied
justify	justified	vary	variation
magnify	magnificent	victory	victorious
necessary	necessarily	worry	worried

Rule 2. If a word ends in "y" preceded by a consonant, retain the "y" when adding a suffix beginning with "i."

accompany	accompanying	satisfy	satisfying
carry	carrying	signify	signifying
hurry	hurrying	supply	supplying

Rule 3. If a word ends in "y" preceded by a vowel, *generally* retain the "y" when adding any suffix or the letter "s."

annoy	annoyance	delay	delayed
attorney	attorneys	journey	journeys
convey	conveyance	pay	payable

Exceptions: pay   paid   say   said

A. Consult your dictionary for the pronunciation and meaning of the following words:

classification   compliance   qualification   testimonial

B. Write a sentence for each of the words in A.

C. Add a suffix to each of the following words and give the rule involved:

apply	buy	cry	heavy	pity
beauty	copy	duty	joy	try

This list contains the most frequently misspelled words in Lessons 35 to 39 inclusive. Review the meanings of the suffixes used in these lessons.

Attaching suffixes to words ending in "e"

abridgment
acknowledgment
advising
argument
chargeable
competing
dining
disbursement
enforcement
extremely

inducement
judgment
loosely
ninety
noticeable
pursuing
truly
vagueness
wholesome
writing

Attaching suffixes to words ending in a consonant

committee
continental
controllable
deference
equipped
formality
habitual

knitted
marvelous
preference
reference
remittance
slippery
traveling

Attaching suffixes to words ending in "y"

accompanying
attorneys
business
carriage
conveyance

magnificent
necessarily
necessities
significant
variation

Review of rules relating to suffixes

A. Add the suffix *able* or *ible* to each of the following words, giving the rule that applies. Use your dictionary if you are in doubt.

access	enforce	observe
approach	expend	prefer
avoid	express	receive
collapse	impression	reduce
contempt	love	reverse
deduct	objection	sense

B. Form words by adding the appropriate suffix *sion* or *tion* to the parts given below. What rules apply?

associa_____   organiza_____
atten_____   produc_____
commis_____   protec_____
divi_____   provi_____
exten_____   televi_____

C. Add the suffix *ize, ise, yse,* or *yze* to each of the following words. What rules apply?

civil	legal
economy	magnet
equal	moral
fertile	special
ideal	union

D. Add the suffix *er* or *or* to the following words, giving the rules that apply.

act	contract
advise	edit
believe	learn
brew	originate
call	sing

What this Language needs is more FLEXIBILITY!

A. Give the meanings of the following prefixes: *per, pre, pro.* Give five words illustrating each prefix.

B. Words ending with the suffixes *sede, ceed,* or *cede* will not bother you if you remember that only one English word ends in *sede*: *supersede.* Only three words end in *ceed*: *exceed, proceed,* and *succeed.* In all other words ending in this sound, use the spelling *cede.* Complete the following words:

pre_____	super_____
con_____	ex_____
pro_____	inter_____
re_____	se_____
suc_____	

C. Give the rule governing the spelling of the suffixes in the following words:

comical	article
practical	icicle
theoretical	monocle
prettiest	oculist
hungriest	chemist
shortest	botanist
longest	machinist

D. Write a sentence for each of the words in B.

E. Write a sentence for each of the following words:

botanist   chemist   monocle   oculist   theoretical

Plurals resemble suffixes in that they are word endings which modify meaning. By the word "suffix," however, we usually mean a syllable, whereas the letters used to indicate plurals—*s* and *es*—may not be pronounced as a syllable. In the word *peaches,* for example, the plural (es) is a syllable, but in the word *pears,* we have the plural (s) as part of a syllable.

The singular form of a noun is changed to the plural form usually by adding *s* to the singular form. Consider the following words: cat—cats; book—books; invitation—invitations; rail—rails; magazine—magazines. These words belong to the general category of nouns whose plurals are formed by the addition of *s*.

There are, however, some nouns that form the plural in slightly different ways, and in Lessons 43 through 48 we shall consider the rules that govern these exceptions.

Rule 1. With nouns ending in *s, x, ch,* or *sh,* we indicate the plural by adding *es.*

church—churches   lash—lashes
mass—masses   tax—taxes

Rule 2. With nouns ending in *y* preceded by a consonant, we form the plural by changing the *y* to *i* and adding *es.*

army—armies   lady—ladies
party—parties

Rule 3. In nouns ending in *y* preceded by a vowel, we form the plural in the usual way; i.e., by adding *s.*

attorney—attorneys   journey—journeys
valley—valleys

After learning the rules in this lesson for forming plurals, copy the following words, adding the plural for each one:

alloy	company	flash	lunch
blotter	country	glass	mix
box	courtesy	guess	navy
brush	cross	heart	pass
bunch	dance	hunch	punch
buoy	desk	industry	sex
church	diary	inquiry	story
class	ferry	leash	tax

Rule 4. Nouns ending in *o* preceded by a vowel form the plural by adding *s*.

radio—radios
curio—curios
rodeo—rodeos

Rule 5. Most nouns ending in *o* preceded by a consonant (especially nouns related to music) form the plural by adding *s*.

piano—pianos   alto—altos
piccolo—piccolos   burro—burros
soprano—sopranos

Rule 6. Some nouns ending in *o* preceded by a consonant form the plural by adding *es*.

potato   potatoes
echo   echoes
Negro   Negroes

A. Copy the following words and write the plural form of each one:

albino	domino	mosquito	studio
alto	dynamo	motto	tobacco
banjo	echo	mulatto	tomato
calico	embargo	palomino	tornado
cameo	embryo	piano	torpedo
cargo	hero	radio	trio
curio	zero	ratio	veto
desperado	kimono	solo	volcano

B. From the preceding list substitute the plural form of the word that corresponds to each of the following definitions:

1. Gem carved in relief
2. Group of three
3. Person having a deficiency of color
4. A loose robe worn by the Japanese
5. Oblong piece used in a game
6. Rare or curious article
7. Individual famous for courage
8. Well-known saying
9. Instrument of power
10. Person of mixed ancestry

Rule 7. Most nouns ending in *f* or *fe* form the plural by adding *s,* but a few change *f* or *fe* to *v* and *es,* as in *life—lives.* There is no rule that governs these exceptions; the plural form must be learned for each word.

proof—proofs
calf—calves
wife—wives

Rule 8. Some nouns have the same form for both the singular and the plural.

corps—corps
Chinese—Chinese
deer—deer

A. Write the plural forms of the following words:

bailiff	fish	rice
beef	half	roof
calf	handkerchief	rye
cheese	hoof	safe
Chinese	knife	salmon
cuff	leaf	scarf
deer	life	sheep
elf	loaf	thief
elk	proof	wolf
fife	rebuff	yourself

B. From the preceding list substitute the plural form of the word that fits the blank.

1. Mary Jenkins has the (   ) of the class pictures.
2. We are planning to drive to the mountains when the (   ) are changing color.
3. Two (   ) make a whole.
4. The sound of pounding (   ) was common in the Old West.
5. "Honor among (   )" has been disproved many times.

C. Write five nouns ending in *f* or *ff* that form the plural by adding *s.* Use each of these words in a sentence.

Rule 9. Some nouns of Latin, Greek, or French origin retain their original plurals, although in some cases an English form is acceptable. In this lesson, words with two acceptable plural forms are marked with an asterisk.

	Original Plural	*English Plural*
alumna [1]	alumnae [3]	(none)
alumnus [2]	alumni [4]	(none)
*beau	beaux	beaus
*formula	formulae	formulas
*index	indices	indexes
*memorandum	memoranda	memorandums

A. Write the plurals of the following words:

alumnus
analysis
*appendix
axis
bacterium
basis
*beau
crisis

*criterion
*curriculum
datum
diagnosis
emphasis
*formula
hypothesis
*index
*medium

*memorandum
parenthesis
phenomenon
stimulus
stratum
*syllabus
synopsis
*tableau
thesis

B. Give a synonym for each of the words in the list above.

C. Write a sentence containing the English plural of each of the words preceded by an asterisk in the list above.

---

[1] Feminine form (a female graduate).
[2] Masculine form (a male graduate).
[3] Feminine form plural.
[4] Masculine form plural.
Note: For a group of graduates comprised of both men and women, use the masculine form, *alumni.*

Rule 10. There are some nouns for which the plural is formed irregularly. These nouns and their plurals, such as those given below, must be learned individually.

child—children	man—men
foot—feet	mouse—mice
goose—geese	ox—oxen
louse—lice	tooth—teeth
madam—mesdames	woman—women

Rule 11. In forming the plural of a proper noun (name of a person or a place), separate the *s* from the name by an apostrophe. This same rule holds for symbols and figures. The apostrophe preserves the original form of the word or symbol and thereby prevents confusion.

There are four Mary's in the class.
There are two Kansas City's in the United States.
The four A's in this class were all earned by boys.

Rule 12. Compound nouns written without a hyphen usually form the plural regularly—that is, by adding *s* to the singular form, as in *football, footballs; blueprint, blueprints; classroom, classrooms;* and *judge advocate, judge advocates.*

Exceptions: There are occasional exceptions, as in

manservant	menservants
spoonful	spoonsful

Hyphenated nouns, however, usually form the plural by adding *s* to the principal part of the word—the principal part of the word is not necessarily the first part of the word, but it often is.

court-martial	courts-martial
mother-in-law	mothers-in-law

A. Write the plural forms of the following words:

aide-de-camp	halftone	self-starter
attorney-at-law	handful	sellout
attorney general	heir apparent	set-to
breakdown	homecoming	sister-in-law
bylaw	looker-on	spoonful
by-product	man-of-war	stepson
cross-examination	mother-in-law	switchboard
cupful	namesake	takeoff
daughter-in-law	passerby	textbook
dumbwaiter	president-emeritus	trademark
ex-president	runner-up	trade union
governor-general	secretary-elect	write-up

B. Why, in your opinion, is the *s* added to the second half of hyphenated words such as **cross-purposes, forget-me-nots,** and **self-starters?**

Rule 13. Some nouns such as *economics, mathematics,* and *molasses* seem to be plural because they end in *s,* but actually these words are singular in form, in the same way that collective nouns are considered to be singular. Note the following sentences:

Economics is (not *are*) his favorite subject.

Mathematics is (not *are*) a difficult field to master.

Molasses has (not *have*) high food value as well as pleasing flavor.

Rule 14. On the other hand, some nouns and expressions ending in *s* always require a plural verb:

assets	grounds
belongings	headquarters
clothes	pajamas
glasses	scissors
golf links	sugar tongs
goods	tidings
trousers	

Rule 15. A third group of nouns may take either the singular or the plural form of the verb, according to the meaning of the writer. When the noun is used as a collective noun, the singular form of the verb is used. When the items or persons represented by the noun are considered individually, the noun is considered to be plural and it takes the plural verb.

This reindeer has just been added to the zoo.
These reindeer are used in MGM's new picture.

The committee is in agreement about the campaign.
The committee are on vacation at present.

The council is comprised of ten members.
The council are making house-to-house calls on taxpayers to get their opinions.

A. Copy the following sentences, choosing the correct verb:

1. When the game was over, the team (was, were) photographed.
2. The council (has, have) come to blows over the matter.
3. The Board of Directors (is, are) filing a protest.
4. The Committee on Foreign Affairs (is, are) not in agreement about the money to be sent to Pakistan.
5. The American delegation (has, have) been divided into three committees by the president of the council.

B. List as many collective nouns as you can.

C. Write ten sentences in which a collective noun is properly followed by a third-person singular form of the verb "to be," present tense or past tense (*is,* or *was*).

57

Copy the following sentences, substituting for the blanks the plural, or the appropriate verb form, of the words in parentheses.

1. We have one doctor and two (attorney) _____ in our family.
2. My brother caught three (trout) _____ in an hour.
3. All the (workman) _____ gave up their lunch hour to help Harry.
4. The fertile (valley) _____ contribute to the country's wealth.
5. The jury (*has* or *have*) _____ given a decision.
6. The jury (*is* or *are*) _____ divided in opinion about this case.
7. Marvin took a picture of the four (deer) _____.
8. He has taken many (journey) _____.
9. All the (child) _____ and the (grandchild) _____ returned.
10. One of the four (Mary) _____ in the class was absent.
11. We appreciate the (courtesy) _____ extended to us.
12. She has a collection of (motto) _____.
13. John received two (B) _____ on his report card.
14. There are (potato) _____ and (tomato) _____ in the stew.
15. The six (Smith) _____ went to the shore together.
16. (Chinese) _____ do not wear (kimono) _____.
17. She was given two (cameo) _____ by the family.
18. She is willing to sing with the (soprano) _____.
19. I always seem to get (handkerchief) _____ for Christmas.
20. The State College (Alumnus) _____ Association sent us two (memorandum) _____ about the Jamboree.
21. There are many (formula) _____ for success.
22. When you have gathered all the (datum) _____, you can write the report.
23. The Texas State College for Women (Alumna) _____ honored the poet at a dinner.
24. Most of the (Pittsburgh) _____ in the United States have dropped the *h* from the name.
25. His headquarters (is, are) _____ in Washington, D. C.
26. Three students lost their confidential (diary) _____.
27. Two (spoonful) _____ of lemon juice will improve the flavor.
28. The student body (is, are) _____ debating the issue this morning.
29. Do not take shortcuts through the (alley) _____.
30. In this room, (echo) _____ resound from wall to wall.
31. At the picnic we played (domino) _____ and told (story) _____, little realizing that the (mosquito) _____ were having the best time of all.
32. These (banjo) _____ should be given to someone.
33. The four (passerby) _____ were witnesses to the crime.
34. In considering (curriculum) _____ for John, we must think first of all of his native (ability) _____.
35. Have you had the (chimney) _____ repaired?
36. Two photographers have (studio) _____ in our town.
37. Add two (cupful) _____ of sugar to the batter.
38. The two (daughter-in-law) _____ were more helpful than the daughters.
39. The two (class) _____ combined talents to present the program.
40. Representatives of the three (army) _____ were present.

In Lessons 50 through 52, we are going to learn the rules concerning the possessive case of nouns, both proper and common, with occasional reference to pronouns.

Rule 1. Nouns not ending in *s* (that is, singular nouns such as *man* and plural nouns such as *children*) form the possessive case by adding an apostrophe and *s*.

Examples: I have the children's bathing suits.
Do you have the doctor's bag?
Are these the stenographer's notes?

Rule 2. The possessive form of a noun ending in *s* differs according to whether the noun is singular or plural.

a. The possessive of a singular noun ending in *s* is formed by adding an apostrophe and *s*, unless the additional *s* makes the word difficult to pronounce.

The hostess's greeting was cordial.
Jones's secretary is to be married soon.

b. The possessive of a plural noun that ends in *s* is formed by adding an apostrophe only.

The boys' books are here.
This is a millionaires' country club.

Rule 3. In proper names of associations, the apostrophe in a possessive is often omitted, as in the *Eastern Business Teachers Association*.

Rule 4. Possessive pronouns do not take the apostrophe because the words in themselves are possessive in meaning and no further indication is necessary.

Examples: *his, hers, yours, ours, theirs, its, whose.*

A. Write the possessive singular and the possessive plural of these nouns:

acquaintance	European	Polynesian
agency	friend	resident
American	hour	Scandinavian
arm	Japanese	soldier
attorney	Korean	student
century	man	subscriber
Chinese	millionaire	tourist
day	minute	woman
decade	moment	workman
enemy	pioneer	year

B. Write a sentence for each of five words in A, using the plural possessive form of the noun.

C. Write a sentence for each of the following possessives:

soldier's   tourist's   centuries'   days'   hour's

Rule 5. Singular nouns ending in *s*, *x*, and *z* form the possessive by adding *'s*, unless the addition of the extra *s* sound makes pronunciation awkward or difficult. In that case, only the apostrophe is used.

As a matter of fact, it is not incorrect to form the possessive of words ending in *s*, *x*, and *z* by adding the apostrophe only, although modern usage prefers the *'s*. It is therefore correct to say or write "Keats' poems," but some authorities consider it preferable to use the *'s*, "Keats's poems."

Examples: Mr. Hughes' book.   Mr. Cox's thesis.
           Mr. Corliss's office.   Cortez's armies.

Rule 6. Compound words form the possessive by adding *'s* to the last word.

Examples: sister-in-law . . . sister-in-law's . . . commander-in-chief . . . commander-in-chief's.

Note: For plural possessives of compound words, use an *of* phrase to indicate possession.

The decisions of the commanders-in-chief. . . .
The estates of the sisters-in-law. . . .

Rule 7. An abbreviated word forms the possessive by adding *'s* after the period.

Examples: Markle Corp.'s financial statements. . . .
Y. M. C. A.'s program of activities. . . .

Rule 8. Joint ownership or authorship is indicated by making the last noun possessive; separate possession is indicated by making each noun possessive.

Examples: Lewis and Clark's expeditions. . . .
Browning's and Shelley's poetry. . . .

A. In the following sentences, fill in the possessive form of the words written in parentheses:

1. The (boys) _____ locker room is always open until 6 p. m.
2. The (dog) _____ collar was too loose.
3. No one disagreed with the (school board) _____ recommendation.
4. Everyone wanted to hear the (park ranger) _____ lecture.
5. Mr. Schwab followed his (attorney) _____ advice.
6. Mrs. Walsh complains she is always stumbling over her (grandchildren) _____ toys.
7. Mr. (Cox) _____ store has a complete line of clothes.
8. The team listened carefully to the (coach) _____ "chalk talk."

B. Write the singular possessives for the following:

aide-de-camp	notary public	John Smith, Jr.
attorney general	passerby	U. S. A.
mother-in-law	Markle Corp.	U. S. Rubber Co.

60

Rule 9. The possessive form of a noun or a pronoun is used with the gerund. (A *gerund* is a verb form used as a noun.)

Examples: The train's *being* late was the cause of our missing the plane.

My *calling* his story a falsehood created a bad situation.

Your *being* in the wrong group caused the misunderstanding.

A. Point out the possessives and the gerunds in the following sentences:

1. I cannot understand his rejecting your sensible suggestion.
2. Because of Bill's attacking the referee, the game was canceled.
3. Mary's admitting her laziness was a surprise to all of us.

B. *Review.* Correct all errors in the following sentences. Some sentences are correct.

1. This paper is your's.
2. I told Mr. and Mrs. Randall that the luggage was theirs.
3. Has the council announced its decision?
4. Do you have Marys' coat?
5. The club will give it's proceeds from the bazaar to the Orphan's Home.
6. Jo Ellen's dress is at the cleaners.
7. We have the childrens' toys.
8. Did she say that the wallet was her's?
9. This is a years work, and I have only three month's time to devote to it.
10. This books' pages are still uncut.
11. Is this Mrs. Jones's house?
12. The room's proportions are not pleasing to the eye.
13. The commander-in-chiefs' decision saved us from catastrophe.
14. In less than a minutes time, he was there.
15. John's arguing with the keeper of the animals frightened the children.
16. The decision should be their's, not ours.
17. Mr. Smiths' shoes need cleaning.
18. That committee has not completed it's work.
19. There were six lunch's in the picnic basket.
20. The evening's coolness was pleasant after the heat of the day.

Using the apostrophe in contractions

In the foregoing lessons we have been writing the apostrophe to indicate possession. The apostrophe is also used to show contraction.

Sometimes when we write two words together, we leave out one or more letters, using an apostrophe to show the omission. These words are called *contractions*.

Examples: can't (cannot)   they're (they are)
that's (that is)   it's (it is)

Note: be sure that you understand the use of *it's* and *its*.

A. Combine each of the following pairs of words into one word by use of the apostrophe to indicate contraction:

I am	I will	I would	can not
you are	you will	you would	would not
he is	he will	he would	was not
we are	we will	we would	is not
they are	they will	they would	could not

B. Use ten of the contractions in A in sentences.

C. *Won't* is the contraction of *will not*. Explain this irregularity (use your dictionary).

54 Hyphenated words

Hyphenated words are usually adjectives or nouns (although there are a few hyphenated verbs). There are more hyphenated adjectives than nouns because of our custom of coining adjectives by combining two or more words into a descriptive word, as in *ten-gallon* hats, *up-and-coming* businessman.

The following rules to be learned about hyphenated words are easy to understand and to apply:

Rule 1. Compound numbers below one hundred are written as hyphenated words, as in twenty-six, seventy-five, eighty-three.

Rule 2. When an adjective is comprised of a word indicating a number, followed by the word *class* or *rate*, the adjective is hyphenated.

Examples: *first-class* ticket, *second-rate* show, *first-rate* performance.

Rule 3. Words with *ex* and *elect* are usually hyphenated. Words with *vice* are hyphenated.

Examples: The president-elect had two conferences with the ex-president.
The vice-president could not attend the meeting.

Rule 4. When two or more words are used together as a word to express a single idea, the words are hyphenated.

Examples: *silver-tongued* diplomats

happy-go-lucky students

Rule 5. Prefixes are usually joined to the main part of the word, as in *misspell, prepay, subgroup.* Some exceptions to this rule are: semi-indirect, anti-intellectual, co-worker.

Rule 6. If in adding a suffix to a word, a letter occurs three times consecutively, use a hyphen to separate the word from a suffix, as in *wall-less, bell-like.*

Rule 7. The hyphen is sometimes necessary in the formation of words to indicate meaning and to distinguish between otherwise identical words. For example, the sentence, "We are going to re-cover the sofa," is quite different in meaning from "We are going to recover the sofa."

Rule 8. The prefix *self* is always followed by a hyphen.

Examples: *self-addressed* envelopes

a man's *self-esteem*

Rule 9. When a prefix is inserted before a proper noun, a hyphen is used to keep the proper noun intact.

Examples: *pro-American, trans-Atlantic, pro-Eisenhower.*

Rule 10. When a verb is coined from two or more words, it should be hyphenated, just as nouns and adjectives are.

Examples: Have you *double-checked* your answer?

I have never tried to *dry-clean* clothes.

A. Write a sentence for each of the following hyphenated nouns:

sisters-in-law   brothers-in-law   ex-presidents   courts-martial
self-esteem

B. Write the following sentences, underscoring the words that should be hyphenated and inserting the hyphen or hyphens.

1. To do first class work in this job, a man must be able bodied and quick witted.
2. There were several absent minded digressions in his after dinner speech, but fortunately the guests were broad minded and kind hearted.
3. My happy go lucky brother in law drives a broken down jalopy that provides a never to be forgotten thrill for his brave hearted passengers.
4. Our next door neighbors are middle aged but not old fashioned.
5. Some up and coming businessmen believe that tailor made clothes increase self confidence in money making activities.
6. That hit and run driver, a bad tempered fellow, was quite cold blooded and self possessed when he faced the broken hearted parents of the victim.

(Continued)

7. Some low priced houses, particularly those with labor saving devices, are first class investments for young couples.
8. He is always high spirited on week end trips, but during the week he is ill mannered and far from good natured.
9. Since he has been playing on coast to coast hookups, he has been wearing high priced custom made clothes and his wife has rented several safe deposit boxes for interest bearing bonds and other valuable investments.
10. She is a tender hearted, God fearing woman, and her kindness is revealed in her care of poverty stricken human beings and any four footed creatures that need her care.

55 Compound words written without a hyphen

Most compound words are written without a hyphen, as in the following list:

bondholder	makeshift	standpoint
breakdown	masterpiece	steamship
countryman	meantime	streetcar
earthquake	namesake	sunburned
football	newspaper	switchboard
furthermore	overdue	textbook
headquarters	pocketbook	undertake
homesick	roommate	underwear
housework	secondhand	viewpoint
however	snowstorm	withhold
keepsake	somewhat	workman

There are few expressions that are more frequently misspelled than "all right." Be sure you write it as two words.

Each of the following expressions is also written as two words:

all right	fire escape
dress coat	ice cream

A. Consult your dictionary for the pronunciation and meaning of the following words:

foregoing   heretofore   postmarked   straightforward

B. From the preceding lists select the word that should accompany each of the following definitions:

1. A temporary expedient
2. To refrain from granting; to restrain
3. Besides, moreover
4. Unpaid beyond the proper time
5. Center of operations and authority
6. Something made with extraordinary skill
7. In some degree or measure
8. A panel for controlling electric connections
9. To set about; to contract
10. A collapse

Although it is better not to divide words at the end of the writing line (a practice stemming from the old-fashioned idea that there should be an "even" right-hand margin in letters and other papers), there are nevertheless occasions when the division of a word at the end of a line is advisable or even necessary. Since a word should be divided only between syllables, and since a dictionary is not always at hand, the general rules of syllabication should be known.

What is a syllable? A syllable has been defined as several letters forming one sound uttered by a single impulse of the voice. Following this definition, we realize that *formed* is a one-syllable word because it is uttered with one impulse of the voice, whereas *seated*, a word with the same number of letters, is a two-syllable word because two impulses of the voice are required in its pronunciation.

Rule 1. Syllabication is determined by the pronunciation of the word. Let us take, for example, the word *occurrence*. Because we know that *ence* is a suffix, we might sensibly divide the word *oc-curr-ence*. However, we do not pronounce the word that way; we pronounce it *oc-cur-rence,* and the word is therefore syllabified that way. *In words accented on the first syllable,* the pronunciation of the word gives an excellent clue as to syllabication, for if the vowel sound is *long,* the syllable usually ends with the vowel; if the vowel sound is *short,* the vowel usually is followed by a consonant that will "close the syllable." Note the illustration of this rule in the following words:

mi-ser	mis-er-y
na-ture	nat-u-ral
e-vil	ev-i-dent
ro-bust	rob-ber
mu-sic	mus-lin

Notice that in the first column the first syllables end with vowels because the vowel sounds are long. In the second column, the syllables are "closed" by a consonant since the vowel sound is short.

Rule 2. Suffixes beginning with the sound of *sh—cion, cious, cian, cial, tion, tious, tial, sion, scious, sial*—cannot be divided.

Examples: ra-tion
con-scious
spe-cial

(Continued)

Rule 3. Double consonants within a word—that is, two *m's*, *s's*, *r's*, *t's*, etc.,—should be divided so that one consonant ends a syllable and the following consonant begins the next syllable, *unless the root word ends with a double consonant.*

Examples: per-mis-sion (root word is *permit*)
slum-ming (root word is *slum*)

but

cross-ing (root word is *cross*)
pass-able (root word is *pass*)

Rule 4. When two consecutive vowels within a word are pronounced separately, they should be divided into syllables.

Examples: re-al-i-ty   co-ag-u-late   cre-ate

Rule 5. Usually a prefix (or the last syllable of the prefix) is separated from the root word.

Examples: circum-vent   pre-dict
con-test   over-work
under-write

Rule 6. Usually a suffix (or the first syllable of the suffix) is separated from the root word.

Examples: home-less   kind-ness
spec-u-la-tive   grace-ful

Rule 7. Hyphenated words should be divided only at the hyhen.

Rule 8. Do not divide (a) titles or initials from a name, (b) the given name from the surname, or (c) the name of the month from the day of the month.

Wrong: . . . . . Mr.   Wrong: . . . . . September
Anderson   8
. . . . . T. L.
Jones

The reason for this rule is that misreading can easily occur when these important units of information are divided.

Rule 9. Do not divide from the rest of the word a one-letter or two-letter syllable at the end of the word or at the beginning of the word.

Rule 10. In case of doubt, check with the dictionary. This is a good rule to follow until you are accustomed to applying the rules.

Assume that you have come to the end of a writing line with three or four letters of each of the following words. Indicate the syllabication of the words and the points at which you would divide the words:

examination   experience   illusions   insinuation
intelligent   investigation   suggestion

4/28/69

A. Observe the words in the columns below. What relationship do you notice between their spelling and pronunciation? Give the rules involved.

most difficult

Letter *G*

change	giant	gate	ego
rage	ginger	agate	goat
huge	gist	regal	forego
gesture	nostalgic	legal	got
gelatin	ranging	toga	goal

Letter *C*

lace	racing	cat	coat
ceiling	medicine	called	raccoon
center	acid	broadcast	percolate
recent	facial	candy	second
racer	facility	practical	cocoa

B. List three words for each of the following prefixes: *ante, anti, ad, bene, bi, com, con, de, dia, en, dis, ex, fore, in, mis, per, pre, pro, re, sub, trans, un, under.*

C. List three words for each of the following suffixes: *able, ible, age, al, ant, ar, en, er, ful, or, ory, ary, ery, ious, ive, ness, tion.*

D. List five words that have both a prefix and a suffix, such as *enchantment, commendation.*

E. Correct the following sentences:

1. Jeans light hearted manner conceals a searching mind.
2. The food at Antoines is excellent, but the service is slow.
3. We stayed only at first class hotels, some with ill mannered guests.
4. Traveling to Capri by boat was a never to be forgotten experience.
5. Never-the-less, I would repeat the experience.
6. I was annoyed at him leaving so early.
7. Were you responsible for them giving the money away?
8. Mary says that the scarfs are her's.
9. In-as-much-as we knew the plans before they were launched, we should share the responsibility for the outcome.
10. The television's loud speaker should be replaced.
11. All of our data is here; were waiting for up to the minute facts and figures from Crawleys.
12. I heard that you hadnt left the country when word was received of Harolds death.
13. The Student Council is comprised of twenty five representatives from student organizations.
14. The council have announced their plan to increase the number from twenty five representatives to thirty five.
15. We believe that his continual arguing with his brother affected his health.

Many men and women who are aware of the importance of appearance are not aware of the importance of their speech. We have all known individuals who were careful about their dress and grooming, but who ruined that favorable first impression by slovenly speech, distinguished by words thoughtlessly selected and carelessly pronounced.

In the following lessons we are going to review the pronunciation and spelling of many names and words often mispronounced. It will be worth your while to master these words, because they are working words that you hear often and should be able to use correctly.

58 Relationship of pronunciation to spelling

We mentioned before that correct pronunciation aids in spelling. Some words are misspelled because letters are omitted in pronouncing them. Thus, "surprise" is sometimes spelled "suprise" and "candidate" is sometimes spelled "canidate," because the writer omits a sound in pronouncing them. Other words are misspelled because of the addition of extra sounds in pronouncing them. Thus, "height" is sometimes misspelled "heighth" because an "h" sound is added in pronouncing the word. "Athletic" is sometimes misspelled "athaletic" or "atheletic" because the extra syllable is added in pronouncing the word. Still other words are misspelled because certain letters are transposed in pronouncing them. Thus, "prescription" is sometimes misspelled "perscription," and "perform" is misspelled "preform" because they are pronounced incorrectly. Some words are misspelled because one letter is substituted for another in pronunciation. Thus, "congratulate" is sometimes spelled "congradulate" because a *d* is substituted for the *t* in pronunciation.

Another source of difficulty is the accent of the word. Sometimes two words which are spelled the same are pronounced differently. For example, *convert* is pronounced convert' when it is used as a verb and con'vert when it is used as a noun. Similarly, the noun *defect* is accented on the first syllable, whereas the verb *defect* is accented on the second syllable. This difference is typical of the distinction made in the pronunciation of two-syllable words used as both nouns and verbs. However, not all words are differentiated in this way; the word *address,* for instance, should be accented on the second syllable when it is used either as a noun or a verb. (And how many times we hear the accent on the first syllable!) These minor refinements of speech distinguish the person who speaks well from the mediocre speaker.

The most commonly mispronounced words in the English language are included in the following lessons. Practice pronouncing each word carefully, syllable by syllable, before pronouncing it fluently as a word;

then concentrate on the spelling of the word. If you are not sure of the correct pronunciation of a word, consult the dictionary. Do not guess about the pronunciation.

Some Basic Rules

Rule 1. Vowels in one-syllable words ending with consonants are usually short. Examples: *bag, but, get, sit, top.*

Rule 2. In open accented syllables, the vowel is usually long. This rule includes one-syllable words ending with vowels (*a, e, i, o, u, y*). Examples: *by, me, no, way, you.* Also: nō-tā-tion.

Rule 3. In one-syllable words, final ē lengthens the preceding vowel if only one consonant separates the final vowel from the preceding vowel.

bit—bite	glad—glade	plan—plane
cap—cape	kit—kite	rat—rate
cub—cube	met—mete	rob—robe
cut—cute	not—note	tap—tape

Rule 4. When a suffix beginning with a vowel is to be added to a one-syllable word ending with a consonant in which the short sound of the preceding vowel is to be retained, the final consonant is doubled.

cut—cutter, cutting
fit—fitter, fitting, fitted
get—getting
plan—planner, planning, planned
rob—robber, robbing, robbed

Rule 5. In two-syllable words, the final consonant is doubled before a suffix beginning with a vowel only if the accent is on the second syllable.

control—controlled, controller, controlling
patrol—patrolled, patrolling
regret—regretted, regretting

When the accent is on the first syllable the final consonant need not be doubled.

cancel—canceled, canceling
jewel—jeweled, jeweler
travel—traveled, traveling

Diphthongs and Digraphs

There has been brief mention of diphthongs and digraphs in other lessons.

The diphthongs are *oi, oy, ou, ow.* Closely related to diphthongs are vowel combinations such as *ya* (*yacht*) and *eu* (*engenics*). *I* and *au* are sometimes listed as diphthongs.

(Continued)

Digraphs include both vowel combinations and consonant combinations. The sounds of the vowel digraphs are *ai, ay, ei, ie, oa, oe, ow, ue, ew, ee, ea.* The sounds of the consonant digraphs are *sh, ch, tch, ck, th, wh, nk, ng;* some authorities call these "consonantal diphthongs."

In vowel digraphs, the first vowel is long and the second vowel is silent, as in:

beat	slay	lie	week	foe
rain	roast	cue	plea	low

That Troublemaker *ie* vs. *ei*

This is the place for our old jingle:

> "*I* before *e* except after *c*
> Save when pronounced as *a*
> As in *neighbor* or *weigh*."

The *ie* digraph often has the sound of ē, as in *niece, piece, fiend.* After *c*, the *ei* digraph has the sound of ē. Unrelated to the letter *c*, the *ei* digraph is frequently pronounced ā, as in *reign, neighbor, freight.* The digraph *ie* after *c* gives *c* the *sh* sound, as in *efficient, proficient, deficient.*

Syllabicate the following words, and then analyze the spelling of the syllables in relation to their pronunciation.

MR. TOPMAN told me to watch the SPELLING and he'd watch the FIGURES!

ache	humane
advantage	incomplete
adventure	inculcate
advice	independent
afraid	induce
again	nature
agitation	niece
airplane	parade
alike	past
alone	plain
alphabet	potato
also	procedure
appear	procure
beach	pumpkin
beginning	reign
bestow	reinstate
celebrate	reprieve
deficient	shining
despise	size
divide	speak
echo	story
escrow	supersede
excite	typewriter
hero	village
huge	weigh

Be sure you accent the right syllable. One of the most frequently occurring mistakes in pronunciation is that of accenting the wrong syllable. The following list contains the words most commonly mispronounced in this way.

abdomen	(ăb′ dō mĕn)	*n.* Section of body containing stomach.
address	(ăd drĕss′)	*n.* Speech; location.
		v. To speak to.
admirable	(ăd′ mĭ rȧ ble)	*adj.* Excellent.
adult	(ă dŭlt′)	*adj.* Mature.
		n. Matured person.
ally	(ăl′ lȳ)	*n.* Associate.
	(ăl lȳ′)	*v.* To join.
applicable	(ăp′ plĭ cȧ ble)	*adj.* Capable of being applied.
askance	(ȧ skănce′)	*adv.* Sideways.
comparable	(cŏm′ pȧ rȧ ble)	*adj.* Capable of being compared.
decoy	(dḗ coy′)	*n.* A lure, snare.
		v. To lure.
defect	(dē′ fĕct)	*n.* Deficiency, imperfection.
	(dḗ fĕct′)	*v.* To forsake; desert.
deficit	(dĕf′ ĭ çĭt)	*n.* A shortage.
discharge	(dĭs′ chärġe)	*n.* Unloading.
	(dĭs chärġe′)	*v.* To relieve of charge.
discourse	(dĭs′ cōurse)	*n.* Conversation.
	(dĭs cōurse′)	*v.* To speak.
exquisite	(ĕx′ qui ş̣ĭte) kwĭ	*adj.* Pleasing.
formidable	(fôr′ mĭ dȧ ble)	*adj.* Threatening.
hospitable	(hŏs′ pĭ tȧ ble)	*adj.* Welcoming to others.
infamous	(ĭn′ fȧ moŭs)	*adj.* Of bad report.
irreparable	(ĭr′ rĕp′ ȧ rȧ ble)	*adj.* Beyond repair.
positively	(pŏş′ ĭ tĭve lȳ)	*adj.* Definitely.
preferable	(prĕf′ ĕr ȧ ble)	*adj.* More desirable.
research	(rḗ sēarch′)	*n.* Diligent investigation.
		v. To seek out.
superfluous	(sṹ pēr′ flu oŭs)	*adj.* Surplus.

A. Consult your dictionary for the pronunciation and meaning of the following words:

    contrary   equitable   grimace   irrevocable   lamentable

B. Form sentences containing the following words:

    comparable deficit formidable infamous irreparable preferable

C. Which words in this lesson were unfamiliar to you? Write a sentence for each of these unfamiliar words.

Do not sound a letter or a syllable that does not exist. The words in this lesson are frequently mispronounced.

across	(à crŏss′)	adj.	On the other side.
athlete	(ăth′ lēte)	n.	A contender in physical games.
bracelet	(brāçe′ lĕt)	n.	Band worn about the arm.
broadcast	(brôad′ căst′, past tense, **not** broadcasted)	v.	Scattered; spread widely.
burst	(bûrst, past tense, **not** bursted)	v.	Exploded; broke suddenly.
crucial	(cru̧′ cial) shăl	adj.	Decisive; conclusive.
dreary	(drēar′ y̆)	adj.	Sad; gloomy.
drowned	(drowned) dround	v.	Past tense of drown; suffocated in water.
elm	(ĕlm, **not** el um)	n.	A tree.
evening	(ēve′ nĭng)	n.	Latter part of the day.
facial	(fā′ cial) shăl	adj.	Pertaining to the face.
film	(fĭlm, **not** fil um)	n.	A thin layer.
foundry	(foun′ dry̆)	n.	A building for casting.
grievous	(griēv′ ŏus)	adj.	Distressing; severe.
heartrending	(heärt′ rĕnd′ ĭng, **not** rendering)	adj.	Causing grief.
hindrance	(hĭn′ drănce)	n.	That which hinders; obstacle.
laundry	(laun′ dry̆)	n.	A washing; place for washing.
lightning	(līght′ nĭng)	n.	Discharge of electricity from clouds.
mischievous	(mĭs′ chĭe voŭs)	adj.	Naughty.
once	(once) wŭns	adv.	At one time.
racial	(rā′ cial) shăl	adj.	Pertaining to a race.
remembrance	(ré̆ mĕm′ brănce)	n.	Recollection; a reminder.
rigmarole	(rĭg′ mȧ rōle)	n.	Foolish statements; rambling talk.
toward	(tō′ ward) ērd	prep.	In the direction of.
umbrella	(ŭm brĕl′ lȧ)	n.	A guard against rain.

A. Consult your dictionary for the pronunciation and meaning of the following words:

disastrous   ingenious   lozenge   palatial   transient

B. Form sentences containing the following words:

burst   crucial   grievous   hindrance   mischievous

Sound every letter and every syllable that should be sounded. Practice the pronunciation of these words, sounding every syllable and letter distinctly.

abominable	(à bŏm′ ĭ nà ble)	*adj.*	Detestable; loathsome.
actually	(ăc′ tŭ ăl *lў*)	*adv.*	In fact; really.
arctic	(ärc′ tĭc)	*adj.*	Relating to the north pole.
bachelor	(băch′ ĕ lŏr)	*n.*	A man who has not married.
bakery	(bāk′ ĕr ў)	*n.*	A place for baking.
boundary	(bound′ à rў)	*n.*	That which fixes a limit.
collegiate	(cŏ*l* lē′ ġĭ ate)	*adj.*	Pertaining to a college.
	ĭt		
definitely	(dĕf′ ĭ n*ĭte* lў)	*adv.*	Distinctly; certainly.
delivery	(dé lĭv′ ĕr ў)	*n.*	Act of delivering.
deteriorate	(dé tēr′ ĭ ō rāte)	*v.*	To grow worse.
elementary	(ĕl′ ĕ mĕn′ tà rў)	*adj.*	Pertaining to first principles.
family	(făm′ ĭ lў)	*n.*	Parents and children.
February	(Fĕb′ ru ar′ ў)	*n.*	Second month of the year.
	rŏŏ ĕr′		
government	(gŏv′ ĕrn mĕnt)	*n.*	Direction of affairs of state.
literature	(lĭt′ ĕr à tŭre)	*n.*	Literary productions.
regular	(rĕg′ ŭ lär)	*adj.*	Conforming to rule or rules.
statistics	(stà tĭs′ tĭcs)	*n.*	Facts classified in number.
strength	(strĕngth, **not** strenth)	*n.*	Force, power.
temperament	(tĕm′ pĕr à mĕnt)	*n.*	Disposition.
variegated	(vâr′ ĭ ĕ gāt′ ĕd)	*adj.*	Having different colors.

The British clip some words short, as "cemetry" for "cemetery." The following words are also clipped by the British. You should use the full American pronunciation.

dictionary	(dĭc′ tion ar′ ў)	*n.*	A book containing words.
	ĕr′		
interested	(ĭn′ tĕr ĕst ĕd)	*adj.*	Having an interest.
military	(mĭl′ ĭ tar′ ў)	*adj.*	Pertaining to soldiers.
	tĕr′		
secretary	(sĕc′ ré tar′ ў)	*n.*	One who attends to letters.
	tĕr′		
territory	(tĕr′ *r*ĭ tō′ rў)	*n.*	An extent of land.

After checking the pronunciation and meaning of the following words in the dictionary, use them in sentences:

boisterous	invariably	liable	poinsettia	theory
conduit	ivory	miniature	quandary	vegetable

Do not sound silent letters. All the words in this lesson contain silent letters, that is, letters that are not pronounced. Silent letters are printed in italics. Be careful not to pronounce these letters when saying the words.

almond	(äl' mȯnd)	*n.*	A tree; a nut.
alms	(älms)	*n.*	A gift to the poor.
asthma	(ăşth' må)	*n.*	A disease characterized by difficulty of breathing.
buffet	(buf fet') boŏ fä'	*n.*	A sideboard; a cupboard.
chasten	(chās' *t*en)	*v.*	To discipline; to punish.
chestnut	(chĕs*t*' nŭt)	*n.*	A tree; a nut.
christen	(chrĭs' *t*en)	*v.*	To baptize; to name.
cupboard	(cŭ*p*' boărd)	*n.*	Closet for dishes.
epistle	(ĕ pĭs' *t*le)	*n.*	A letter.
forehead	(fŏre' hĕad)	*n.*	The face above the eyes.
glisten	(glĭs' *t*en)	*v.*	To sparkle or shine.
hasten	(hās' *t*en)	*v.*	To urge forward; to hurry.
herb	(*h*ĕrb)	*n.*	A plant used for flavor.
indict	(ĭn dīc*t*')	*v.*	To charge with an offense.
kiln	(kĭl*n*)	*n.*	A furnace for burning or drying.
moisten	(mois' *t*en)	*v.*	To make moist.
often	(ôf' *t*ĕn)	*adv.*	Frequently.
parliament	(pär' lĭ*a* mĕnt)	*n.*	A legislative body.
raspberry	(răs*p*' bĕr r*y̆*)	*n.*	A berry and its plant.
salmon	(să*l*m' ȯn)	*n.*	A large fish.
solder	(sŏ*l*' dẽr)	*n.*	A metal used to join other metals.
subtle	(sŭ*b*' tle)	*adj.*	Cunning; crafty; artful.
vehicle	(vē' *h*ĭ cle)	*n.*	A conveyance.
Wednesday	(Wĕd*n*eş' da*y̆*)	*n.*	The fourth day of the week.
yolk	(yō*l*k)	*n.*	The yellow part of an egg.

A. Consult your dictionary for the pronunciation and meaning of the following words:

    corps   debris   debut   qualm   victuals

B. Form sentences containing the following words:

    buffet   epistle   indict   subtle   vehicle

C. Write ten sentences containing words in which a consonant is silent. In each sentence underscore the word containing the silent consonant(s).

Be careful about the sounds of your vowels. In each of the following words a vowel is frequently mispronounced. In some words a short vowel is given a long sound; in others a long vowel is given a short sound. Pronounce each word correctly a number of times.

again	(ȧ gain´) gĕn´	*adv.* Another time.
alias	(ā´ lĭ ȧs)	*n.* An assumed name.
apparatus	(ăp´ pȧ rā´ tŭs)	*n.* A complex instrument.
apricot	(ā´ prĭ cŏt)	*n.* A fruit.
aviator	(ā´ vĭ ā´ tŏr)	*n.* Pilot or other person flying a plane.
bayou	(ba´ you)	*n.* Inlet from gulf, lake, or river.
bouquet	(bou quet´) bī´ ōo	*n.* A bunch of flowers.
	bōō kā´	
brooch	(brōoch)	*n.* Ornamental dress clasp.
can	(căn, **not** kin)	*v.* Able to.
catch	(cătch, **not** ketch)	*v.* Take captive.
column	(cŏl´ ŭm*n*)	*n.* Anything pillar-shaped.
coupon	(cou´ pŏn) kōō´	*n.* A section of a certificate or ticket.
creek	(crēēk)	*n.* A small stream of water.
data	(dā´ tȧ)	*n.* Facts.
deaf	(dĕaf)	*adj.* Unable to hear.
de luxe	(dĕ́ luxe´) lōoks´	*adj.* Luxurious.
demise	(dĕ́ mīṣe´)	*n.* Death.
discretion	(dĭs crē̆´ tion)	*n.* Prudence; caution.
err	(err, pronounced ûr, **not** air)	*v.* To make a mistake.
finance	(fĭ nănce´)	*n.* Money management.
food	(fōōd)	*n.* Edibles.
genuine	(ġĕn´ ū ĭne)	*adj.* Not counterfeit; real.
granary	(grăn´ ȧ rў̆)	*n.* A storehouse for grain.
gratis	(gră´ tĭs)	*adj.* For nothing; free.

A. Consult your dictionary for the pronunciation and meaning of the following words:

apropos   buoy   cinema   donor   homage

B. Form sentences containing the following words:

alias   data   de luxe   demise   finance

C. Write ten sentences containing words in which a vowel is frequently mispronounced. In each sentence, underscore the word in which a vowel causes difficulty in pronunciation.

This lesson is a continuation of the previous lesson, advising you to *be careful about the sounds of your vowels*. In each of the following words a vowel is frequently mispronounced. Practice the correct pronunciation of the words.

inquiry	(ĭn quir′ ў) kwĭr′	*n.*	A question; an investigation.
just	(jŭst, **not** jest)	*adj.*	Fair.
liaison	(li′ āi ̤ôn′) lē′	*n.*	Connection.
lingerie	(lin′ ge rie′) lăn′ zh′ rē′	*n.*	Underwear for women.
long-lived	(lŏng′-līved′)	*adj.*	Having a long life.
menu	(mĕn′ ū)	*n.*	Bill of fare.
naïve	(nä ïve′) ĕv′	*adj.*	Simple; artless.
pathos	(pā′ thŏs)	*n.*	That quality which excites pity.
penalize	(pē′ năl īze)	*v.*	To exact a penalty.
peony	(pē′ ŏ nў)	*n.*	A flower.
radiator	(rā′ dĭ ā′ tŏr)	*n.*	That which radiates (heat or cool air).
reptile	(rĕp′ tĭle)	*n.*	Animal that crawls on its stomach.
robot	(rō′ bŏt)	*n.*	Mechanical man.
roof	(ro͞of)	*n.*	Cover of a building.
status	(stā′ tŭs)	*n.*	State; condition.
subsidiary	(sŭb sĭd′ ĭ ar′ ў) ĕr′	*n.*	An auxiliary.
suburb	(sŭb′ ûrb)	*n.*	Outskirts of city.
supple	(sŭp′ ple)	*adj.*	Soft; flexible; yielding.
tepid	(tĕp′ ĭd)	*adj.*	Lukewarm.
textile	(tĕx′ tĭle)	*n.*	A woven fabric.
verbatim	(vĕr bā′ tĭm)	*adv.*	Word for word.

A. Consult your dictionary for the pronunciation and meaning of the following words:

> morale   mousse   patronize   strata   ultimatum

B. Use the following words in sentences:

> long-lived   pathos   penalize   reptile   suburb

This list contains the most frequently mispronounced and misspelled words in Lessons 58 to 64 inclusive. Review the pronunciation as well as the spelling of these words.

admirable	granary
apparatus	hasten
arctic	indict
asthma	inquiry
athlete	irreparable
boisterous	irrevocable
boundary	kiln
bouquet	laundry
buffet	literature
chestnut	lozenge
column	mischievous
comparable	parliament
conduit	pathos
corps	poinsettia
coupon	qualm
cupboard	quandary
data	raspberry
debris	rigmarole
deficit	statistics
deteriorate	status
donor	supersede
epistle	temperament
equitable	textile
finance	transient
foundry	ultimatum

66 Words often mispronounced (Continued)

Watch your consonants! The words below contain consonants that sometimes give trouble: notice that *g* followed by *i*, *e*, or *y* usually has the *j* sound; *g* followed by *a* or *u* has the *gay* sound. Notice that *ch* sometimes has the *k* sound, sometimes the *sh* sound, and then again the regular *ch* sound.

agenda	(ȧ ġĕn′ dȧ)	*n.* List of things to be done.
archipelago	(är′ c*h*ĭ pĕl′ ȧ gō)	*n.* Group of islands.
architect	(är′ c*h*ĭ tĕct)	*n.* One who plans buildings.
archives	(är′c*h*īves)	*n.* Public records.
brochure	(brṓ chure′) shŏŏr′	*n.* A pamphlet.
chandelier	(chan′ dĕ liēr′) shăn′	*n.* A light fixture.
chiropodist	(c*h*ī rŏp′ ṓ dĭst)	*n.* One who treats hands and feet.
congratulate	(cŏn grăt′ ṹ lāte)	*v.* To wish joy.
diphtheria	(dĭph thē′ rĭ ȧ)	*n.* A disease of the throat.
giblets	(ġĭb′ lĕts)	*n.* Gizzard, heart, and liver of fowl.
gigantic	(ġī găn′ tĭc)	*adj.* Huge.
gist	(ġĭst)	*n.* The main point.
kindergarten	(kĭn′ dẽr gär′ tĕn)	*n.* School for small children.
length	(lĕngth, **not** lenth)	*n.* State of being long in space or time.
naphtha	(năph′ thȧ)	*n.* A flammable liquid.
niche	(nĭche)	*n.* Recess in a wall, usually for a statue.
picture	(pĭc′ tṹre)	*n.* Representation in art or words.
quantity	(quan′ tĭ tў̆) kwŏn′	*n.* An amount; a portion.
sword	(s*w*ōrd)	*n.* Weapon; rapier.
towards	(tō′ wards) ẽrds	*prep.* In the direction of.

A. Consult your dictionary for the pronunciation and meaning of the following words:

chaotic **diphthong** **fungi** **regime** **specie**

B. Form sentences containing the following words:

agenda **brochure** **chiropodist** **gist** **naphtha**

C. Copy each of the following words and underscore the letter sometimes omitted in error:

aqueduct	**climactic**	**government**	**recognize**
cataract	**February**	**library**	**surprise**

Watch the vowels, consonants, and accents in the following miscellaneous list of words that are frequently mispronounced.

auxiliary	(aux ĭl′ ia rў) ôg zĭl′ yà	*adj.* Helping. *n.* An assistant.
blasé	(blä se′) zā′	*adj.* Surfeited; indifferent.
boudoir	(bou′ doir) bōō′ dwär	*n.* A lady's bedroom.
carillon	(cär′ ĭl lŏn)	*n.* A set of bells.
cello	(cel′ lō) chĕl′	*n.* A musical instrument.
combatant	(cŏm′ bàt ănt)	*n.* A fighter.
connoisseur	(cŏn′ noĭs seûr′)	*n.* A critical judge of art.
consommé	(côn′ sŏm me′) mä′	*n.* A light-colored clear soup.
corsage	(côr sage′) säzh′	*n.* A bouquet worn by a girl or a woman.
decade	(dĕc′ āde)	*n.* A period of ten years.
drought	(drou*gh*t)	*n.* Dry weather; lack of rain.
facsimile	(făc sĭm′ ĭ lē)	*n.* An exact copy.
fiancé	(fĭ′ än cé′) fē′ sā′	*n.* Man engaged to be married.
fiancée	(fĭ′ än cée′) fē′ sā′	*n.* Woman engaged to be married.
finale	(fĭ nä′ le) fé′ lá′	*n.* Concluding part.
licorice	(lĭc′ ŏ rĭçe)	*n.* A dried root and its extract.
maintenance	(māin′ tĕ nănçe)	*n.* Act of maintaining; support.
massacre	(măs′ sà cre) kĕr′	*n.* Wholesale slaughter.
oblique	(ŏb lique′) lēk′	*adj.* Slanting; inclined.
pianist	(pĭ ăn′ ĭst)	*n.* One who plays the piano.
prestige	(prĕs tige′) tēzh′	*n.* Weight; influence.
rendezvous	(ren′ dez vous) rän′ dĕ vōō	*n.* A place of meeting.
route	(route) rōōt	*n.* The way or path to be traveled.
suede	(suede) swād	*n.* A kind of leather.
tacit	(tăç′ ĭt)	*adj.* Unspoken; implied.
theater	(thē′ à tēr)	*n.* A place for dramatic performances.
zoology	(zŏ ŏl′ ŏ ġў)	*n.* The science of animals.

A. Consult your dictionary for the pronunciation and meaning of the following words:

askance	buoy	encore	massage	quay
bouillon	cuisine	idea	naïve	risqué

B. Form sentences containing the following words:

auxiliary	boudoir	finale	oblique	tacit
blasé	cello	maintenance	prestige	theater

Each of the following words, when accented on one syllable, is used as one part of speech; but, when accented on another syllable, is used as a different part of speech.

absent	(ăb′ sĕnt)	*adj.* Not present.
	(ăb sĕnt′)	*v.* To withdraw (oneself).
accent	(ăc′ çĕnt)	*n.* A mark of emphasis.
	(ăc çĕnt′)	*v.* To emphasize.
compound	(cŏm′ pound)	*adj.* Not simple. *n.* A mixture.
	(cŏm pound′)	*v.* To mix.
concert	(cŏn′ çērt)	*n.* A musical entertainment.
	(cŏn çērt′)	*v.* To plan together.
conduct	(cŏn′ dŭct)	*n.* Behavior.
	(cŏn dŭct′)	*v.* To guide.
conflict	(cŏn′ flĭct)	*n.* A struggle.
	(cŏn flĭct′)	*v.* To oppose.
contract	(cŏn′ trăct)	*n.* An agreement.
	(cŏn trăct′)	*v.* To agree; to reduce.
escort	(ĕs′ côrt)	*n.* A guard.
	(ĕs côrt′)	*v.* To accompany.
export	(ĕx′ pōrt)	*n.* Something sent out.
	(ĕx pōrt′)	*v.* To send out.
extract	(ĕx′ trăct)	*n.* An essence.
	(ĕx trăct′)	*v.* To draw out.
import	(ĭm′ pōrt)	*n.* Something brought in.
	(ĭm pōrt′)	*v.* To bring in.
increase	(ĭn′ crēase)	*n.* An addition.
	(ĭn crēase′)	*v.* To enlarge.
object	(ŏb′ jĕct)	*n.* A tangible thing.
	(ŏb jĕct′)	*v.* To oppose.
permit	(pẽr′ mĭt)	*n.* Permission.
	(pẽr mĭt′)	*v.* To allow.
progress	(prŏg′ rĕss)	*n.* Forward movement.
	(prŏ grĕss′)	*v.* To advance.
rebel	(rĕb′ ĕl)	*adj.* Rebellious. *n.* One in rebellion.
	(rĕ bĕl′)	*v.* To revolt.
record	(rĕc′ ŏrd)	*n.* Something written.
	(rĕ côrd′)	*v.* To write.
subject	(sŭb′ jĕct)	*adj.* Liable; prone. *n.* One under authority.
	(sŭb jĕct′)	*v.* To expose to.
transfer	(trăns′ fẽr)	*n.* A removal.
	(trăns fẽr′)	*v.* To change from.

A. Consult your dictionary for the pronunciation and meaning of the following words:

abstract	compact	digest	invalid	refuse

B. Complete each sentence by filling in a word from this lesson. Be careful to accent the right syllable.

1. He acted as her (   ) to the dance.
2. The secretary will (   ) the motion.
3. You should ask for a (   ) when you leave the bus.
4. The dentist will (   ) the tooth.
5. Coffee is an (   ) from Brazil.
6. The cold weather made the iron bar (   ).
7. Does the school expect an (   ) in its enrollment?
8. Ask the manager for a (   ) to visit the plant.
9. The people will (   ) against such tyranny.
10. You should (   ) the second syllable.
11. He offered to (   ) Jim through the factory.
12. He is likely to (   ) himself from the meeting.

69   Words having two pronunciations (Continued)

Here are a number of additional words that are used as one part of speech when accented on one syllable, but as a different part of speech when accented on another syllable.

collect	(cŏl′ lĕct)	n. A prayer.
	(col lĕct′)	v. To gather.
console	(cŏn′ sōle)	n. An architectural ornament.
	(cŏn sōle′)	v. To comfort.
content	(cŏn′ tĕnt)	n. That which is contained.
	(cŏn tĕnt′)	adj. Satisfied.
contest	(cŏn′ tĕst)	n. A struggle.
	(cŏn tĕst′)	v. To struggle.
convict	(cŏn′ vĭct)	n. One under prison sentence.
	(cŏn vĭct′)	v. To find guilty.
convoy	(cŏn′ voy)	n. An escort.
	(cŏn voy′)	v. To escort.
desert	(dĕṣ′ ẽrt)	n. A solitary place.
	(dĕ́ ṣẽrt′)	v. To leave; to abandon.
ferment	(fẽr′ mĕnt)	n. Tumult; fermentation.
	(fẽr mĕnt′)	v. To undergo fermentation.
forecast	(fōre′ càst′)	n. A prophecy.
	(fōre càst′)	v. To foretell.
imprint	(ĭm′ prĭnt)	n. Something printed.
	(ĭm prĭnt′)	v. To impress or print.
incline	(ĭn′ clīne)	n. An inclined plane.
	(ĭn clīne′)	v. To lean or bend.
insert	(ĭn′ sẽrt)	n. A thing placed between.
	(ĭn sẽrt′)	v. To place between.
insult	(ĭn′ sŭlt)	n. An affront.
	(ĭn sŭlt′)	v. To affront.
perfume	(pẽr′ fūme)	n. A pleasant odor.
	(pẽr fūme′)	v. To fill with a sweet odor.
present	(prĕṣ′ ĕnt)	n. A gift.
	(prĕ́ ṣĕnt′)	v. To offer as a gift.

(Continued)

produce	(prŏd′ ūçe)	*n.* Agricultural products.
	(prŏ dūçe′)	*v.* To make.
project	(prŏj′ ĕct)	*n.* A plan.
	(prŏ jĕct′)	*v.* To extend.
protest	(prō′ tĕst)	*n.* A declaration against.
	(prŏ tĕst′)	*v.* To declare against.
refuse	(rĕf′ ūṣe)	*n.* Rubbish.
	(rĕ fūṣe′)	*v.* To decline.
reprint	(rē′ prĭnt′)	*n.* A second or later printing.
	(rē prĭnt′)	*v.* To print again.

An "s" is added to each of the following words when the word is given the meaning indicated by the first definition:

confines	(cŏn′ fīneṣ)	*n.* Boundaries.
	(cŏn fīne′)	*v.* To keep within limits.
proceeds	(prō′ çēedṣ)	*n.* The results from a transaction.
	(prŏ çēed′)	*v.* To move forward.

A. Consult your dictionary for the pronunciation and meaning of the following words:

attribute   consort   entrance   incense   purport

B. Complete each of the following sentences by filling in a word from this lesson. Be careful to accent the right syllable.

1. This book is a (   ) of the first edition.
2. The workmen gathered the (   ) that was scattered around the lawn.
3. Most of the European nations agreed to the (   ).
4. Be sure to (   ) a circular in each envelope.
5. The (   ) was sunk by a submarine.
6. The retailer bought his (   ) from a farmer.
7. The minister tried to (   ) the widow.
8. What is the weather (   ) for the week?
9. I will (   ) my talk to ten minutes.
10. The merchant was (   ) with the profit he made.
11. Every effort was made to capture the escaped (   ).

The following words may be pronounced in more than one way. Authorities differ as to the preferred pronunciation.

abdomen	(ăb' dŏ mĕn)	or (ăb dō' mĕn)	n.
advertisement	(ăd' vĕr tīse' mĕnt)	or (ăd vĕr'tĭse mĕnt)	n.
centenary	(çĕn tĕn' à rў)	or (çĕn' tế nār' ў)	adj. and n.
chaperon	(çhăp' ẽr ōn)	or (çhăp' ẽr ôn)	n. and v.
contemplate	(cŏn'tĕm plāte)	or (cŏn tĕm' plāte)	v.
depot	(dĕ' pōt)	or (dĕ' pŏt)	n.
envelope	(ĕn' vĕ lōpe)	or (en' vĕ lōpe) or (ĕn vĕl' ȯpe)	n. and v.
		ŏn'	
extraordinary	(ĕx traôr' dĭ nār' ў)	or (ĕx' trà ôr' dĭ nĕr' ў)	adj.
hygiene	(hў' ġiene)	or (hў' ġĩ ēne)	n.
illustrate	(ĭl' lŭs trāte)	or (ĭl lŭs' trāte)	v.
isolate	(ī' sŏ lāte)	or (ĭs' ō lāte)	v.
juvenile	(jụ' vế nĭle)	or (jụ' vế nĭle)	adj. and n.
leisure	(lēi' sure)	or (lei' sure)	n. and adj.
	zhẽr	lĕzh' úre	
lenient	(lē' nĭ ĕnt)	or (le' ni ent)	adj.
		lēn' yĕnt	
ordeal	(ôr dēal')	or (ôr dē'ăl)	n.
patronage	(pā' trȯn age)	or (păt' rȯn age)	n.
	ĭj	ĭj	
prelude	(prĕl' ūde)	or (pre' lūde)	n. and v.
		prā'	
recess	(rē' çĕss)	or (rế çĕss')	n. and v.
turbine	(tûr' bĭne)	or (tûr' bīne)	n.

A. Consult your dictionary for the pronunciation and meaning of the following words. Which of the two pronunciations for each word is preferred by your dictionary?

economics   lever   strategic   surveillance   valet

B. Complete each of the following sentences by filling in a word from this lesson.

1. The boy was tried in the (   ) court.
2. I saw the price in a newspaper (   ).
3. Does the teacher (   ) resigning?
4. We met in a railroad (   ).
5. Harry seems to have a great deal of (   ) time.
6. The letter was enclosed in an (   ).
7. She was invited to (   ) the school party.
8. The picture will be used to (   ) the story.
9. The Senator was in control of the political (   ).
10. War is always a terrible (   ).
11. While in school, she studies home (   ).
12. The suspected criminal was kept under close (   ).

This lesson contains the most frequently mispronounced and misspelled words in Lessons 66 to 70 inclusive.

Words often mispronounced

agenda	brochure	drought	naphtha
aqueduct	chandelier	encore	oblique
archipelago	chaotic	facsimile	rendezvous
architect	chiropodist	kindergarten	suede
auxiliary	climactic	maintenance	tacit
bouillon	connoisseur	massacre	zoology

Words having two pronunciations

Be sure you know the meaning of each word in the following list (1) when it is accented on the first syllable, and (2) when it is accented on the second syllable.

absent	convict	import	progress
accent	convoy	incense	project
attribute	entrance	invalid	protest
conduct	escort	perfume	purport
conflict	extract	permit	refuse
consort	forecast	proceeds	transfer

Use the following words in sentences.

advertisement	extraordinary	isolate	lenient
chaperon	hygiene	juvenile	patronage
envelope	illustrate	leisure	recess

72 Names of well-known persons of the twentieth century *

Only names that are likely to be mispronounced are included in this list of well-known men and women who have lived in the twentieth century, or whose life-span has overlapped this century.

Baruch, Bernard	(Bä ruch′) rōōk′	American economist.
Brandeis, Louis	(Brăn′ deīs)	American jurist.
Callas, Maria	(Căl′ lăs)	Greek soprano.
Chiang Kai-shek	(Chi äng′ Kaī′-shĕk′) jĕ	Chinese general and statesman.
Curie, Marie	(Cŭ riē′)	French (Polish born) chemist.
Dostoevski, Feodor	(Dŏs to ev′ skĭ) tŭ yĕf′	Russian novelist.

---

* With one exception—Alfred Nobel belongs to the nineteenth century, but his name lives on because of the Nobel Peace Prize.

Freud, Sigmund	(Freud) froid	Austrian neurologist; father of phychoanalysis.
Gandhi, Mohandas	(Gän′ d*h*ĭ)	Indian political and religious leader.
Hirohito	(Hi rŏ hi′ tō) hē hē′	Emperor of Japan (1926-).
Jung, Carl	(Jung) yŏong	Swiss psychiatrist.
Klee, Paul	(Klee) klā	Swiss painter.
Khrushchev, Nikita	(Khrush′ chev) krŏŏsh′ chŏf	Political leader, U. S. S. R.
Mao Tse-tung	(Mä′ ŏ Tse′-tung′) dzĕ′ dŏong′	Chinese communist leader.
Maugham, W. Somerset	(Maugham) môm	English dramatist and novelist.
Mussolini, Benito	(Mus sŏ li′ ni) mŏŏ lē′ nĕ	Italian Fascist leader.
Nehru, Jawaharlal	(Neh′ ru) nä′ rŏŏ	First prime minister of India.
Nobel, Alfred	(Nŏ bĕl′)	Swedish inventor, donor of the Nobel Peace Prize.
Paderewski, Ignace	(Pä dĕ rew′ skĭ) rĕf′	Polish pianist.
Pavlova, Anna	(Păv′ lŏ và)	Russian ballerina.
Peron, Juan	(Pe rôn′) pä	President of Argentina (1946-1955).
Proust, Marcel	(Proust) prŏŏst	French novelist.
Roosevelt, Franklin D.	(Roose′ vĕlt) rŏ′ zĕ	President of the United States (1933-1945).
Sibelius, Jean J.	(Sĭ be′lĭ us) bā′ ŏŏs	Finnish composer.
Stalin, Josef	(Stä′ lĭn)	Russian communist leader.
Tagore, Rabindranath	(Tä′ gŏre)	Indian poet, novelist, and dramatist.
Tito, Marshal	(Ti′ tō) tē′	Yugoslav communist leader.
U Thant	(U Thànt)	Secretary General of the United Nations (1961-).
Yeats, William Butler	(Yeāts)	Irish poet.

Substitute names in this lesson for blanks in the following sentences. Practice reading the sentences, making sure that you can pronounce the names correctly.

1. Have you ever heard C_____ sing?
2. Some art critics believe that K_____ is one of the greatest Swiss painters.
3. *Crime and Punishment,* written by D_____, is one of the best-known Russian novels.
4. G_____, the great Hindu mystic, will doubtless be considered by historians as one of the great men of our century.
5. F_____ is sometimes called the father of modern psychiatry.
6. B_____, the American economist, has been adviser to many presidents of the United States.
7. K_____, leader of the Soviet regime, was a farmer before he entered politics.
8. Judge B_____ helped many young men to achieve distinction as lawyers and jurists.
9. U T_____ succeeded Dag Hammersjkold, Swedish Secretary General of the United Nations, killed in Africa.
10. The beautiful music of Jean S_____ suggests the tranquil beauty of Finland.

Aesop	(Aē′ sŏp)	Greek writer of fables (620-560 B.C.).
Aristotle	(Ăr′ ĭs tŏt le)	Greek philosopher (384-322 B.C.).
Descartes, Rene	(Des cärt*es*′) dā	French philosopher and mathematician (1596-1650 A.D.).
Goethe (von), Johann	(von Goe′ *th*ĕ) fôn gŭ′	German author (1749-1832 A.D.).
Gogh (van), Vincent	(văn Gō*gh*)	Dutch painter (1853-1890 A.D.).
Michelangelo	(Mī *ch*ĕl ăn′ ġĕ lō)	Italian sculptor, artist (1475-1564 A.D.).
Omar Khayyam	(Ō′ mär Khay yäm′) kī	Persian poet (? -1123 A.D.).
Pasteur, Louis	(Păs teûr′)	French chemist (1822-1895 A.D.).
Plato	(Plā′ tō)	Greek philosopher (427-347 B.C.).
Pepys, Samuel	(Pēpys)	English writer (1633-1703 A.D.).
Sappho	(Sap′ *ph*ō) săf′	Greek poetess (? -600 B.C.).
Shakespeare, William	(Shāk*e*′ spēare)	English dramatist, poet (1564-1616 A.D.).
Socrates	(Sŏc′ rà tēş)	Greek philosopher; Plato's teacher (469-399 B.C.)
Stradivari, Antonio	(Strä di vä′ ri) dĕ rĕ	Italian violinmaker (1644-1737 A.D.).
Vinci (da), Leonardo	(dä Vin′ ci) vĕn′ chĕ	Italian artist, engineer, and scientist (1452-1519 A.D.).
Wagner, Richard	(Wag′ nēr) väg′	German composer, originator of the music drama (1813-1883 A.D.).

Insert the appropriate names in the following sentences:

1. The French philosopher, D_____, was interested in proving the existence of God by scientific methods.
2. S_____ was a Greek poetess who lived on the island of Lesbos.
3. We can drink milk without fear of contamination, thanks to Louis P_____.
4. Tourists from every part of the world go to Rome to see M_____'s paintings in the Sistine Chapel.
5. P_____'s *Dialogues* are read widely by rulers in every country, as well as by philosophers.
6. S_____'s plays have been translated into all of the major languages.
7. O_____ K_____, urging us in his poetry to enjoy today and to forget tomorrow's worries, gives us good poetry but poor advice.
8. S_____, the Greek philosopher, is remembered for his method of teaching by questioning.
9. Vincent v_____ G_____ was a prolific painter, but he led a tragic life.
10. Richard W_____'s operas combine music and drama to the advantage of both.

The following names of places are well known to men and women who have traveled or read widely, but they are likely to be mispronounced or misspelled. Learn their pronunciation and the location of the places. (These words are all proper nouns.)

Within the United States and its possessions

Albuquerque	(Ăl′ bŭ quer′ que)	City in New Mexico.
	kûr′ kḗ	
Annapolis	(Ăn năp′ ỏ lĭs)	Capital of Maryland; location of the U. S. Naval Academy.
Arkansas	(Är′ kăn sas)	South-central state of the United States.
	sô	
Asheville	(Ăshe′ vĭlle)	City in North Carolina.
Baton Rouge	(Băt′ on Rouge′) rōōzh′	Capital of Louisiana.
Bayonne	(Bā yŏnne′)	City in New Jersey.
Boise	(Boi′ se)	Capital of Idaho.
	boy′ sĭ	
Cape Canaveral	(Cāpe Cà năv′ ĕr ăl)	Missile-launching base in Florida.
Chattanooga	(Chăt′ tà nōō′ gà)	City in Tennessee.
Cheyenne	(Chey ĕnne′) shī	Capital of Wyoming.
Cincinnati	(Cĭn cĭn năt′ ĭ)	City in Ohio.
Des Moines	(Dĕs moines′)	City in Iowa.
Detroit	(Dĕ troit′)	Industrial city in Michigan.
Duquesne	(Du quesne′) dōō kān′	City in Pennsylvania.
El Paso	(Ĕl Păs′ ō)	City in Texas.
Gloucester	(Glouces′ tĕr)	City in Massachusetts.
Greenwich	(Grēen′ wĭch)	City in Connecticut.
Hawaii	(Hä waī′ ĭ)	State of the U. S. located in the Pacific.
	ḗ	
Honolulu	(Hō′ nỏ lu′ lu)	Capital of Hawaii.
	lōō′ lōō	
Illinois	(Ĭl′ lĭ nois′)	Midwestern state.
Iowa	(Ī′ ỏ wà)	Midwestern state.
Los Angeles	(Lŏs Ăn′ ġĕ lēs)	Largest city in California.
Miami	(Mī ăm′ ĭ)	City in Florida.
Mojave	(Mỏ ja′ vĕ)	Desert in western part of the United States.
	hä′	
Nevada	(Nĕ văd′ à)	Western state.
New Orleans	(New Ôr′ lḗ ănş)	City in Louisiana.
Palo Alto	(Păl′ ō Ăl′ tō)	City in California.
Pittsburgh	(Pĭtts′ bûrgh)	Industrial city in Pennsylvania.
Poughkeepsie	(Pōugh keep sĭe)	City in New York.
	kĭp	
Pueblo	(Pú ĕb′ lō)	City in Colorado.
Puerto Rico	(Puer′ tō Ri′ cō)	Island in West Indies.
	pwĕr′ rē′	
Reading	(Rĕad′ ĭng)	City in Pennsylvania.
San Jose	(Săn Jo se′) hō zā′	City in California.
Schenectady	(Sche nĕc′ tà dy)	City in New York.
	skĕ dē	
Spokane	(Spō′ kăne)	City in Washington.
Terre Haute	(Tĕr′rĕ Haute)	City in Indiana.
	hōt	
Tucson	(Tuc sŏn′)	Resort city in Arizona.
	tōō	
Worcester	(Worces′ tĕr)	City in Massachusetts.
	wŏŏs′	
Yosemite	(Yỏ sĕm′ ĭ tḗ)	National park in California.

In the previous lesson, we reviewed the names of some well-known cities and states in the United States. In this lesson, we shall consider the names of some places in foreign lands frequently mentioned in books and in conversation.

Names of places in foreign lands

Acapulco	(Ä′ cä pul′ cŏ) pōōl′	Resort city in Mexico.
Arctic	(Ärc′ tĭc)	Northernmost ocean; northernmost region.
Brazzaville	(Brăz′ zà vĭlle)	Capital of French Equatorial Africa.
Buenos Aires	(Bue′ nos Ai′ res) bwä′ nŭs âr′ ĕz	Capital of Argentina.
Cairo	(Caī′ rō)	Capital of Egypt and the United Arab Republic.
Calcutta	(Căl cŭt′ tà)	City in India.
Caribbean	(Căr ĭb bē′ ăn)	Arm of Atlantic Ocean between the West Indies and Central and South America.
Ceylon	(Çéy lŏn′)	Island in Indian Ocean.
Chile	(Chĭl′ é)	Country in South America.
Congo	(Cŏn′ gō)	Nation in Equatorial Africa.
Copenhagen	(Cŏ′ pĕn hä′ gĕn)	Capital of Denmark.
Czechoslovakia	(Czech′ ŏ slŏ vä′ kĭ à) chĕk′	Country in Europe.
Danzig	(Dăn′ zĭg)	City in Poland.
Edinburgh	(Ed′ ĭn burgh) bû rŏ	Capital of Scotland.
Ghana	(Ghä′ nà)	A country in Africa.
Iran (Persia)	(Ī rän′) é	Country in Asia.
Iraq	(Ī raq′) räk′	Country in southwestern Asia.
Istanbul	(Ĭs′ tan bul′) tăm bōōl′	Largest city in Turkey.
Juarez	(Jua′ rez) hwä′ rĕs	City in Mexico.
Kenya	(Kĕn′ yà)	Nation in East Africa.
Kobe	(Kō′ bĕ)	City in Japan.
Le Havre	(Lē Hä′ vre)	City in France.
Leopoldville	(Lē′ ŏ pōld vĭlle′)	Capital of the Belgian Congo.
Lima	(Li′ mà) lē′	Capital of Peru.
Moscow	(Mŏs′ cow)	Capital of the U. S. S. R.
Nice	(Nice) nēs	Resort city on French Riviera.
Nuremberg	(Nür′ ĕm bûrg)	City in Germany.
Philippines	(Phĭl′ ĭp pines) pēnz	Group of islands in the Pacific, now a Republic.
Prague	(Prägue′)	Capital of Czechoslovakia.
Rio de Janeiro	(Ri′ ō dĕ Jà nei′ rō) rē′ nä′	Capital of Brazil.
Riviera	(Ri vie′ ra) rĭv′ ĭ âr′ à	Beautiful region along the Mediterranean Sea.
Saigon	(Saī gŏn′)	Capital of Vietnam.
San Juan	(Săn Juan′) hwän′	Capital of Puerto Rico.
Tanganyika	(Tăn găn yi′ kà) yē′	Country in East Africa.
Tel Aviv	(Tĕl′ A viv′) vēv	City in Israel.
Thailand (Siam)	(Thaī′ lănd)	Country in Asia.
Tokyo	(Tō′ kў ō)	Capital of Japan.
Trieste	(Tri ĕste′) trē	City in Italy.
Venezuela	(Vĕn′ é zue′ là) zwē	Country in South America.
Vietnam	(Vi ĕt′ näm′) vĕ	Country in Southeast Asia.
Wiesbaden	(Wies′ bä dĕn) vēs′	Resort city in Germany.
Yugoslavia	(Yu gŏ slä′ vĭ à) yōō	Country in Europe.

In this lesson we shall learn some French words and expressions that have become part of the English language, but that present pronunciation problems for many Americans.

à la carte	(ä' là cärte')	From the menu.
à la mode	(ä' là mōde')	In the fashion: topped with ice cream.
apropos	(ăp' rŏ pō*s*')	Relevant; appropriate.
attaché	(ăt' *t*à ché') shā'	Person attached to embassy staff.
au gratin	(au grä' tin) ō tăn	With a browned crust of bread crumbs, often mixed with butter or cheese.
au revoir	(au' rĕ voir') ō' vwär'	Farewell.
beaux arts	(beaux arts') bō zär'	Fine arts.
bête noire	(bete' noire') bāt' nwär'	Person or thing strongly feared; black beast.
blasé	(blä se') zā'	Bored; apathetic to pleasure.
bon jour	(bôn' jour') zhōōr'	Good morning.
bon soir	(bôn' soir') swär'	Good evening; good night.
bon voyage	(bôn' voy age') vwä yàzh'	Good voyage.
café	(cà' fé') fā'	Coffeehouse; restaurant.
camaraderie	(cä' mà rä' dĕ riē)	Good-fellowship.
camouflage	(căm' ou flage) ōō fläzh	Disguise.
carte blanche	(cärte' blanche') blänsh'	Unconditional power.
chaise longue	(chaise' lôngue') shāz'	Long chair with a raised back support.
chef	(chef) shĕf	Cook.
chic	(chic) shēk	Fashionable, stylish.
cloisonné	(cloi' şŏn né') nā'	Enamel decoration.
cuisine	(cui sine') kwē zēn'	Type of cooking.
debonair	(dĕb' ŏ nàir')	Lighthearted; courteous.
debris	(dĕ bris') brĕ'	Rubbish.
debut	(de' bū*t*) dā'	First formal appearance before the public.

From the list of words and expressions in this lesson, select a word or expression to replace each of the blanks in the following sentences:

1. For dessert, please bring me apple pie (   ).
2. The (   ) cooked a delicious dinner; the potatoes (   ) were the best I ever ate.
3. Mary is making her (   ) as soon as she returns from Europe.
4. The (   ) on the corner of South and Main Streets is famous for its (   ).
5. It is generally cheaper to order a full dinner than to order (   ).
6. The Club presented him with a (   ) gift and best wishes for a good journey.
7. This suit is (   ) and practical, too.
8. He has (   ) to set up the sales program as he sees fit.
9. Mathematics has always been my (   ); for some reason, my answers are always wrong.
10. He is an (   ) at the French Embassy.

This lesson will conclude our study of French words and expressions. Our list is by no means a complete one, but it contains many of the most widely used words.

elite	(e lite') á lēt'	Choice part.
encore	(en cōre') än	Demand for repetition.
ennui	(en' nui) än' wē	Feeling of weariness, boredom.
esprit de corps	(ĕs prit' dĕ côr*ps*') prē'	Group spirit.
exposé	(ĕx' pŏ sé') zā'	Exposure of something discreditable.
faux pas	(faux' päs') fō'	Mistake. Embarrassing error.
finesse	(fĭ nĕs*se*')	Strategy; cunning.
glacé	(glà'cé') sā'	Iced; smooth.
hors d'oeuvres	(*h*ôrs d'oeu' vres') dûrv'	Appetizers served at beginning of meal.
joie de vivre	(joie dĕ vivre') zhwà vēvr'	Joy of living.
laissez-faire	(lais' sez-fàire') lĕ' sā	Noninterference.
maître d'hôtel	(mâi' tr*e* d'hô'tĕl') dō'	Chief employee in a hotel or restaurant.
motif	(mŏ tif') tēf	Theme; pattern.
mousse	(mousse) mōōs	Frozen dessert made with whipped cream.
née	(née) nā	Born; referring to maiden name.
nonchalance	(nŏn' cha lănce') shà	Indifference.
nouveau riche	(nou' veau' riche') nōō' vō' rēsh'	Newly rich.
piquant	(pi' quant) pē' kănt	Sharp; stimulating to the taste.
protégé	(prō' té gé) tĕ zhā	One under the special care of another.
raison d'être	(rái' şôn' d'être) dâ'tr	Reason for existing.
rendezvous	(ren' dĕ*z* vous) rän' vōō	A meeting place; meeting by appointment.
résumé	(ré' su mé') rā' zŭ mā'	Summary.
risqué	(rĭs' qué') kā'	Verging on impropriety.
savoir faire	(sà' voir' fàire') vwàr'	Sophistication; knowing how to act.
table d'hôte	(tà' bl*e* d'hôte') dōt'	Complete meal served in a restaurant or hotel.
tête-à-tête	(tête'-à-tête') tāt' á tāt'	Intimate conversation.

From the list of words and expressions in this lesson, select a word or expression to replace each of the blanks in the following sentences:

1. I did not like to interrupt their (　　　　) because they seemed to be discussing something important.
2. Henry is the (　　　　) of Mr. Delettre, who will make a first-class musician of him.
3. What is the name of the poet who wrote of his (　　　　) with Death?
4. This sauce is (　　　　), just right for bland fruits like pears.
5. Was the dinner served (　　　　) or did you have to order à la carte?
6. After a delicious steak with salad, we had pineapple (　　　　).
7. Not knowing that she had married again, I made the (　　　　) of calling her by her former name.
8. We spent two hours before dinner drinking juice and eating (　　　　).
9. She has such (　　　　) in handling embarrassing situations.
10. Call the (　　　　) this evening for our luncheon reservation.

In this lesson we shall study a few of the Latin words and expressions that have become part of the English language.

ad hoc	(ăd′ hŏc)	For this purpose only.
ad infinitum	(ăd′ ĭn′ fĭ nī′ tŭm)	Limitless.
affidavit	(ăf′ fĭ dā′ vĭt)	A sworn statement in writing.
agenda	(à gĕn′ dà)	List of things to be done.
alma mater	(ăl′ mà mā′ tẽr)	College or school from which one has been graduated.
alumna	(à lŭm′ nà)	Female graduate of a college or university.
alumnae	(à lŭm′ naē)	Female graduates of a college or university.
alumni	(à lŭm′ nī)	Male (or male and female) graduates of a college or university.
alumnus	(à lŭm′ nŭs)	Male graduate of a college or university.
anno Domini	(ăn′nō Dŏm′ ĭ nī)	In the year of our Lord.
bona fide	(bō′nà fī′ dḗ)	In good faith; genuine.
data	(dā′ tà)	Facts.
de luxe	(dḗ luxe′) lōōks′	Luxurious; sumptuous.
et cetera	(ĕt çĕt′ ẽr à)	And other things.
finale	(fi nä′ lḗ) fḗ	Concluding part; ending.
in toto	(ĭn tō′ tō)	In its entirety.
ipso facto	(ĭp′ sō făc′ tō)	By the fact itself.
non sequitur	(nŏn se′ qui tŭr) sĕk′ wĭ	An inference that does not follow from the premises.
per annum	(pẽr ăn′ num)	By the year.
per capita	(pẽr căp′ ĭ tà)	By the head; poll.
per diem	(pẽr dī′ ĕm)	By the day.
per se	(pẽr sē)	In itself.
pro rata	(prō rā′ tà)	In proportion to.
pro tempore	(prō tĕm′ pō rḗ)	For the time being.
status quo	(stā′ tŭs quo) kwō	Existing state of affairs.
sub rosa	(sŭb rō′ sà)	Furtive; secret.
tempus fugit	(tĕm′ pŭs fū′ ġĭt)	Time flies.
ultimatum	(ŭl′ tĭ mā′ tŭm)	Final proposition; last word.
via	(vī′à)	By way of.
vice versa	(vī′ çḗ vẽr′ sà)	The reverse.
vox populi	(vŏx pŏp′ ú lĭ)	Voice of the people.

Select a word or expression from this lesson to replace each of the blanks in the following sentences:

1. Keep this (   ) with the other legal papers on this case.
2. The (   ) of the Chatham College for Women are having a drive for funds to aid needy students.
3. The (   ) of the University of California include many men and women prominent in every walk of life.
4. Do you have the (   ) for the meeting?
5. His salary is $8,500 a year and, in addition, he receives $18 (   ) for traveling expenses.
6. All voters in our state pay a (   ) tax.
7. Is Princeton your (   )?
8. She has always resisted change, and her mother is a great believer in the (   ).
9. Helen will serve as secretary (   ).
10. Jim's father laid down an (   ) concerning the use of the family car.

This list contains some of the frequently misspelled words in Lessons 72 to 78 inclusive. Check the names to be sure that you can pronounce and spell them. Be prepared to write from dictation sentences containing these names.

Names of well-known persons

Baruch, Bernard
Chiang Kai-shek
Gandhi, Mohandas
Khrushchev, Nikita
Maugham, W. Somerset

Pasteur, Louis
Roosevelt, Franklin D.
Vinci (da), Leonardo
Wagner, Richard
Yeats, William Butler

Names of places at home and abroad

Albuquerque
Buenos Aires
Cincinnati
Hawaii
Iran

Istanbul
Philippines
Poughkeepsie
Rio de Janeiro
Thailand

Foreign words and expressions

Be prepared to read the following list of foreign words and expressions, pronouncing them properly. Be prepared to define each one and use it in a sentence.

agenda
alma mater
alumni
carte blanche
cuisine
debris
debut
elite
esprit de corps
faux pas

hors d'oeuvres
non sequitur
per annum
protégé
raison d'être
résumé
risqué
status quo
table d'hôte
vice versa

Part 4 ◢ SPECIAL WORDS

Homonyms

Three words that every student of language should understand are *homonyms, synonyms,* and *antonyms. Homonyms* are words that sound alike, but have different meanings. *Synonyms* are words that are related in meaning but do not sound alike (*begin* and *commence,* for instance). *Antonyms* are direct opposites in meaning, as *hot— cold*; *white—black.*

Take, for example, the common words *to, too,* and *two,* pronounced exactly alike but by no means interchangeable in writing. To be sure that you choose the correct spelling for any one of these, you must know the meaning of all three so that you will not be led into a wrong choice by a feeling of vagueness and uncertainty. It is easy to remember that *two* refers to number, *too* means *more than enough* and *also,* and that *to* is the busy little runabout used with verbs (*to* do, *to* see, etc.) and also with nouns and pronouns (*to* town, *to* you, *to* Jim Jones).

In Lessons 80 through 83, we shall learn the specific meanings and exact spelling of the homonyms that cause so much difficulty. Then we shall be able to check and double-check our use of them until we are sure of accuracy. In Lessons 85 through 87, we shall examine pairs of words that are somewhat alike in sound, but not entirely so.

Use of Words

Your ability to use words correctly depends, first of all, upon your possession of a large vocabulary. You may know the meanings of many words, however, and still be careless in using them. If you are to express your ideas effectively and appealingly, you must select words that convey the exact meanings you desire.

Certain pairs of words are very commonly misused, even by those who have had a good education. A good example of such a pair is "amateur" and "novice." Perhaps you want to convey the idea that another person is unskilled and call him an "amateur." As a matter of fact, an amateur may be highly skilled. Thus, an amateur tennis player may be the world's champion. *Amateur* means one who is not a professional. The word you should have used is "novice," for this word suggests that the other person is a beginner, that he lacks skill. Similar pairs of words that are commonly misused are presented in Lessons 89 through 93.

Inexactness may result from the overuse of general terms. Definite words give definite mental images. "She wore a *bright-colored* dress," does not give the clear mental picture that one receives from "She wore a *red* dress." Some misused words, such as "dumb," "awful," and "cute," are especially overworked. Lessons 99 through 102 present a number of exact words that may be substituted to advantage for some of the more general expressions.

Words Pertaining to Time

In Lessons 103 and 104 are words pertaining to time which are commonly used in our daily conversation and in writing letters. You should master their spelling, pronunciation, and use.

States, Territories, and Cities

In Lessons 105 through 109, we shall learn (1) the names, capitals, and abbreviations of states; and (2) the names of cities that are difficult to spell.

Abbreviations

Most of the commonly used abbreviations are presented in the last three lessons of this part.

The words in the following groupings are alike in sound, but are unlike in spelling and meaning.

ascent	(ăs çĕnt′)	n. The act of rising; a high place.
assent	(ăs sĕnt′)	v. To agree. n. Consent.
base	(bāse)	n. Foundation. adj. Lacking higher value.
bass	(bāss)	n. A deep tone. adj. Of low pitch.
berth	(bĕrth)	n. A place in which to sleep.
birth	(bĭrth)	n. Act of coming into life.
cannon	(căn′ nŏn)	n. A piece of artillery.
canon	(căn′ ȯn)	n. A rule or law.
canvas	(căn′ vȧs)	n. A strong cloth used for tents.
canvass	(căn′ vȧss)	v. To solicit. n. Act of soliciting.
capital	(căp′ ĭ tăl)	adj. Chief; prominent. n. Property; wealth.
capitol	(căp′ ĭ tŏl)	n. Statehouse.
carat	(căr′ ăt)	n. Unit of weight.
caret	(căr′ ĕt)	n. Proofreader's mark.
carrot	(căr′ rot) ŭt	n. Plant with edible root.
coarse	(cōarse)	adj. Common; unrefined.
course	(cōurse)	n. A passage; a sequence of subjects.
kill	(kĭll)	v. To deprive of life.
kiln	(kĭln)	n. A furnace.
mantel	(măn′ tel)	n. A shelf above a fireplace.
mantle	(măn′ tle)	n. A loose garment. v. To overspread.
miner	(mīn′ ĕr)	n. One who mines.
minor	(mīn′ ŏr)	adj. Less. n. A person under legal age.
plain	(plāin)	adj. Simple. n. Level land.
plane	(plāne)	adj. Flat. n. A flat surface; a tool.
raise	(rāise)	v. To elevate.
raze	(rāze)	v. To lay level with the ground.

A. Consult your dictionary for the pronunciation and meaning of the following words:

cereal	serial	freeze	frieze
coolie	coolly	root	route

B. Copy the following sentences, substituting the correct words for the blank spaces.

1. The building contractor used (   )-dried lumber.
2. Please reserve a lower (   ) on the Chicago Express.
3. He sang (   ) in the choir.
4. She threw a (   ) over her shoulders.
5. Red Cross workers will (   ) from house to house.
6. The (   ) belongs to the carpenter.
7. Has the principal given his (   ) to the request?
8. Such a procedure is contrary to a church (   ).
9. They began to (   ) the old building today.
10. What (   ) are you taking in school?

Below are additional groups of words that are alike in sound, but unlike in spelling and meaning.

bolder	(bōld′ ẽr)	*adj.* More courageous.
boulder	(bōuld′ ẽr)	*n.* A large, detached rock.
brake	(brāke)	*n.* A device for stopping. *v.* To retard.
break	(breāk)	*v.* To separate into parts. *n.* A gap.
bridal	(brīd′ ăl)	*adj.* Pertaining to bride or marriage.
bridle	(brī′ dle)	*n.* Restraint; curb. *v.* To curb.
core	(cōre)	*n.* The central part of anything. *v.* To remove the center.
corps	(cōr*p*s)	*n.* A body of persons.
gilt	(gĭlt)	*n.* Goldlike material.
guilt	(guĭlt)	*n.* State of having violated a law.
knead	(*k*nēad)	*v.* To work into a mass.
need	(nēed)	*n.* Want. *v.* To require.
marshal	(mär′ shăl)	*n.* An officer. *v.* To direct.
martial	(mär′ tial) shăl	*adj.* Pertaining to war.
mean	(mēan)	*v.* To intend. *adj.* Inferior. *n.* Middle point.
mien	(miēn)	*n.* Appearance; bearing.
principal	(prĭn′ çĭ păl)	*adj.* Highest in rank; chief. *n.* Leader.
principle	(prĭn′ çĭ ple)	*n.* Fundamental truth.
right	(rīght)	*adj.* Correct; opposite of left.
rite	(rīte)	*n.* A ceremony.
wright	(*w*rīght)	*n.* A workman.
write	(*w*rīte)	*v.* To express in writing; to compose.
serge	(sērġe)	*n.* A twilled woolen fabric.
surge	(sûrġe)	*n.* A large wave. *v.* To rise and fall.
to	(to)	*prep.* Indicates direction or action.
too	(tōō)	*adv.* More than enough. *conj.* Also.
two	(two)	*adj.* Number after one. *n.* One plus one.

A. Consult your dictionary for the pronunciation and meaning of the following words:

dyeing	dying	complement	compliment
suite	sweet	vain	vane vein

B. Copy the following sentences, substituting the correct words for the blank spaces.

1. A large ( ) crashed down the mountain side.
2. He claimed to be a ship ( ) by trade.
3. A religious ( ) was held in the church.
4. His dignified ( ) attracted much attention.
5. The baker will ( ) the dough.
6. They employ a large ( ) of stenographers.
7. There was a ( ) of spectators over the field.
8. The ( ) suit needed relining.
9. ( ) music filled the air.
10. The picture frame was painted with ( ).

aisle	(aīsle)	n. A passage in a church or an auditorium.
isle	(īsle)	n. A small island.
altar	(al′ tar) ôl′ tĕr	n. Place for sacrifices.
alter	(al′ ter)	v. To change.
bail	(bāil)	v. To set free on security. n. Security.
bale	(bāle)	n. A large bundle. v. To make into a bundle.
board	(bōard)	n. A piece of timber sawed rather thin.
bored	(bōred)	v. Uninterested; wearied.
cede	(çēde)	v. To yield; to give up.
seed	(sēed)	n. That from which plants spring.
ceiling	(çĕil′ ĭng)	n. Overhead covering of a room.
sealing	(sēal′ ĭng)	v. Marking or closing with a seal.
cession	(çĕs′ sion)	n. A yielding or surrender.
session	(sĕs′ sion)	n. The sitting of a court or a legislature.
council	(coun′ çĭl)	n. Assembly for deliberation.
counsel	(coun′ sĕl)	n. Advice. v. To give advice.
forth	(fōrth)	adv. Forward.
fourth	(fōurth)	adj. Next after third.
guessed	(guĕssed)	v. Surmised; suspected.
guest	(guĕst)	n. A visitor.
indict	(ĭn dīct′)	v. To charge with an offense.
indite	(ĭn dīte′)	v. To compose; to write.
lessen	(lĕss′ en)	v. To reduce; to decrease.
lesson	(lĕs′ son)	n. An exercise assigned to students.
serf	(serf) sûrf	n. Slave.
surf	(surf)	n. Swell of sea breaking on shore.
stair	(stâir)	n. Any step of a series.
stare	(stâre)	v. To gaze fixedly.
stake	(stāke)	n. A pointed piece of wood or iron.
steak	(steāk)	n. A slice of meat.

A. Consult your dictionary for the pronunciation and meaning of the following words:

| choir | quire | currant | current |
| mail | male | pair | pare | pear |

B. Copy the following sentences, substituting the correct words for the blank spaces.

1. The prisoner was released on $1,000 (   ).
2. Everyone was (   ) with the long story.
3. I saw him (   ) at the stranger.
4. The grand jury is sure to (   ) him.
5. Mexico was asked to (   ) the territory.
6. The hostess welcomed the (   ).
7. The bill was passed at the last (   ).
8. It was difficult to paper the (   ).
9. We drove a (   ) in the ground.

allowed	(ăl lowĕd')	*adj.* Permitted.
aloud	(à loud')	*adv.* Loudly.
aught	(aught) ôt	*n.* In arithmetic, a cipher.
ought	(ou*gh*t)	*v.* Should.
census	(çĕn' sŭs)	*n.* Official enumeration of population.
senses	(sĕn' sĕs)	*n.* Special faculties of sensation.
		v. To become aware of.
cite	(çīte)	*v.* To summon.
sight	(sī*gh*t)	*n.* Spectacle.
		v. To see.
site	(sīte)	*n.* Local position of edifice, monument, etc.
correspondence	(cŏr' rĕ spŏnd' ĕnçe)	*n.* Communication by letters.
correspondents	(cŏr' rĕ spŏnd' ĕnts)	*n.* Individuals writing letters.
fair	(fâir)	*n.* Bazaar.
		adj. Pleasing; free from defect.
fare	(fâre)	*n.* Price of transportation.
		v. To go forth.
foreword	(fōre' wôrd')	*n.* Preface.
forward	(fôr' wărd)	*adj.* Onward.
		v. To advance; send onward.
hear	(hēar)	*v.* Listen to.
here	(hēre)	*adv.* At this place.
loan	(lōan)	*n.* That lent or borrowed.
		v. To lend.
lone	(lōne)	*adj.* Solitary; without company.
medal	(mĕd' ăl)	*n.* Commemorative award.
meddle	(mĕd' *d*le)	*v.* To interfere.
morning	(môrn' ĭng)	*n.* Early part of the day.
mourning	(mōurn' ĭng)	*n.* Sorrowing; lamentation.
pain	(pāin)	*n.* Distressing feeling.
		v. To distress.
pane	(pāne)	*n.* Compartment of glass.
peace	(pēaçe)	*n.* Tranquillity; quiet.
piece	(piēçe)	*n.* Fragment of whole.
		v. To repair, "make do."
presence	(prĕş' ĕnçe)	*n.* State of being present.
presents	(prĕş' ĕnts)	*n.* Gifts.
rain	(rāin)	*n.* Water falling in drops from clouds.
		v. To pour.
reign	(reign) rān	*n.* Royal authority; period of rule.
		v. To govern; to prevail.
stationary	(stā' tion ăr' ў)	*adj.* Motionless.
stationery	(stā' tion ĕr' ў)	*n.* Writing paper.
wade	(wāde)	*v.* To move forward against resistance.
weighed	(weighed) wād	*adj.* Measured as to weight.
waive	(wāive)	*v.* To remove; reject.
wave	(wāve)	*n.* Inundation; swelling motion.
		v. To flutter; to signal.

A. Consult your dictionary for the pronunciation and meaning of the following words:

| blew | blue | cast | caste | peer | pier |
| tear | tier | their | there | they're | |

B. Underscore the correct word in parentheses in each of the following sentences:

1. The (site, sight, cite) of the plant has been chosen, and construction will soon begin.
2. We expect to stay (here, hear) if we are (allowed, aloud) to attend the (fair, fare).
3. There are ten (correspondence, correspondents) in that department taking care of the (morning's, mourning's) (male, mail).
4. Can you (wave, waive) the mathematics requirement without a petition?
5. We sensed the (presence, presents) of an unexpected visitor when we saw a stranger in (mourning, morning).
6. To be awarded the Carnegie (medal, meddle) for bravery is one of the finest compliments society can bestow.
7. He was obviously in (pane, pain), yet he was at (piece, peace) with the world.
8. Is your name on your personal (stationery, stationary)?
9. We will go (forward, foreword) with the project without delay.
10. Have you (wade, weighed) the luggage you are planning to take?

84 Review

A. Copy the following sentences, correcting any errors you detect:

1. Our city counsel will meet tonight to discuss the traffic problem.
2. These bridle flowers will be attractive on the mantle.
3. Have you ever seen the Capital Building in our nation's capital?
4. It is against my principals to let Alice assume these responsibilities while she is a miner; she's to young for such a burden.
5. The flowers on the alter were arranged in tears with the blew ones alternating with the white.
6. The cite of there house is, in many ways, the best along the shore, but of coarse the serf is sometimes a problem.
7. Mr. Adams, Principle of Norwood High School, told the entire caste of the senior play that there special requests were in vein.
8. Helen's fiancé, a playwright, gave her a one-caret diamond ring as an engagement present.
9. He took a photograph of the bridle party as they walked up the isle.
10. I think you should wave the educational requirements for this job because they are to high.

B. Use each of the following words in a sentence:

alter—altar	council—counsel
capitol—capital	martial—marshal
principle—principal	

C. Define each word in the following sets of homonyms and use each one in a sentence:

cereal—serial	medal—meddle
choir—quire	pier—peer
currant—current	root—route

The following pairs of words are somewhat alike in sound, but not entirely so.

advice	(ăd vīçe′)	*n.*	Recommendation.
advise	(ăd vīṣe′)	*v.*	To give advice to.
commence	(cŏm mĕnçe′)	*v.*	To begin.
comments	(cŏm′ *m*ĕnts)	*n.*	Remarks; criticisms.
complement	(cŏm′ plĕ mĕnt)	*n.*	That which completes.
		v.	To complete.
compliment	(cŏm′ plĭ mĕnt)	*n.*	Flattering remark.
		v.	To commend; praise.
cooperation	(cō ŏp′ ēr ā′ tion)	*n.*	Collective action.
corporation	(côr′ pŏ rā′ tion)	*n.*	A body of persons.
decease	(dĕ çease′)	*n.*	Death. *v.* To die.
disease	(dĭṣ ēaṣe′)	*n.*	Illness.
deference	(dĕf′ ēr ĕnçe)	*n.*	Courteous yielding.
difference	(dĭf′ *f*ēr ĕnçe)	*n.*	State of being unlike.
allusion	(ăl lū′ sion) zhŭn	*n.*	Reference to.
elusion	(ĕ lū′ sion) zhŭn	*n.*	Evasion.
illusion	(ĭl lū′ sion) zhŭn	*n.*	An unreal image.
eminent	(ĕm′ ĭ nĕnt)	*adj.*	Prominent.
imminent	(ĭm′ *m*ĭ nĕnt)	*adj.*	Threatening to occur.
incite	(ĭn çīte′)	*v.*	To arouse; to provoke.
insight	(ĭn′ sī*ght*)	*n.*	Mental vision.
persecute	(pēr′ sĕ cūte)	*v.*	To annoy; to afflict.
prosecute	(prŏs′ ĕ cūte)	*v.*	To carry on; to sue.
precede	(prē cēde′)	*v.*	To go before.
proceed	(prō cēed′)	*v.*	To go forward.
prophecy	(prŏph′ ĕ çў)	*n.*	A foretelling.
prophesy	(prŏph′ ĕ sȳ)	*v.*	To foretell.

A. Consult your dictionary for the pronunciation and meaning of the following words:

confidant   confident   ingenious   ingenuous

B. Copy the following sentences, substituting the correct words for the blank spaces.

1. A mirage is an (   ).
2. He attempted to (   ) the mob to violence.
3. It is wrong to (   ) a man because of his religion.
4. What do you (   ) me to do?
5. It is difficult to (   ) the outcome.
6. Dr. Nolan is an (   ) educator.
7. The (   ) finally caused his death.
8. A storm is (   ).
9. There was splendid (   ) among the members.
10. He wrote (   ) on the margins of the book.
11. The clerk showed (   ) to his employer's wishes.
12. Notice of his (   ) appeared in the obituary column.

Be sure that you know the meaning of the words in this lesson and that you can pronounce them correctly.

accept	(ăc çĕpt′)	v. To receive what is offered.
except	(ĕx çĕpt′)	prep. With the exclusion of.
access	(ăc′ çĕss)	n. Means of approach; admission.
excess	(ĕx çĕss′)	n. That which exceeds.
adverse	(ăd vẽrse′)	adj. Acting against; opposed.
averse	(à vẽrse′)	adj. Having an aversion; reluctant.
affect	(ăf fĕct′)	v. To influence.
effect	(ĕf fĕct′)	n. A result. v. To bring about.
extant	(ĕx′ tănt)	adj. In existence; not destroyed.
extent	(ĕx tĕnt′)	n. The size; the length.
formally	(fôr′ măl lў)	adv. In order; regularly.
formerly	(fôr′ mẽr lў)	adv. In time past.
human	(hū′ măn)	adj. Belonging or relating to man.
humane	(hú māne′)	adj. Benevolent.
loose	(lōōse)	adj. Not fastened.
lose	(loṣe)	v. To suffer a loss.
personal	(pẽr′ sȯn ăl)	adj. Pertaining to a person; private.
personnel	(pĕr′ sȯn nĕl′)	n. A body of persons.
practicable	(prăc′ tĭ cà ble)	adj. Capable of being done.
practical	(prăc′ tĭ căl)	adj. Opposed to theoretical; useful.
propose	(prṓ pōṣe′)	v. To offer; to state.
purpose	(pûr′ pȯse)	v. To intend. n. An intention.
respectfully	(rḗ spĕct′ ful lў)	adv. With regard for.
respectively	(rḗ spĕc′ tĭve lў) fŏŏl	adv. Each to each.

A. Consult your dictionary for the pronunciation and the meaning of the following words:

eruption   irruption   farther   further

B. Copy the following sentences, substituting the correct words for the blank spaces.

1. The accountant said that there was an (   ) of $5,000.
2. What is the (   ) of this meeting?
3. He showed a (   ) attitude toward the wounded enemy.
4. To what (   ) will this plan be adopted?
5. Jewelry is considered as (   ) property.
6. The superintendent will (   ) resign this week.
7. I am glad to (   ) your offer.
8. I am not (   ) to doing the work.
9. What (   ) will this have on the outcome?
10. How will this (   ) the outcome?
11. The student had (   ) to the library.
12. The electrician found a (   ) connection.
13. He is (   ) in his judgments and always glad to help others.
14. You live two miles (   ) from the College than I do.
15. Do you have anything (   ) to say?

101

adapted	(à dăpt' ĕd)	*adj.* Made suitable; adjusted.
adopted	(à dŏpt' ĕd)	*adj.* Taken voluntarily as one's own.
addition	(ăd dĭ' tion)	*n.* Increase; increment.
edition	(ĕ dĭ' tion)	*n.* One of several issues of a printed work.
anecdote	(ăn' ĕc dōte)	*n.* Brief, amusing story.
antidote	(ăn' tĭ dōte)	*n.* Remedy.
appraise	(ăp prāiṣe')	*v.* To judge as to quality, status, etc.
apprise	(ăp prīṣe')	*v.* To inform.
censor	(çĕn' sōr)	*n.* Overseer of morals.
		v. To subject to moral judgment.
censure	(çĕn' sure) shēr	*n.* Adverse criticism.
		v. To criticize adversely.
command	(cŏm mănd')	*v.* To order.
		n. An order given.
commend	(cŏm mĕnd')	*v.* To applaud; to praise.
contest	(cŏn' tĕst)	*n.* Competition.
context	(cŏn' tĕxt)	*n.* Section in which a word or passage occurs.
credible	(crĕd' ĭ ble)	*adj.* Believable.
creditable	(crĕd' ĭt à ble)	*adj.* Praiseworthy.
exceed	(ĕx çēēd')	*v.* To go beyond.
accede	(ăc çēde')	*v.* To attain (to); to agree (to).
immoral	(ĭm môr' ăl)	*adj.* Contrary to conscience.
immortal	(ĭm môr' tăl)	*adj.* Imperishable, abiding.
moral	(môr' ăl)	*n.* Lesson to be drawn from a story.
		adj. Right and proper.
morale	(môr àle')	*n.* Spirit of cooperation.
ordinance	(ôr' dĭ nănçe)	*n.* Rule; law.
ordnance	(ôrd' nănçe)	*n.* Military supplies.
plaintiff	(plāin' tĭff)	*n.* The complaining party in a lawsuit.
plaintive	(plāin' tĭve)	*adj.* Sorrowful.
poplar	(pŏp' lär)	*n.* A shade tree.
popular	(pŏp' ú lär)	*adj.* Approved by the people.
quiet	(qui' ĕt)	*adj.* Still, hushed. *n.* Repose.
	kwī'	*v.* To calm.
quite	(quite) kwīt	*adv.* Completely.
weather	(wĕath' ēr)	*n.* State of atmosphere.
		v. To expose to air; to endure.
whether	(whĕth' ēr)	*conj.* Indication of choice or doubt.

A. Give the adjectival forms for the following nouns and write a sentence for each adjective:

addition   anecdote   command   context

B. Write the noun forms for the following adjectives and give a sentence for each noun:

adapted   adopted   immortal   popular

C. Underscore the correct word in parentheses in each of the following sentences:

1. We have (adapted, adopted) the story to meet college standards.
2. Do you believe that we should (accede, exceed) last year's budget?
3. Dr. Evans' amusing (anecdotes, antidotes) are better than medicine.
4. Please (precede, proceed) with your part of the program.
5. Have you (appraised, apprised) him of his victory?

From the words in Lessons 85 through 87, select a word to substitute for each of the blanks in the following sentences:

Lesson 85

1. Since you have asked my (   ), I shall have to say that I think the investment is unsound.
2. Did Henry (   ) you to make this investment?
3. I hear that our (   ) is going to announce an extra dividend on its common stock.
4. Dr. Hollinger had enough (   ) into human nature to know that Jack's (   ) to his teacher's wishes was not sincere.
5. John Kane can unintentionally (   ) more trouble in a classroom than any three boys I know.
6. An (   ) lawyer was engaged to (   ) the young man accused of murder.
7. Many public officials (   ) that war is (   ), but I believe that peace is still possible.
8. Mrs. Brewer has been suffering for months under the (   ) that her friends and relations were trying to (   ) her.

Lesson 86

9. I am happy to (   ) your invitation.
10. When did he (   ) his wallet?
11. The (   ) of his criticism was deadly; she made no further effort to improve.
12. Did the wage increase (   ) the price of the product?
13. Mr. and Mrs. John Anderson have (   ) announced their daughter's engagement.
14. Jack is (   ) in planning projects; he always foresees difficulties.
15. I do not believe the plan to be (   ).
16. Sacramento is a (   ) city in its provision for an animal shelter for stray animals.
17. Before her marriage, Jack's wife did not realize the (   ) to which he was involved in civic affairs.

Lesson 87

18. What (   ) of the magazine are you seeking?
19. The (   ) of the office employees is at a low level.
20. The colonel's task was to (   ) the private who unofficially left the base.
21. The humorist injected many funny but meaningful (   ) into his talk.
22. Before the group (   ) its new constitution, many of the provisions had to be (   ) to reflect the organizational changes.
23. Sometimes there may be danger in quoting a word or words out of (   ).
24. The critics will (   ) your recital if you repeat today's rehearsal.
25. The cold, icy (   ) of last winter did not damage the beautiful, towering (   ).

In each of the groups of words given in Lessons 89 through 93, one word is frequently misused for the other. Be sure you understand the exact meaning of each word and can use the word in a sentence.

courtesy	(coûr′ tĕ sў)	*n.* Politeness.
curtesy	(cûr′ tĕ sў)	*n.* Husband's interest in estate of deceased wife.
curtsy	(cûrt′ sў)	*n.* Gesture of respect.
divers	(dī′ vẽrş)	*adj.* Various.
diverse	(dī vẽrse′)	*adj.* Different.
emerge	(é mẽrġe′)	*v.* To rise out of.
immerge	(ĭm mẽrġe′)	*v.* To sink into.
emigrant	(ĕm′ ĭ grănt)	*n.* A person leaving one country for another.
immigrant	(ĭm′ mĭ grănt)	*n.* Person coming into one country from another.
envelop	(ĕn vĕl′ op) ŭp	*v.* To enclose; surround.
envelope	(ĕn′ vĕ lōpe)	*n.* Paper wrapper.
ingenious	(ĭn ġēn′ ious) yŭs	*adj.* Inventive.
ingenuous	(ĭn ġĕn′ úoŭs)	*adj.* Frank.
last	(lăst)	*adj.* After all others.
latest	(lāt′ ĕst)	*adj.* Most recent.
leave	(lēave)	*v.* To move away.
let	(lĕt)	*v.* To permit.
lightening	(līght′ ĕn ĭng)	*v.* Making lighter.
lightning	(līght′ nĭng)	*n.* Electric flash from clouds.
may	(māy)	*v.* To be permitted.
can	(căn)	*v.* To be able.
raise	(rāişe)	*n.* A pay increase. *v.* To lift.
rise	(rīşe)	*v.* To ascend. *n.* An upward slope.

A. Distinguish the meanings of the following groups of words:

    (local   native   indigenous)   (audience   spectators)

B. Underscore the correct words in parentheses:

1. Tonight's speaker is an (ingenious, ingenuous) economist whose (last, latest) book on foreign aid closes with a criticism of overseas personnel.
2. (Let, Leave) me pay this bill so that there will be no argument.
3. (Can, May) I have this morning's paper after you have read it?
4. In the winter, the fog (raises, rises) around ten o'clock.
5. Few financial (magnets, magnates) are humorous.
6. I've lost the letter, but here is the (envelop, envelope).
7. (Immigrants, Emigrants) from the Far East are usually diligent workers.
8. We seldom have thunder or (lightening, lightning) in California.
9. He (emerges, immerges) from crises with no sign of strain.
10. (Divers, Diverse) views are almost certain to be (divers, diverse) in nature.

adjacent	(ăd jā′ çĕnt)	*adj.* Near.
adjoining	(ăd join′ ĭng)	*adj.* In contact with; touching.
allude	(ăl lūde′)	*v.* To refer indirectly.
elude	(ē lūde′)	*v.* To avoid.
apparent	(ăp păr′ ĕnt)	*adj.* Seeming to be so.
evident	(ĕv′ ĭ dĕnt)	*adj.* Obviously so.
averse	(à vĕrse′)	*adj.* Disinclined.
adverse	(ăd vĕrse′)	*adj.* Unfavorable.
cite	(çīte)	*v.* To mention a person or passage as authority.
quote	(quote) kwōt	*v.* To repeat the exact words used by another.
crime	(crīme)	*n.* Felony; serious offense against human rights.
sin	(sĭn)	*n.* Misbehavior; transgression. Usually less serious than crime.
eligible	(ĕl′ ĭ ġĭ ble)	*adj.* Qualified to be chosen.
legible	(lĕġ′ ĭ ble)	*adj.* Easy to read.
famous	(fā′ moŭs)	*adj.* Celebrated; renowned.
infamous	(ĭn′ fà moŭs)	*adj.* Of very bad reputation.
ineligible	(ĭn ĕl′ ĭ ġĭ ble)	*adj.* Not qualified.
illegible	(ĭl lĕġ′ ĭ ble)	*adj.* Undecipherable.
marital	(măr′ ĭ tăl)	*adj.* Pertaining to marriage.
martial	(măr′ tial) shăl	*adj.* Pertaining to war.
noted	(nōt′ ĕd)	*adj.* Eminent; famous.
notorious	(nŏ tō′ rĭ oŭs)	*adj.* Widely and unfavorably known.

A. Distinguish the meanings of the following groups of words:

(urban   suburban   rural)   (fatal   fateful)

B. Underscore the correct words in parentheses:

1. His neglect of himself is a (sin, crime), but his neglect of his children is a (sin, crime).
2. Many of us are (adverse, averse) to physical exercise.
3. (Adverse, Averse) criticism is not necessarily hostile; it may be helpful.
4. The fact that she had associated with (noted, notorious) criminals did not prevent her falling in love with a (noted, notorious) artist.
5. Gene checked his (marital, martial) status as "single."
6. She is evidently trying to (elude, allude) her responsibilities as committee chairman.
7. Bill (quotes, cites) long passages from Sandburg verbatim.
8. Judge Samuels is a (noted, notorious) jurist, recipient of many honors.

aggravate	(ăg′ grȧ vāte)	v. To make worse; to intensify.
exasperate	(ex as′ pĕr āte) ĕg zăs′	v. To arouse the anger of.
answer	(àn′ swẽr)	n. A response to a question or a letter. v. To respond.
reply	(rḗ plȳ′)	n. A formal response, as in a debate. v. To respond formally.
continual	(cŏn tĭn′ ū̇ ăl)	adj. Occurring in rapid succession.
continuous	(cŏn tĭn′ ū̇ oŭs)	adj. Occurring without break.
envious	(ĕn′ vĭ oŭs)	adj. Desiring what is another's.
jealous	(jĕal′ oŭs)	adj. Intolerant of rivalry in matters of affection.
ignorant	(ĭg′ nȯ́ rănt)	adj. Lacking knowledge.
illiterate	(ĭl lĭt′ ẽr ȧte)	adj. Unable to read or write.
majority	(mȧ jŏr′ ĭ tȳ̌)	n. More than half.
plurality	(plụ răl′ ĭ tȳ̌)	n. An excess of votes over those for any other candidate.
orthodontist	(ôr′ thȯ́ dŏn′ tĭst)	n. Dentist dealing with irregularity of teeth.
orthopedist	(ôr′ thȯ́ pē′ dĭst)	n. Doctor dealing with correction or prevention of deformities.
pediatrician	(pē′ dĭ ȧ trĭ′ cian) shŭn	n. Physician specializing in treatment of children.
chiropodist	(chi rŏp′ ȯ́ dĭst) kī	n. Specialist in treatment of ailments of the feet.
perquisite	(pĕr′ qui sĭte) kwĭ	n. An added advantage.
prerequisite	(prḗ req′ ui ṣite) rĕk′ wĭ	n. Preliminary requirement.
perspective	(pĕr spĕc′ tĭve)	n. View in correct proportion.
prospective	(prȯ́ spĕc′ tĭve)	adj. Expected.
receipt	(rḗ çēi pt′)	n. A written acknowledgment.
recipe	(rĕç′ ĭ pē)	n. A formula or prescription.
surprise	(sûr prīṣe′)	v. To take unawares.
astonish	(ăs tŏn′ ĭsh)	v. To strike with wonder.

A. Consult your dictionary for the pronunciation and meaning of the following words:

(pupil   scholar   student)   (decoration   ornament)

B. Choose the correct word from the pairs of words in parentheses:

1. Your letter will (aggravate, exasperate) your employer.
2. The senator made the (answer, reply) to the charge.
3. As he was (ignorant, illiterate), he could not read the note.
4. Sherwood received fifty-two votes of the seventy cast, and thus won by a (majority, plurality) of seventeen.
5. You will soon meet your (prospective, perspective) father-in-law.
6. Competence in mathematics is a (prerequisite, perquisite) to success in engineering.

accelerate	(ăc çĕl′ ẽr āte)	*v.* To hasten, quicken.
exhilarate	(ex hil′ à rāte) ĕg zĭl′	*v.* To enliven.
adapt	(à dăpt′)	*v.* To make suitable.
adept	(ă dĕpt′)	*adj.* Proficient.
adopt	(à dŏpt′)	*v.* To take as one's own.
compensate	(cŏm′ pĕn sāte)	*v.* To pay for loss or injury.
remunerate	(rḗ mū′ nẽr āte)	*v.* To pay for services.
credible	(crĕd′ ĭ ble)	*adj.* Worthy of belief.
credulous	(crĕd′ ū loŭs)	*adj.* Believing readily.
elicit	(ḗ lĭç′ ĭt)	*v.* To draw forth.
illicit	(ĭl lĭç′ ĭt)	*adj.* Unlawful.
exalt	(ex alt′) ĕg zôlt′	*v.* To raise high; lift up.
exult	(ex ult′) ĕg zŭlt′	*v.* To be in high spirits; rejoice.
exceptionable	(ĕx çĕp′ tion à ble)	*adj.* Objectionable.
exceptional	(ĕx çĕp′ tion ăl)	*adj.* Unusual.
feasible	(fēa′ ṣĭ ble)	*adj.* Capable of being done.
plausible	(plạu′ ṣĭ ble)	*adj.* Apparently true.
healthful	(hĕalth′ fụl)	*adj.* Promoting health.
healthy	(hĕalth′ ў̆)	*adj.* Having good health.
later	(lāt′ ẽr)	*adj.* More late. *adv.* By and by; subsequently.
latter	(lăt′ *t*ẽr)	*adj.* More recent; coming after something.
luxuriant	(lŭx ū′ rĭ ănt)	*adj.* Showing profuse growth.
luxurious	(lŭx ū′ rĭ oŭs)	*adj.* Pertaining to luxury.
momentary	(mō′ mĕn tar′ ў̆) tẽr′	*adj.* Continuing only a moment.
momentous	(mṓ mĕn′ toŭs)	*adj.* Important; weighty.
oculist	(ŏc′ ū lĭst)	*n.* Ophthalmologist or optometrist.
ophthalmologist	(ŏph′ thăl mŏl′ ō gĭst)	*n.* Doctor of Medicine specializing in diseases of the eyes.
optometrist	(ŏp tŏm′ ĕ trĭst)	*n.* Specialist in fitting glasses, not a Doctor of Medicine.
prescribe	(prḗ scrībe′)	*v.* To give as a rule.
proscribe	(prṓ scrībe′)	*v.* To outlaw; to condemn.
psychiatrist	(*p*sȳ c*h*ī′ à trĭst)	*n.* Physician specializing in treatment of mental and emotional disorders.
psychologist	(*p*sȳ c*h*ŏl′ ṓ g̣ĭst)	*n.* Specialist in study of man's mind and emotions; not a physician, as a rule.

(Continued)

restful	(rĕst′ fu̯l)	adj. Quiet; relaxed.
restive	(rĕs′ tĭve)	adj. Inactive; uneasy.
sample	(săm′ ple)	n. A representative portion of a whole.
specimen	(spĕç′ ĭ mĕn)	n. A particular item, representative of the group.
stature	(stăt′ ûre)	n. Height. Status gained by achievement.
statute	(stăt′ ūte)	n. A law.
talent	(tăl′ ĕnt)	n. Superior aptitude; gift.
ability	(à bĭl′ ĭ tў)	n. Power to perform; competence.

A. Consult your dictionary for the pronunciation and meaning of the following words:

(amateur novice)
(blemish defect fault) (colleague partner)

B. Look up the words *just* and *jest* in your dictionary. Then write a sentence using *just* correctly and a sentence using *jest* correctly.

C. Choose the correct word from the pairs of words in parentheses:

1. The railroad will (compensate, remunerate) him for the loss of his hand.
2. He told a (credible, credulous) story about being shipwrecked.
3. She has (exceptionable, exceptional) ability as a singer.
4. Do you think the building of a bridge at that place is (feasible, plausible)?
5. The college is located in a (healthful, healthy) climate.
6. The meadow was covered with a (luxuriant, luxurious) growth of grass.
7. Ask the physician to (prescribe, proscribe) for the disease.
8. Dr. Hauser, an outstanding (ophthalmologist, optometrist), helped with the surgery.
9. He broke a (stature, statute) when he burned the house.
10. John is a man of no special (talent, ability), but he is a good employee because he is diligent and reliable.
11. (Accelerated, Exhilarated) training has an (accelerating, exhilarating) effect upon superior students.
12. She has a (momentary, momentous) decision to make about her responsibility in this matter.
13. Tom is (adapt, adept) at getting information from top-level sources.
14. Louise will be (restive, restful) as long as she has to cope with this difficult situation.
15. Do you think that we will be able to (illicit, elicit) the facts and figures we need for this story?

among	(ȧ mŏng′)	*prep*. Mixed with more than two things.
between	(bĕ twēēn′)	*prep*. In the space that separates two things.
character	(chăr′ ăc tēr)	*n*. One's real nature.
reputation	(rĕp′ ū tā′ tion)	*n*. One's supposed nature.
compare	(cŏm pâre′)	*v*. To examine for resemblances.
contrast	(cŏn trăst′)	*v*. To examine for differences.
custom	(cŭs′ tŏm)	*n*. An action characteristic of most people in a culture.
habit	(hăb′ ĭt)	*n*. A settled action of one person.
discover	(dĭs cŏv′ ēr)	*v*. To obtain knowledge of something for the first time.
invent	(ĭn vĕnt′)	*v*. To make for the first time; to devise.
educated	(ĕd′ ū cāt′ ĕd)	*adj*. Enlightened through systematic instruction.
intelligent	(ĭn tĕl′ lĭ ġĕnt)	*adj*. Having a great capacity to learn.
evidence	(ĕv′ ĭ dĕnçe)	*n*. Anything that proves a fact.
testimony	(tĕs′ tĭ mō′ nўy)	*n*. The declaration of a person to prove a fact.
famous	(fā′ mŏŭs)	*adj*. Celebrated or renowned in a good sense.
notorious	(nṓ tō′ rĭ oŭs)	*adj*. Generally known in a bad sense.
hardly	(härd′ lўy)	*adv*. With difficulty; by hard work.
scarcely	(scârçe′ lўy)	*adv*. Lacking in quantity; with scant margin.

A. Consult your dictionary for the pronunciation and meaning of the following words:

(arbitrate   conciliate   pacify)   (conscious   aware)
(consistently   constantly)

B. Choose the correct words from the pairs of words in parentheses in the following sentences:

1. There was a warm friendship (among, between) the three students.
2. He had a (character, reputation) for paying his debts promptly.
3. (Compare, Contrast) the temperature of the equatorial region with that of the arctic region.
4. It was his (custom, habit) to arise at six o'clock.
5. Many attempts were made to (discover, invent) a better engine.
6. His knowledge of the classics showed him to be an (educated, intelligent) man.
7. Have you given your (evidence, testimony) at the trial?
8. The man proved to be a (famous, notorious) gambler.
9. His leg was so stiff that he could (hardly, scarcely) climb the stairs.
10. Take your choice (among, between) the two seats that are still available.

The following pairs of misused words are taken from Lessons 89 to 93. Be especially careful to review the meanings of these words.

aggravate	hardly
exasperate	scarcely
among	healthful
between	healthy
character	ignorant
reputation	illiterate
compare	later
contrast	latter
compensate	last
remunerate	latest
continual	majority
continuous	plurality
educated	may
intelligent	can
emigrant	noted
immigrant	notorious
exceptionable	sample
exceptional	specimen
feasible	surprise
plausible	astonish

Be prepared to give sentences for the following words:

amateur
novice
conscious
aware
fatal
fateful
local
native
indigenous
pupil
scholar
student

Not only is the letter *e* the most frequently used letter in the English language, it is also the greatest trouble maker in spelling. The vowels *i* and *e* seem to have an attraction for each other, for they are frequently found in *ie* and *ei* combinations. When the letter *c* precedes these letters, you may have trouble.

You know the rule:

"Use *i* before *e*
Except after *c*;
Or when sounded like *a*,
As in *neighbor* or *weigh*."

Now this rule in itself causes trouble because it is incomplete. It is true that in a word such as *receive*, the *e* precedes the *i* because these letters follow *c*. The rule holds when the two letters have the long *e* sound.

There are many words, however, in which *i* precedes *e* after *c*; words such as effi*ci*ent have the *cie* combination, but note the difference in pronunciation. When *ie* follows *c*, the *ci* has the *sh* sound; the *i* not only "softens" the *c*, but adds the *h* sound.

There are some exceptions to these rules: *either*, *neither*, *weird*, *seize*, *heifer*, *forfeit*, *counterfeit*, and *leisure*. Some of these words— *either*, *neither*, and *leisure*, for example—were at one time pronounced with the *ā* sound; the pronunciation of the words changed, but the spelling of the words remained the same.

A. What rules apply to the spelling of the following words?

ancient	efficient	proficient
conceit	eight	receive
conscious	freight	sufficient
deceit	neighbor	veil
deceive	perceive	weight

B. Copy the following sentences, correcting any misspelled words:

1. Mary's neice was visiting her over the weekend.
2. Mrs. Jones always keeps her reciepted bills.
3. We believed our football team would win.
4. I was deceived by his masquerade.
5. Did you get a reciept for your money?
6. Niether of the girls is ready to go.
7. They are good neighbors, and very efficeint.
8. She recieved three handkerchiefs for her birthday.
9. How much does this carton weigh?
10. We visited friends in Rome last year, and while there, we saw many ancient buildings.

C. Write five words in which *ei* is pronounced *ā*; five words in which *cient* is pronounced *shĕnt;* and five words in which *cei* is pronounced *sē*.

A. Syllabicate each of the following words, indicating the syllable or syllables most likely to cause trouble:

accommodate
accurate
advice
all right
already
assistance
business
calendar
complimentary
convenient
correspondence
criticism
description
experience
incidentally
maintenance
occasion
occurred
personnel
principal
privilege
procedure
repetition
scarcity
separate
similar
territory
undoubtedly
unnecessary
wholly

B. 1. Why is there a final *e* in *envelope,* when *develop* does not have a final *e*?

2. Why are there two *r's* in *occurred*? Why are there two *m's* in *accommodate*?

3. From what adjective is the word *business* derived?

C. Why do the words *familiar* and *similar* differ in ending? Do the words have the same suffix? Explain.

A. Copy the following words and underscore the part of each word most likely to cause misspelling.

acquaintance	fourth
across	government
already	governor
among	inconvenient
analysis	it's
analyze	its
apparent	laboratory
appearance	legitimate
arrangement	loose
beginning	maintenance
brilliant	mortgage
calendar	omission
collateral	omitted
coming	pamphlet
committee	practical
confident	preferred
controversy	procedure
criticize	professor
difference	reference
endeavor	repetition
especially	seized
exceed	stationary
except	strictly
experience	surprise
explanation	their

B. Use the following words in sentences:
apparent   collateral   committee   it's   its   legitimate   mortgage

C. List the prefixes to be found in the words given in A.

Have you kept a record of your errors in your notebook? Is there a pattern to your errors? Do you transpose letters? Are your mistakes made on word beginnings, word endings? Are your mistakes due to failure to syllabicate words, to lack of knowledge of phonetics?

Whatever the reasons for your mistakes, consider a method of conquering them. One way is to pronounce a word the way it is spelled and associate this pronunciation with the correct pronunciation. Example: accident-ally—accidentally; Wed-nes-day—Wednesday.

Another way is to associate troublesome words with other words. Example: all right—all wrong. Rudolf Flesch gives the following examples of this type of association.[1]

Dr. Flesch's Own Spelling Associations

accidentally. There's a *tally* in *accidentally.*
accurate. *Accuracy* is the only *cure* for mistakes.
address. On second-class mail, the *address* is the *ad dress.*
adviser. Even an advis*er* may *err.*
aging. Drinking *gin* speeds *aging.*
all right—already. The *two* of them are *all right*; they're *already together.*
battalion. The *battalion* fought like *a lion.*
bogey. Keep your *eye* on the ball.
Britain. *Britain* wanted to *retain* her empire.
buses. *Buses* have many *uses.*
collar. A *collar* in a *large* size.
colossal. *Colossal* movies are in *color.*
comparison. The *comparison* shopper went to *Paris.*
compliment. *Compliments* flatter the ego—the *I.*
costume. *Costumes cost* money.
counsel. A *counsel sells* his advice.
custom. Don't *cuss* when you go through *customs.*
dependent. *Dependents* must be taken to the *dentist.*
describe. The *description* is on your *desk.*
diary. In a *diary,* the *I* comes first.
dumfounded. I was so *dumfounded* I lost a *b.*
embarrass. *Embarrassment* is a *barrier* to conversation.
exhilarating. It's ex*hilar*ating to walk up a *hill.*
forty. *Forty* soldiers held the *fort.*
gorilla. The dead *gorilla* was a *gory* sight.
gypsy. *I'm* not a *gypsy.*
hangar. A han*gar* is an airplane *gar*age.
harass. *Harassed* as a hunted *hare.*
hypocrisy. Hypo*crisy* can produce a *crisis.*
imminent. It can happen any *minute.*
incidentally. There's a *tally* in *incidentally.*
indispensable. As indispen*sable* as *sable.*
loose. A *moose* let *loose.*
mantel. There's a *telephone* on the man*tel.*
mortgage. *Mortals* are apt to die before the *mortgage* is paid off.
mustache. His *mustache* was *musty* and dusty.
nickel. It cost a nick*el* to ride the old *el.*
obbligato. A steady *obbligato* of *b—b—b—b.*
paid. To be *paid* is an *aid.*

---

[1] Rudolf Flesch, "How to Be a Perfect Speller," *Saturday Review* (January 14, 1961), p. 41.

parallel. *All el* tracks are par*allel.*
pendant. My *aunt* wore a pend*ant.*
playwright. Some play*wrights* are carpenters rather than *writers.*
pygmy. *I'm* not a *pygmy.*
resin. They decided to *re-sin.*
sacrilegious. Sac*rileg*ious is the opposite of *relig*ious.
separate. To *separate* means to set *apart.*
sibyl. The sib*yl* lived near*by.*
siege. The besi*eg*ed city was down to one *egg.*
sieve. They used a si*eve* for the *eve*ning meal.
stationary. He made *nary a move.*
stationery. *One* pen, *one* pencil, *one* sheet of paper.
succeed—success. He *succeed*ed in *doubling* his fortune.
supersede. When you're being super*seded,* take a *sed*ative.
surprise. A *burp* gives *rise* to *surprise.*
their. *Their* house was left to an *heir.*
there. *There* is not *here.*
villain. That's the *villa in* which the *villain* lives.

It may not be profitable to spend much time on an analysis of your errors, unless you are especially interested in such analysis, but you should be aware of the difficulties that prevent you from becoming accurate in your spelling.

Syllabicate the following words commonly used in business correspondence, marking any syllables likely to cause trouble:

accept	incidentally
accommodate	lose
accumulate	magazine
advise	necessary
affect	noticeable
all right	occasion
already	occurrence
attendance	opportunities
benefited	personal
business	possession
conscientious	principle
conveniently	proceed
definite	processes
description	psychology
develop	quantity
disappoint	questionnaire
effect	receive
eligible	recommendations
embarrass	respectfully
equipped	respectively
existence	schedule
extension	stationery
foreign	superintendent
height	thorough
immediately	useful

The effectiveness of our speech and writing is determined to a great extent by our ability to find the one word that precisely suits our purpose. There are many synonyms in the English language—that is, words with similar meanings—but few words with identical meanings. It has been said that "begin" and "commence" have almost exactly the same meaning and that few other synonyms are so closely related. Be that as it may, we know that to use words exactly, we must have exact knowledge of the meaning of many words plus the patience to search for the best words to express our meaning.

Take, for example, the common words *discover* and *invent*. Was atomic energy discovered or invented? Was electricity discovered or invented? What is the exact meaning of these words? Likewise, consider the words *amateur* and *novice*. Is a beginner an amateur? If so, what is a novice? When does one cease to be a novice and/or an amateur? These are just a few of the questions that come to mind in comparing and contrasting these words. Unfortunately, some of us do not bother to "pin down" our understanding of words; we use them fuzzily and then wonder why our comments are misunderstood and misquoted.

Inexactness results also from the overuse of general terms. Some general words are sadly overworked—words such as *nice, terrible, awful, funny, good, bad*. These words have been so used, overused, and misused that they lack meaning. This is also true of slang so widely used that it has lost meaning. Only definite words give definite mental images. For example, one gets only a fuzzy impression from the comment that "Helen wears awful clothes to the office." *Awful* may refer to the quality of the clothes, their condition, their appearance on Helen, their suitability to the occasion, etc. How much more definite is the comment that "Helen wears bright, sleeveless dresses to the office," or "Helen wears her old evening clothes, slightly altered, to the office," or "Helen's clothes never fit her." We could go on indefinitely interpreting the word "awful" in the original comment.

A. Complete each of the following sentences by filling in a word, in its proper form, from the list of 15 below.

Words Related to *Make*

build	design	generate
compose	develop	manufacture
construct	erect	originate
convert	fashion	produce
create	forge	weave

1. In colonial days, cloth was (   ) in homes and (   ) into durable garments.
2. Turbines are (   ) so that they may be used to (   ) the power of waterfalls into electricity.

3. My teacher has (   ) several songs that have been published.
4. Because of assembly-line methods, automobiles are (   ) in such numbers that they are available to most families.
5. Increased interest in television has (   ) new problems for the motion-picture industry.
6. John is a skilled draftsman who (   ) very accurate blueprints.
7. After the blade has been (   ) in the blacksmith's shop, it is ground and polished.
8. The grandstand and bleachers were (   ) by a reliable lumber company.
9. Improved methods of physical training should (   ) a nation of athletes.
10. Russel Wright (   ) glasses as well as pottery.

B. *Nice* is one of our overused adjectives, also misused to the point where it has lost its original meaning of *precision, discrimination*. Following are a few of the words that might be suggested by *nice* in certain contexts: *amiable, attractive, comfortable, considerate, delicate, delightful, exciting, fastidious, luscious,* and *refreshing*. In the expressions below, substitute the preceding words for the word *nice*:

nice chair	nice fruit
nice housekeeper	nice game
nice evening	nice girl
nice friend	nice fragrance

C. *Go* and its past tense, *went*, are too much with us. Usually a more descriptive word could be used to advantage. Substitute for each blank in the following sentences the correct form of the most appropriate word from the list of more exact words:

dash	saunter
jump	scamper
leap	scurry
limp	shuffle
meander	trek
run	walk

1. When I turned on the light in the barn, I saw the rats (   ) across the floor.
2. On bright mornings he would (   ) slowly along the garden paths, a fox terrier (   ) at his heels.
3. After emerging from the foothills, the two streams (   ) sluggishly over the fields.
4. The pioneers had to (   ) hundreds of miles over the desert to reach fertile land.
5. With a languid air, the comedian would (   ) across the stage and stare mournfully at the audience.
6. Harry (   ) into the room without a greeting and then (   ) out as though demons were pursuing him.
7. Many city dwellers (   ) ten or twelve blocks every night before going to bed.

In this lesson, we shall find substitutes for the overused and too general words *awful, expert,* and *noise,* before proceeding to more exacting exercises.

	awful		
discordant	nauseating	serious	ugly
monotonous	odious	terrible	unsavory

A. In the following expressions, substitute words taken from the foregoing group for the word "awful."

awful accident
awful battle
awful discourse
awful food

awful hat
awful music
awful sensation
awful task

	expert		
accomplished	dexterous	proficient	shrewd
apt	facile	ready-witted	stealthy

B. In the following expressions, substitute words taken from the foregoing group for the word "expert."

expert debater
expert musician
expert painter
expert politician

expert sewer
expert student
expert teacher
expert thief

	noise		
buzz	murmur	rumble	whistle
howl	patter	sputter	whiz

C. In the following expressions, substitute words taken from the foregoing group for the word "noise."

noise of bees
noise of hot fat
noise of rain
noise of the arrow

noise of the brook
noise of the locomotive
noise of the wolf
noise of thunder

Avoid long words that may be unfamiliar to the reader or listener. The best words to use are the words that everyone understands. Do not say that a man is *impecunious*; say that he is *poor.* It is usually better to speak of *standards* rather than *criteria,* of *pen names* rather than *pseudonyms*, of *spelling* rather than *orthography*. Another way of stating this rule is to say that whenever possible, the writer or speaker should use words of Anglo-Saxon origin, with relatively few words of Latin or Greek origin.

D. Copy the following sentences, inserting the most suitable words from those suggested:

1. *manufacture, produce, construct*
   (a) The use of organic fertilizer enables land to (   ) more healthful crops.
   (b) Our company (   ) educational toys.
   (c) A competent carpenter can (   ) a prefabricated house with little difficulty.

2. *income, wages, salaries*
   The (   ) of workmen have increased threefold whereas the (   ) of white-collar workers have increased but slightly. Moreover, the average white-collar worker, like the average workman, has no (   ) from other sources.

3. *valuable, expensive*
   John's education was (   ) but not particularly (   ) to him because he does not seem to have profited from it. Arthur's education, on the contrary, was not (   ), since he attended a state college and lived at home during his college years; but his degree has proved to be (   ) to him both from a personal standpoint and from a vocational point of view.

E. Underscore the word in parentheses that is most closely related to the word outside the parentheses. Then, use each of the "outside words" in a sentence.

1. affability (sense of humor, pretense, sociability, credulity)
2. annihilate (kill, erase, destroy, excuse)
3. antagonistic (hostile, ambitious, envious, jealous)
4. arid (dry, hot, spicy, deserted)
5. chronic (long-lasting, timely, diseased, elusive)
6. defray (unload freight, pay, untangle)
7. expedite (explain, walk, rush, pretend)
8. matriculate (graduate, enroll, ensue, murder one's mother)
9. mien (bearing, nastiness, smallness, middle)
10. monogamous (tiresome, attractively lettered, gifted in speaking, having but one mate)

Here are five words that are much overworked. Below each of the five words are listed eight words that are far more descriptive than the general terms. Learn to spell and to pronounce every word in this lesson.

bunch			
assembly	bundle	drove	retinue
bouquet	collection	gang	swarm

A. In the following expressions, substitute words taken from the foregoing group for the word "bunch."

bunch of deputies   **bunch of old coins**   **bunch of sticks**
bunch of flowers   **bunch of oxen**   **bunch of thieves**
bunch of locusts   **bunch of servants**

cut			
carve	divide	mutilate	sever
cleave	mow	reduce	split

B. In the following expressions, substitute words taken from the foregoing group for the word "cut."

cut branches   **cut the body**   **cut the roast**
cut hairs   **cut the bone**   **cut the spoils**
cut prices   **cut the lawn**

funny			
awkward	freakish	preposterous	unaccountable
eccentric	old-fashioned	remarkable	unconventional

C. In the following expressions, substitute words taken from the foregoing group for the word "funny."

funny achievement   **funny house**   **funny storm**
funny action   **funny person**   **funny taste**
funny charge   **funny situation**

120

pretty			
artistic	dainty	plaintive	sparkling
becoming	graceful	silvery	stirring

D. In the following expressions, substitute words taken from the foregoing group for the word "pretty."

pretty bird call	pretty lace	pretty room
pretty dress	pretty march	pretty water
pretty fawn	pretty moonlight	

grand			
delicious	gallant	mild	rare
elaborate	inimitable	ornate	winning

E. In the following expressions, substitute words taken from the foregoing group for the word "grand."

grand banquet	grand soldier	grand weather
grand food	grand storyteller	grand wild flower
grand furniture	grand team	

102   Exact words vs. general words (Concluded)

A. Contrast each of the words in parentheses with the word outside the parentheses. Then use the words in sentences to show their exact meaning. Note that we start with general words that you might use to describe some of your associates, and then proceed to more specific words.

1. friendly (affable, convivial, genial, gregarious, generous)
2. industrious (capable, conscientious, creative, energetic, untiring)
3. clever (shrewd, brilliant, scheming, witty, entertaining)
4. courageous (daring, fearless, foolhardy, idealistic, selfless)
5. sophisticated (cultivated, cynical, poised, tactful, worldly-wise)

B. Write a sentence for each of the following words, highlighting their differences in meaning:

adroitness	cleverness	finesse	originality
competence	cunning	ingenuity	skill

C. 1. Give a synonym for each of the following words:

callous	casual	destitute	diligent
candid	concise	detain	diverse
		dubious	

2. Use six of the above words in sentences.

Everyone is interested in time. This is shown by our talking about such things as our "last summer's vacation," or our "future plans," or the "football season."

afternoon	(àft′ ẽr no͞on′)	*n.*	Between noon and evening.
ancient	(ān′ cient) shĕnt	*adj.*	Belonging to times past.
annually	(ăn′ *n*ū̆ ăl lў̆)	*adv.*	Yearly.
autumn	(au′ tŭm*n*)	*n.*	Between summer and winter.
biannual	(bī ăn′ *n*ū̆ ăl)	*adj.*	Occurring twice a year.
biennial	(bī ĕn′ *n*ĭ ăl)	*adj.*	Occurring every two years.
contemporary	(cŏn tĕm′ pŏ́ rar′ ў̆) rĕr′	*adj.*	Existing at the same time.
decade	(dĕc′ āde)	*n.*	Ten consecutive years.
epoch	(ĕp′ ŏc*h*)	*n.*	A period of time; an era.
eternal	(ĕ tẽr′ n ă l)	*adj.*	Everlasting.
eventually	(ĕ́ vĕn′ tū̆ ăl lў̆)	*adv.*	Finally; ultimately.
finally	(fī′ năl lў̆)	*adv.*	At the end; ultimately.
forenoon	(fōr*e*′ no͞on′)	*n.*	The early part of the day.
fortnight	(fôrt′ nī*gh*t)	*n.*	Two weeks.
infinity	(ĭn fĭn′ ĭ tў̆)	*n.*	Unlimited extent of time, space, or quantity.
instantly	(ĭn′ stănt lў̆)	*adv.*	Without delay; at once.
intermission	(ĭn′ tẽr mis′ sion) mĭsh′ ŭn	*n.*	Intervening period of time.
midnight	(mĭd′ nī*gh*t′)	*n.*	Twelve o'clock at night.
momentary	(mō′ mĕn tar′ ў̆) tĕr′	*adj.*	Continuing only a moment.
prior	(prī′ ŏr)	*adj.*	Preceding in order of time.
semiannual	(sĕm′ ĭ ăn′ *n*ū̆ ăl)	*adj.*	Occurring every six months.
subsequent	(sŭb′ sĕ́ quĕnt) kwĕnt	*adj.*	Following in time or order.

A. List the names of the months of the year. Consult your dictionary concerning the derivation of these names. Write a sentence for each month, explaining the name of the month.

B. List the names of the days of the week. Get as much information as you can about these names from your dictionary, from your school librarian, and from reference books. Write a short paper giving this information.

C. Consult your dictionary for the pronunciation and meaning of the following words:

antiquity   biennium   century   medieval   millennium

Below are additional words pertaining to time. Why are many of the words in this and the preceding list adverbs?

afterward	(ȧf′ tẽr wȧrd)	*adv.* At a later time.
always	(al′ wāyṣ)	*adv.* At all times.
anniversary	(ăn′ *ni* vẽr′ sȧ rȳ)	*n.* Annual event.
beforehand	(bḗ fōr*e*′ hănd′)	*adv.* In advance.
constantly	(cŏn′ stănt lȳ)	*adv.* Uniformly; continuously.
endure	(ĕn dūre′)	*v.* To last.
eternity	(ḗ tẽr′ nǐ tȳ)	*n.* A totality of infinite time.
everlasting	(ĕv′ ẽr làst′ ĭng)	*adj.* Lasting forever.
forthwith	(fōrth′ wǐth′)	*adv.* Immediately; without delay.
frequent	(frē′ quent) kwĕnt	*adj.* Often.
gradually	(grăd′ ú̇ ăl lȳ)	*adv.* By degrees; slowly.
hastily	(hȧst′ ĭ lȳ)	*adv.* Hurriedly; quickly.
holiday	(hŏl′ ĭ dāy)	*n.* A festival day.
immediately	(ĭ*m* mē′ dǐ át*e* lȳ)	*adv.* Without delay; at once.
meanwhile	(mēan′ while′) hwǐl′	*adv.* In the intervening time.
modern	(mŏd′ ẽrn)	*adj.* Pertaining to the present.
nowadays	(now′ ȧ dāyṣ)	*adv.* At the present time.
perpetual	(pẽr pĕt′ ú̇ ăl)	*adj.* Continuing forever.
preliminary	(prḗ lǐm′ ǐ nar′ ȳ) nẽr′	*adj.* Preceding the main affair.
rapidly	(răp′ ĭd lȳ)	*adv.* Speedily; quickly.
swiftly	(swĭft′ lȳ)	*adv.* Quickly; rapidly.
temporary	(tĕm′ pō̇ rar′ ȳ) rẽr′	*adj.* Lasting for a short time only.
transient	(trăn′ sient) shĕnt	*adj.* Of short duration; brief; passing through.
ultimately	(ŭl′ tǐ mát*e* lȳ)	*adv.* Finally.
yesterday	(yĕs′ tẽr dāy)	*n.* The day before today.

A. Consult your dictionary for the pronunciation and meaning of the following words:

expedite   interim   opportune   pending   premature

B. Use the following words in sentences:

endure   perpetual   preliminary   transient   ultimately

C. What is the difference between a *centenarian* and an *octogenarian*?

D. Use each of the words in A in a sentence.

The names of a few states should not be abbreviated. "Cal." was formerly used as an abbreviation for "California," and "Col." as an abbreviation for "Colorado." So many mistakes resulted, however, from the similarity of the abbreviations, that "Calif." and "Colo." are now preferred.

STATE	ABBREVIATION	CAPITAL CITY
Alabama	Ala.	Montgomery
Alaska		Juneau
Arizona	Ariz.	Phoenix
Arkansas	Ark.	Little Rock
California	Calif.	Sacramento
Colorado	Colo.	Denver
Connecticut	Conn.	Hartford
Delaware	Del.	Dover
District of Columbia	D. C.	Washington
Florida	Fla.	Tallahassee
Georgia	Ga.	Atlanta
Hawaii	H. I.	Honolulu
Idaho		Boise
Illinois	Ill.	Springfield
Indiana	Ind.	Indianapolis
Iowa		Des Moines
Kansas	Kans.	Topeka
Kentucky	Ky.	Frankfort
Louisiana	La.	Baton Rouge
Maine		Augusta
Maryland	Md.	Annapolis
Massachusetts	Mass.	Boston
Michigan	Mich.	Lansing
Minnesota	Minn.	St. Paul
Mississippi	Miss.	Jackson
Missouri	Mo.	Jefferson City
Montana	Mont.	Helena
Nebraska	Nebr.	Lincoln
Nevada	Nev.	Carson City

The name of a state should never be abbreviated unless it is used in connection with the name of a city. Thus, it is correct to write, "He lives in Albany, N. Y."; but it would be incorrect to write, "He lives in N. Y."

STATE	ABBREVIATION	CAPITAL CITY
New Hampshire	N. H.	Concord
New Jersey	N. J.	Trenton
New Mexico	N. Mex.	Santa Fe
New York	N. Y.	Albany
North Carolina	N. C.	Raleigh
North Dakota	N. Dak.	Bismarck
Ohio		Columbus
Oklahoma	Okla.	Oklahoma City
Oregon	Oreg.	Salem
Pennsylvania	Pa.	Harrisburg
Rhode Island	R. I.	Providence
South Carolina	S. C.	Columbia
South Dakota	S. Dak.	Pierre
Tennessee	Tenn.	Nashville
Texas	Tex.	Austin
Utah		Salt Lake City
Vermont	Vt.	Montpelier
Virginia	Va.	Richmond
Washington	Wash.	Olympia
West Virginia	W. Va.	Charleston
Wisconsin	Wis.	Madison
Wyoming	Wyo.	Cheyenne

COMMONWEALTH AND ADMINISTERED REGIONS		
American Samoa		Pago Pago
Canal Zone	C. Z.	Balboa Heights (admin. center)
Commonwealth of Puerto Rico	P. R.	San Juan
Guam		Agaña
Virgin Islands	V. I.	Charlotte Amalie

107   Names of cities that are difficult to spell

The spelling of the names of the following cities frequently causes trouble. Names of cities should never be abbreviated.

NAME OF CITY	LOCATION	NAME OF CITY	LOCATION
Akron	Ohio	Charlottesville	Va.
Alexandria	Va.	Chattanooga	Tenn.
Altoona	Pa.	Chautauqua	N. Y.
Amarillo	Tex.	Cheyenne	Wyo.
Annapolis	Md.	Cleveland	Ohio
Asheville	N. C.	Covington	Ky.
Atchison	Kans.	Du Bois	Pa.
Augusta	Ga.	Dubuque	Iowa
Bayonne	N. J.	Duluth	Minn.
Beaumont	Tex.	El Paso	Tex.
Binghamton	N. Y.	Fresno	Calif.
Birmingham	Ala.	Gloucester	Mass.
Bismarck	N. Dak.	Harrisburg	Pa.
Boulder	Colo.	Hattiesburg	Miss.
Bridgeport	Conn.	Holyoke	Mass.
Cambridge	Mass.	Houston	Tex.

A. List the five largest cities in your state. Write five sentences, one for each city, in which you tell something about that city.

B. List the ten largest cities in the United States, with their respective states.

C. Write a brief paragraph telling the history of the name of your community.

D. List the state capitals given in this lesson and use each of them in a sentence.

If you are in doubt about the pronunciation of any of the names in this lesson, be sure to look them up in the dictionary. Notice that Newark is one word, not two. Notice particularly the number of "s's" in Pasadena and Passaic, and the number of "t's" in Paterson.

NAME OF CITY	LOCATION	NAME OF CITY	LOCATION
Huntington	W. Va.	Montpelier	Vt.
Indianapolis	Ind.	Nashville	Tenn.
Ithaca	N. Y.	New Orleans	La.
Kalamazoo	Mich.	Newark	N. J.
Kankakee	Ill.	Niagara Falls	N. Y.
Keokuk	Iowa	Olympia	Wash.
Knoxville	Tenn.	Omaha	Nebr.
Las Vegas	Nev.	Orlando	Fla.
Louisville	Ky.	Oshkosh	Wis.
Lowell	Mass.	Pasadena	Calif.
Lynn	Mass.	Passaic	N. J.
Macon	Ga.	Paterson	N. J.
Marietta	Ohio	Pawtucket	R. I.
Memphis	Tenn.	Pensacola	Fla.
Miami	Fla.	Peoria	Ill.
Milwaukee	Wis.	Philadelphia	Pa.
Minneapolis	Minn.	Pierre	S. Dak.

A. List the names of five cities in the United States not given in this book that you consider difficult to spell.

B. Write one sentence about each of the cities listed in A.

C. Explain the spelling of "Pierre" in South Dakota. Why should a name pronounced as "Pir" be spelled "Pierre"?

Notice that Pittsburgh, Pennsylvania, ends in an "h"; whereas Pittsburg, Kansas, does not end with "h." "San," which forms part of such names as San Antonio and San Bernardino, is the Spanish for "Saint."

NAME OF CITY	LOCATION	NAME OF CITY	LOCATION
Pittsburg	Kans.	Schenectady	N. Y.
Pittsburgh	Pa.	Scranton	Pa.
Pueblo	Colo.	Seattle	Wash.
Providence	R. I.	Shreveport	La.
Raleigh	N. C.	Sioux City	Iowa
Rochester	N. Y.	Somerville	Mass.
Sacramento	Calif.	Spokane	Wash.
Saginaw	Mich.	Syracuse	N. Y.
St. Louis	Mo.	Tacoma	Wash.
San Antonio	Tex.	Tallahassee	Fla.
San Bernardino	Calif.	Utica	N. Y.
San Diego	Calif.	Waterbury	Conn.
Sandusky	Ohio	Wichita	Kans.
San Francisco	Calif.	Wilmington	Del.
Savannah	Ga.	Yonkers	N. Y.

A. Some of the names above are Indian names. Choose one of these Indian names and learn as much as you can about it.

B. Which of the cities above were named for Christian Saints? Choose one of these names and learn as much as you can about it.

C. Why do so many of the cities in the West have Spanish names, whereas so many of the cities in the East have British names?

This list contains some of the frequently misspelled words in Lessons 95 to 104 inclusive.

accommodate	immediately
analysis	industrious
biannual	maintenance
committee	repetition
correspondence	stationary
defray	subsequent
efficient	sufficient
expedite	transient

Be prepared to write correctly all of the state and territory abbreviations and capitals when they are dictated to you. (Lessons 105 and 106.)

This list contains many of the frequently misspelled city names in Lessons 107 to 109.

NAME OF CITY	LOCATION	NAME OF CITY	LOCATION
Amarillo	Tex.	Minneapolis	Minn.
Annapolis	Md.	Montpelier	Vt.
Asheville	N. C.	Olympia	Wash.
Bayonne	N. J.	Pasadena	Calif.
Binghamton	N. Y.	Passaic	N. J.
Bismarck	N. Dak.	Paterson	N. J.
Charlottesville	Va.	Pittsburgh	Pa.
Cheyenne	Wyo.	Raleigh	N. C.
Dubuque	Iowa	Sacramento	Calif.
Holyoke	Mass.	San Bernardino	Calif.
Indianapolis	Ind.	San Francisco	Calif.
Ithaca	N. Y.	Savannah	Ga.
Kalamazoo	Mich.	Schenectady	N. Y.
Kankakee	Ill.	Sioux City	Iowa
Memphis	Tenn.	Tallahassee	Fla.

As a rule, we use few abbreviations in general writing, but we should recognize many abbreviations since some are commonly used in business writing.

Many abbreviations are composed of the initial letters of foreign words. Thus, the abbreviation "A.M." is formed from the initial letters of the phrase *ante meridiem*, meaning "before noon." In this and the following lessons, the foreign phrases from which some of the abbreviations have been taken are omitted and only the English meanings are given.

ABBREVIATION	ENGLISH MEANING
acct.	account
Asst.	assistant
B.C.	before Christ
C.O.D.	collect *or* cash on delivery
cwt.	hundredweight *(Centum) L*
doz.	dozen *or* dozens
Dr.	Doctor
e.g.	for example *(exemplē gratia) L.*
Esq.	Esquire
et al.	and others *(et alii) L*
etc.	and so forth *et cetera)*
F.O.B.	free on board
ft.	foot *or* feet
gal.	gallon *or* gallons
Hon.	Honorable
hr.	hour *or* hours
ICBM	intercontinental ballistic missiles
i.e.	that is *(id est) L*
Jos.	Joseph *or* Josiah
lb.	pound *or* pounds *libra*
memo.	memorandum
Messrs. *French*	Gentlemen
Mr.	Mister
Mrs.	Mistress
No. *Numero L*	number
oz.	ounce *or* ounces
Ph.D.	Doctor of Philosophy
P.M.	after noon *Post Meridian*
pp.	pages
P.S.	postscript *(written after)*
recd.	received
Rev.	Reverend
S.R.O.	Standing Room Only
U.N.	United Nations
viz.	namely

Such words as "association," "building," and "company" are ordinarily common nouns and are not capitalized unless they refer to specific associations, buildings, or companies. When these words are used as proper nouns—i.e., as parts of names—they are abbreviated only if the organization represented abbreviates the word in its name. The "Adams and Smith Co." determines whether the last unit of its name should be abbreviated or spelled in full.

ABBREVIATION	ENGLISH MEANING
A.B.	Bachelor of Arts
A.D.	in the year of our Lord *(anno Domini)*
amt.	amount
assn.	association
ave.	avenue
bbl.	barrel *or* barrels
B/L	bill of lading
bldg.	building
B.S.	Bachelor of Science
bu.	bushel *or* bushels
chap.	chapter
co.	company
C.P.A.	Certified Public Accountant
D.D.	Doctor of Divinity
dept.	department
H.R.	House of Representatives
in.	inch *or* inches
Jr.	Junior
M.A.	Master of Arts
M.D.	Doctor of Medicine
mdse.	merchandise
Mgr.	manager
mo.	month
pd.	paid
Prof.	professor
qt.	quart *or* quantity
R & D	research and development
St.	street *or* Saint
Supt.	superintendent
U.S.N.	United States Navy
vol.	volume
vs. *versus*	against
v.v.	vice versa
wk.	week
yd.	yard *or* yards

ABBREVIATION	ENGLISH MEANING
anon.	anonymous
A. P.	Associated Press
ARC	American Red Cross
cert.	certificate, certify
c.o.	care of *or* carried over
cr.	credit
D.D.S.	Doctor of Dental Surgery
do.	ditto
doc.	document *or* doctor
D.S.T.	Daylight Saving Time *or* Doctor of Sacred Theology
dup.	duplicate
dz.	dozen
Govt.	government
hdqrs.	headquarters
ibid.	in the same place
invt.	inventory
I.Q.	intelligence quotient
LCL	less than carload lot
loc. cit.	in the place cited
mph	miles per hour
mtge.	mortgage
N.B.	note well
pat.	patent, patented, pattern
pfd.	preferred
p.n.	promissory note
ppd.	prepaid
pph.	pamphlet
pro tem.	for the time being
Q.E.D.	which was to be demonstrated
Rd.	road
r.p.m.	revolutions per minute
R.S.V.P.	Please reply
Ry.	railway
SEC	Securities and Exchange Commission
seq.	the following
tfr.	transfer
U.S.S.R.	Union of Soviet Socialist Republics

Part 5 ◢ WORDS RELATED TO BUSINESS AND ECONOMICS

The business world—always moving and always changing—requires millions of employees to perform thousands of different kinds of jobs. In addition to having a mastery of work skills, men and women who enter the business world must possess an understanding of what business is and how it operates.

What is involved in business? Business is the buying and selling of goods and services in stores, in service establishments, and in offices. Business is financing, for funds are needed to pay employees, to build inventories, to set aside savings for the purchase of new equipment, and to provide for the payment of dividends to stockholders and interest to bondholders. Business is producing and distributing. Raw materials are taken by business, processed, and distributed in the form of food, clothing, shelter, and thousands of other articles to world-wide markets. Through business we are provided with a marketplace where we can secure those goods and services needed for our daily living. Finally, business affords us career opportunities in which we can use our knowledge and skills to earn money to purchase goods and services.

In the lessons that make up Part 5, we shall focus our attention upon those words related to the field of business and economics. These words are commonly encountered by students who take business courses in school, who read current periodicals, who listen to radio and TV newscasts, and who converse with others of the general public. Some terms that are highly specialized and peculiar to a particular field of endeavor have been omitted from these lists, since such words are seldom used by the general public.

Well, you might say I'm an abstractionist in spelling, Mr. Topman— Expressive - individual - original!

acre	(ā′ cre) kēr	n. A measure of land.
alfalfa	(ăl făl′ fȧ)	n. A forage plant.
barren	(băr′ rĕn)	adj. Not producing vegetation.
cultivate	(cŭl′ tĭ vāte)	v. To loosen the soil; to till.
ensilage	(ĕn′ sĭ lage) lĭj	n. Preserved green fodder.
fallow	(făl′ lōw)	adj. Left untilled; uncultivated.
fertile	(fēr′ tĭle)	adj. Rich; productive.
fertilize	(fēr′ tĭ līze)	v. To enrich the soil.
fodder	(fŏd′ dēr)	n. Coarse food for horses and cattle.
forage	(fŏr′ age) ĭj	n. Food for horses and cattle.
fungicide	(fŭn′ ģĭ çīde)	n. Substance for destroying fungi.
harrow	(hăr′ rōw)	n. Tool for smoothing soil. v. To smooth.
harvest	(här′ vĕst)	n. A gathering of crops. v. To gather.
heifer	(hĕif′ ēr)	n. A young cow.
humus	(hū′ mŭs)	n. Decomposed vegetable matter.
husbandry	(hŭş′ bănd rў)	n. Farming.
hybrid	(hў′ brĭd)	n. Plant bred of two species.
implement	(ĭm′ plĕ mĕnt)	n. A tool or utensil.
incubator	(ĭn′ cú bā′ tŏr)	n. An apparatus for hatching eggs.
insecticide	(ĭn sĕc′ tĭ çīde)	n. Preparation for killing insects.
irrigate	(ĭr′ rĭ gāte)	v. To supply land with water by canals.
meadow	(mĕad′ ōw)	n. Grassland.
mulch	(mŭlch)	n. Substance spread upon the ground to protect plant roots.
nursery	(nûrs′ ēr ў)	n. A place for raising young plants.
orchard	(ôr′ chärd)	n. A group of fruit trees.
pasture	(pȧs′ túre)	n. Grassland used for feeding animals.
poultry	(pōul′ trў)	n. Domestic fowl.
prairie	(prâi′ rĭe)	n. Extensive tract of level or rolling land.
scythe	(scȳthe)	n. A tool for cutting grass.
tractor	(trăc′ tŏr)	n. Vehicle used for drawing a plow.
vineyard	(vĭne′ yärd)	n. A plantation of grapevines.

A. Consult your dictionary for the pronunciation and meaning of the following words:

alluvial	citrus	legume	separator	silo

B. 1. What compound word is found in this lesson?
2. Can "acre" be divided at the end of a line? Explain.
3. What is the plural of "nursery"?
4. What is the plural of "silo"?
5. What is the meaning of "or" in "separator"?

C. Form sentences containing the following words:

cultivate	fertile	humus	irrigate	scythe

alphabetic	(ăl′ phȧ bĕt′ ĭc)	*adj.* Making use of the letters of the alphabet.
auxiliary	(aux il′ ia rў̆) ôg zĭl′ yȧ	*adj.* Aid or help.
binary	(bī′ nȧ rў̆)	*adj.* Two-digit system (zero and one).
calculator	(căl′ cú lā′ tŏr)	*n.* Machine for computing arithmetical operations.
centralization	(çĕn′ trăl ĭ zā′ tion)	*n.* Act of bringing to a central point.
circuit	(cir′ cuĭt) sûr′	*n.* The path of an electric current.
compiler	(cŏm pīl′ ẽr)	*n.* One who collects items.
component	(cŏm pō′ nĕnt)	*n.* A part.
console	(cŏn′ sōle)	*n.* A cabinet.
cycle	(çȳ′ cle)	*n.* One round of a regularly recurring succession of events.
disbursement	(dĭs bûrse′ mĕnt)	*n.* Funds paid out.
disc	(dĭsc)	*n.* A metal record used for storing data.
electronical	(é lĕc′ trŏn′ ĭc ăl)	*adj.* Pertaining to electrons.
mnemonic	(mné mŏn′ ĭc)	*adj.* Assisting the memory.
monitor	(mŏn′ ĭ tŏr)	*n.* A warning device.
nomenclature	(nō′ mĕn clā′ túre)	*n.* System of names used in classifications.
interpreter	(ĭn ter′ prĕ tẽr) tûr′	*n.* A translating machine.
phonetic	(phó nĕt′ ĭc)	*adj.* Consisting of speech sounds.
programming	(prō′ grăm mĭng)	*v.* Working out a sequence of operations to be performed.
rotary	(rō′ tȧ rў̆)	*adj.* Pertaining to a calculating machine; as opposed to key-driven.
synchronize	(syn′ chró nīze) sĭng′	*v.* To cause to agree in time.
tabulate	(tăb′ ú lāte)	*v.* To form into a table.
Teletype	(Tĕl′ é tȳpe)	*n.* A special kind of typewriter.
verifier	(vĕr′ ĭ fī′ ẽr)	*n.* A machine used to check accuracy of card punching.

A. Consult your dictionary for the pronunciation and meaning of the following words:

classification   implementation   mimeograph   photostat

B. Form sentences containing the following words:

alphabetic   interpreter   mnemonic   **synchronize**   verifier

Addressograph	(Ad drĕs' sŏ grăph)	n. A machine for addressing letters, etc.
analysis	(à năl' y̆ sı̆s)	n. Separation of anything into its parts.
by-product	(bȳ'-prŏd' ŭct)	n. A secondary or additional product.
collate	(cŏl-lāte')	v. To arrange or collect papers, forms, etc., according to an orderly system.
conversion	(cŏn ver' sion) vûr' shŭn	n. Act of changing from one thing to another.
debugging	(dē bŭg' gı̆ng)	v. Removing defects.
diagram	(dī' à grăm)	n. A drawing that shows arrangement and relations.
digital	(dı̆g' ı̆t ăl)	adj. Pertaining to a system based on ten.
duplicate	(dū' plı̆ cáte)	n. A copy.
electromechanical	(é lĕc' trŏ mé chăn' ı̆ căl)	adj. Electrically controlled.
integrate	(ı̆n' tĕ grāte)	v. To unite so as to form a whole.
keyboard	(kēy' bōard)	n. The arrangement of the keys of a machine.
language	(lan' guage) lăng' gwı̆j	n. A means of communicating thought.
memorandum	(mĕm' ŏ răn' dŭm)	n. An informal record.
modification	(mŏd' ı̆ fı̆ că' tion)	n. Alteration or change.
Multigraph	(Mŭl' tı̆ grăph)	n. A type of small printing press.
numerical	(nú mĕr' ı̆ căl)	adj. Expressed by numbers rather than letters.
parallel	(păr' ă l lĕl)	adj. Running side by side.
photoelectric	(phō' tō é lĕc' trı̆c)	adj. Pertaining to electronic or other electrical effects produced by light.
register	(rĕg' ı̆s tēr)	n. A record containing entries.
requisition	(req' ui sı̆' tion) rĕk' wı̆ zish' ŭn	n. A formal application for items.
schematic	(schĕ măt' ı̆c)	adj. Conformed to an established pattern.
stencil	(stĕn' çı̆l)	n. A perforated sheet used for duplicating.
transcription	(trăn scrı̆p' tion)	n. A typed copy of some material.
translation	(trăns lā' tion)	n. A rendering from one language to another.
variable	(vâr' ı̆ à ble)	adj. Subject to change.

A. Consult your dictionary for the pronunciation and meaning of the following words:

automation   directory   microfilm   sequence   stationery

B. From what verbs are the following nouns derived?

calculator   duplicator   eradicator   fastener   programmer

C. 1. What is the meaning of "graph" in "Addressograph"?
2. What words in this lesson are compounds?
3. Why are "Addressograph" and "Multigraph" capitalized?
4. How may "mimeograph" be divided at the end of a line?

account	(ăc count′)	*n.* A device used for recording changes in assets, liabilities, and proprietorship.
accrual	(ăc crṵ′ ăl)	*n.* An increase in an asset or a liability arising from a contract.
amortization	(á môr′ tĭ zā′ tion)	*n.* The gradual liquidation of a debt.
asset	(ăs′ s̆et)	*n.* Anything of value that is owned.
balance	(băl′ ănçe)	*n.* Difference between two sides of an account.
capital	(căp′ ĭ tăl)	*n.* Excess of assets over liabilities; net worth.
contingent	(cŏn tĭn′ ğĕnt)	*adj.* Dependent on the happening of a future event.
credit	(crĕd′ ĭt)	*n.* An entry on the right-hand side of an account. *v.* To make an entry on the right side.
debit	(dĕb′ ĭt)	*n.* An entry on the left-hand side of an account. *v.* To make an entry on the left side.
depreciation	(dĕ́ prē′ ci ā′ tion) shĭ	*n.* A lessening in value.
double-entry	(dŏŭ′ ble-ĕn′ trў̆)	*adj.* Method of bookkeeping, having two entries for each transaction.
equity	(eq′ ui tў̆) ĕk′ wĭ	*n.* A claim in property.
inventory	(ĭn′ vĕn tō′ rў̆)	*n.* Value of goods on hand.
journal	(joûr′ năl)	*n.* A book of original entry.
ledger	(lĕdğ′ ĕr)	*n.* A book of final entry.
liability	(lĭ′ á bĭl′ ĭ tў̆)	*n.* An amount owed.
payable	(pāy′ á ble)	*adj.* Referring to a note or an account to be paid.
proprietorship	(prō prī′ ĕ tŏr shĭp′)	*n.* Ownership; capital.
receivable	(rĕ́ çeiv′ á ble)	*adj.* Referring to a note or an account to be collected from a debtor.
stockholder	(stŏck′ hōld′ ĕr)	*n.* One who owns stock.
subsidiary	(sŭb sĭd′ ĭ ar′ ў̆) ĕr′	*adj.* Referring to a ledger that is summarized in the general ledger.

A. Consult your dictionary for the pronunciation and meaning of the following words:

audit   dividend   expenditure   intangible   transaction

B. Use each of the following expressions in a sentence:

declare a dividend   increased expenditure   current expenses
take an inventory   unpaid balance

acknowledge (ăc knŏwl′ ĕdġe)   *v.* To certify the receipt of.
airmail (âir′ māil)   *n.* Mail sent by aircraft.
cablegram (cā′ ble grăm)   *n.* A message sent by telegraphic cable.

cipher (çī′ phĕr)   *n.* A method of secret writing.
classified (clăs′ sĭ fīed)   *adj.* Forbidden to be disclosed for matters of security.

code (cōde)   *n.* A system of signals.
collect (cŏl lĕct′)   *adj.* or *adv.* To be paid for by recipient.

dial (dī′ ăl)   *n.* A plate for establishing connection by telephone.

directory (dĭ rĕc′ tŏ rў)   *n.* Book containing names, addresses, and telephone numbers.

enclosure (ĕn clō′ sure) zhĕr   *n.* Material sent with a letter.

envelope (ĕn′ vĕ lōpe)   *n.* A piece of folded paper to enclose a letter.

forward (fôr′ ward) wĕrd   *n.* To send on.
letterhead (lĕt′ tĕr hĕad′)   *n.* Stationery with a printed heading.

messenger (mĕs′ sĕn ġĕr)   *n.* A dispatch bearer.
minimum (mĭn′ ĭ mŭm)   *n.* Lowest service charge.
night letter (nīght lĕt′ tĕr)   *n.* Telegram sent at a special low rate.

postage (pōst′ age) ĭj   *n.* Charge for sending a letter.
postmark (pōst′ märk)   *n.* Cancellation mark on an envelope.

questionnaire (quĕs′ tion nâire′) chŭn   *n.* A set of questions submitted to a group of people.

registered (rĕġ′ ĭs tĕred)   *adj.* Mail that must be signed for by receiver.

stationery (stā′ tion ĕr′ ў)   *n.* Writing paper.
switchboard (swĭtch′ bōard′)   *n.* An apparatus through which telephone calls are transmitted.

telegram (tĕl′ é grăm)   *n.* A telegraphic dispatch.
telephone (tĕl′ é phōne)   *n.* An instrument for reproducing sounds at a distance.

wire (wīre)   *n.* A telegram.
zone (zōne)   *n.* One of the mailing sections into which a large city is divided.

A. Consult your dictionary for the pronunciation and meaning of the following words:

    bulletin   **memorandum**   **special delivery**   **station-to-station**

B. Use each of the following words in a sentence:

    directory   **enclosure**   **postage**   **registered**   **switchboard**

The following sentences contain words in Lessons 114 through 118 that are frequently misspelled. Rewrite each sentence, correcting all misspelled words.

1. The modern farmer sprays his vinyerd with insectacide so that the bugs will not spoil his grapes.
2. The poultry breeder was very unhappy because his new incubater burned to the ground last night.
3. Our office has decided to install an auxilliary fonetic file, in addition to the alfabetic file now in use.
4. The new girl is learning how to operate our rotery calculator very quickly.
5. I wonder why the key board on a Telatype is somewhat different from that on a regular typewriter.
6. The expert who made an analysis of our office routines thinks that we must integrate operations more fully if we are to have a truly efficient office.
7. Arrange these stencils in numberical order, attach this memorandum, and take them to the president's secretary.
8. The corporation is going bankrupt because it has never given thought to the amortazation of its large public debt, which has now fallen due.
9. We are doing very well this year and our ratio of currant assets to currant liabilities is extremely favorable.
10. Richard did well in his bookeeping course in school and it certainly is reflected in the excellent job he is doing for the company.
11. Remember, students, in a double-entry system you must always make the journel entry first and then post to the leger.
12. Please take this message to the switch board operator and have her send this cabelgram immediately.
13. This stationary has such an attractive letter head that I am sure our customers will be impressed.
14. The postege required on airmail packages is very reasonable when we consider the amount of service rendered by our post office.
15. I like to call my mother, who lives in Washington, collect because then my telaphone bill is not so high at the end of the month.
16. The land which was fertilised and planted in alfalffa this year will be used as pasture next year.
17. Prior to programming the recording of cash disbursements, a verafier was used to check the accuracy of the punched cards.
18. To prepare the sales analisis for this period, all the by-product tapes must be colated and translated.
19. Joe correctly answered that the fundamental bookkeeping equation is "Asets equal libilities and proprietership."
20. The switch board operator was instructed to send all classified telagrams and codded cabelgrams to the agency in Berne.

absenteeism	(ăb′ sĕn tēē′ ĭ̧sm)	*n.*	Continual interruption of attendance at place of employment.
apprentice	(ă*p* prĕn′ tĭce)	*n.*	One learning a trade through practical experience.
arbitration	(är′ bĭ trā′ tion)	*n.*	Hearing and determining a dispute between parties.
bargaining	(bär′ gaĭn ĭng)	*v.*	Negotiating over terms of an agreement.
boycott	(boy′ cŏtt)	*v.*	To refrain from using or buying items.
coercion	(cŏ́ er′ cion) ûr′ shŭn	*n.*	Act of constraining by force, law, or authority.
compensation	(cŏm′ pĕn sā′ tion)	*n.*	Payment for services.
demotion	(dĕ́ mō′ tion)	*n.*	Act of reducing to a lower position.
discrimination	(dĭs crĭm′ ĭ nā′ tion)	*n.*	Difference in treatment of workers.
diversification	(dī ver′ sĭ fĭ cā′ tion) vûr′	*n.*	State of doing or producing many different things.
exploitation	(ĕx′ ploi tā′ tion)	*n.*	Making use of others for one's own benefit.
grievance	(griēv′ ănce)	*n.*	A cause of complaint.
mobility	(mŏ́ bĭl′ ĭ tў)	*n.*	Freedom of worker to move from one place to another.
motivation	(mŏ́ tĭ vā′ tion)	*n.*	A force that incites to action.
pension	(pĕn′ sion) shŭn	*n.*	Allowance given for past services.
personnel	(per sŏ*n* nĕl′) pûr	*n.*	Employees of a business.
productivity	(prŏ′ dŭc tĭv′ ĭ tў)	*n.*	Output per unit of effort.
promotion	(prŏ́ mō′ tion)	*n.*	Act of raising in position or rank.
specialization	(spe′ cial ĭ zā′ tion) spĕsh′ ăl	*n.*	Becoming adept in performance of one function at the expense of all others.
vacation	(vā cā′ tion)	*n.*	A period of exemption from work.
vocation	(vŏ́ cā′ tion)	*n.*	One's occupation or profession.

A. Consult your dictionary for the pronunciation and meaning of the following words:

injunction   intervention   mediation   security   unemployment

B. Use each of the following words in a sentence:

arbitration   boycott   grievance   motivation   pension

140

abscond	(ăb scŏnd′)	*v.*	To steal off.
adjudicate	(ăd ju′ dĭ cāte)	*v.*	To settle by judicial decision.
	jōō′		
alias	(ā′ lĭ ăs)	*n.*	An assumed name.
ambiguity	(ăm′ bĭ gū′ ĭ tў)	*n.*	State of being indistinct, uncertain.
apprehend	(ăp′ *p*rě hĕnd′)	*v.*	To lay hold of; to arrest.
assign	(ăs sīgn′)	*v.*	To turn over to another.
attest	(ăt tĕst′)	*v.*	To hear witness to.
bankrupt	(bank′ rŭpt)	*adj.*	Legally discharged from debt.
	băngk′		
bestow	(bě stŏ*w*′)	*v.*	To give or confer.
claimant	(clāim′ ănt)	*n.*	One who asserts a right or title.
codicil	(cŏd′ ĭ çĭl)	*n.*	An added provision.
criminal	(crĭm′ ĭ năl)	*n.*	One guilty of a crime.
deposition	(dĕp ố şĭ′ tion)	*n.*	Written testimony after oath.
executor	(ex ec′ ŭ tor)	*n.*	One who carries out a will.
	ĕg zĕc′ tĕr		
guardian	(guärd′ ĭ ăn)	*n.*	One who cares for the property or the person of another.
incriminate	(ĭn crĭm′ ĭ nāte)	*v.*	To charge with or involve in a crime.
legacy	(lĕg′ ȧ çў)	*n.*	A gift of property by will.
legitimate	(lě ġĭt′ ĭ måte)	*adj.*	Lawful.
magistrate	(măg′ ĭs trāte)	*n.*	Public official.
plaintiff	(plāin′ tĭff)	*n.*	One who brings suit.
subpoena	(sŭb poē′ nȧ)	*n.*	Writ summoning a witness.
testify	(tĕs′ tĭ fў)	*v.*	To give testimony.
valid	(văl′ ĭd)	*adj.*	Having legal force.
warrant	(war′ rănt)	*n.*	An authorization.
	wŏr′		

A. Consult your dictionary for the pronunciation and meaning of the following words:

accessory   clemency   felony   indictment   misdemeanor

B. Use each of the following words in a sentence:

abscond   claimant   deposition   legacy   subpoena   warrant

C. Copy the following sentences, correcting all spelling errors:

1. I must go to Akron to make a depossition about the accident.
2. It isn't convenient for me to go now, but I have to testafy on the date specified.
3. It is fortunate I don't have to incriminnate anybody else.
4. The plaintif contends that the will is not valid because of its ambiguitie, and therefore he is a claimant for the legasy.
5. This young man, traveling under six aliuses, has criminle tendencies, although all the charges against him are classed as misdeamenors.

abeyance	(à bey′ ăņçe) bā′	n. Condition of being undetermined.
acquittal	(ăc quit′ tăl) kwĭt′	n. Act of setting free from the charge of an offense.
affidavit	(ăf′ fĭ dā′ vĭt)	n. A sworn statement in writing.
allegation	(ăl′ lĕ́ gā′ tion)	n. Statement of what one undertakes to prove.
appellate	(ăp pĕl′ lăte)	adj. Having the power to reverse the decision of another tribunal.
assault	(ăs sault′) sôlt′	n. A violent attempt without carrying through the threat.
bailee	(bāil′ ēe)	n. One to whom goods are committed in trust.
bequeath	(bĕ́ queath′) kwē̶th′	v. To leave by will.
chattel	(chăt tĕl′)	n. Property, except real estate.
client	(clī′ ĕnt)	n. One consulting an attorney.
conviction	(cŏn vĭc′ tion)	n. The act of finding a person guilty.
defendant	(dĕ́ fĕnd′ ănt)	n. One who is sued.
duress	(dū′ rĕss)	n. Actual or threatened violence which forces one to do some act.
incorporate	(ĭn côr′ pŏ́ rāte)	v. To unite by law in one body.
justice	(jŭs′ tĭ̧ce)	n. Fairness; rightfulness.
libel	(lī′ bĕl)	n. A defamatory statement.
lien	(li′ĕn) lē′	n. A legal claim against property.
litigation	(lĭt′ ĭ gā′ tion)	n. A suit at law.
penalty	(pĕn′ ăl tў)	n. Punishment.
testator	(tĕs tā′ tor) tĕr	n. One who leaves a will at death.
trustee	(trŭs tēe′)	n. One holding property in trust.

A. Consult your dictionary for the pronunciation and meaning of the following words:

administrator   damages   homicide   precedent   trespass

B. Use each of the following words in a sentence:

affidavit   bailee   conviction   litigation   testator

C. Copy the following sentences, correcting all spelling errors:

1. The prosecuting attorney made some serious allegasions about the reliability of the defendent.
2. When the defendant submitted affadavits from employers, he was reminded of the penalty involved in forging signatures.
3. The case will probably be taken to an appelate court after it is held in abayance for a few months.
4. Litagation is expensive not only in money but also in time and in emotional stress and strain.
5. A testator should bequeathe his property in a way that promotes justice among his heirs.

auction	(auc′ tion) ôk′	*n.* A public sale of property to the highest bidder.
commodity	(cŏm mŏd′ ĭ tў)	*n.* An article of commerce.
competition	(cŏm pḗ tĭ′ tion)	*n.* Striving for the same market.
consumer	(cŏn sūm′ ẽr)	*n.* One who uses goods and services.
customer	(cŭs′ tom ẽr) tŭm	*n.* One who makes purchases from a tradesman.
distribution	(dĭs trĭ bū′ tion)	*n.* The manner in which goods are dispensed to the public.
expenditure	(ex pĕnd′ ĭ tứre) ĕks	*n.* A disbursement.
fashion	(făsh′ ion) ŭn	*n.* Style.
goodwill	(gŏŏd′ wĭll′)	*n.* The benefits to a business arising out of reputation, good location, and similar intangible advantages.
innovation	(ĭn′ nŏ vā′ tion)	*n.* Introduction of something new.
jobber	(jŏb′ bẽr)	*n.* A middleman.
margin	(mär′ ġĭn)	*n.* The difference between cost and selling price.
markup	(märk′ ŭp′)	*n.* The percentage of increase between cost and selling price.
mercantile	(mer′ căn tile) mûr′ tēl	*adj.* Of or pertaining to merchants.
merchandise	(mer′ chăn dīşe) mûr′	*n.* Goods bought or sold in trade.
middleman	(mĭd′ dle măn′)	*n.* A dealer between the producer and the consumer.
overhead	(ō′ vẽr hĕad′)	*n.* Costs other than direct costs of materials and labor; burden; general expense.
patron	(pā′ tron) trŭn	*n.* A customer.
promotion	(prŏ́ mō′ tion)	*n.* Activities that increase the sale of a product or service.
retailer	(rē′ tāil ẽr)	*n.* A merchant who sells directly to the consumer.
transaction	(trăns ăc′ tion)	*n.* An act involving buying and selling.
wholesale	(*w*hōle′ sāle′)	*n.* Selling goods in large quantity, as to retailers.

A. Consult your dictionary for the pronunciation and meaning of the following words:

commission diversification fabrication markdown regional tariff

B. Use each of the following words in a sentence:

competition expenditure goodwill jobber merchandise

accelerator (ăc çĕl′ ĕr ā tor) *n.* The ratio of an increase or de-
               tĕr   crease in investment to an increase
                                       or decrease in income.

bimetallic (bī′ mĕ tăl′ *l*ĭc) *adj.* Using a double metallic stand-
                                       ard for currency.

bullion (bul′ lion) *n.* Uncoined gold or silver in the
        bŏŏl′ yŭn   shape of bars or ingots.

circulation (cir′ cŭ lā′ tion) *n.* The movement of money from per-
         sûr′   son to person.

coinage (coin′ age) ĭj *n.* The act of minting money.

currency (cûr′ *r*ĕn çў) *n.* That which passes from hand to
                              hand as a medium of exchange.

cyclical (çў′ clĭ căl) *n.* Subject to the influence of recur-
                            ring economic fluctuations.

deficit (dĕf′ ĭ çĭt) *n.* Excess of expenditures over in-
                            come.

domestic (dŏ mĕs′ tĭc) *adj.* Relating to one's own country or
                          the country under consideration.

elasticity (ĕ lăs′ tĭç′ ĭ tў) *n.* The manner in which the supply
                          or demand of a commodity varies
                          in relation to its price.

fiscal (fĭs′ căl) *adj.* Pertaining to financial matters.

liquidity (lĭ quid′ ĭ tў) *n.* State of possessing assets readily
        kwĭd′   convertible into cash.

maturity (mȧ tū′ rĭ tў) *n.* The time fixed for payment of an
                        obligation.

monetary (mŏn′ ĕ tar ў) *adj.* Relating to money.
            tĕr

parity (păr′ ĭ tў) *n.* Equality of purchasing power be-
                        tween different kinds of money at
                        a given ratio.

propensity (prŏ pĕn′ sĭ tў) *n.* An innate or inherent tendency.

specie (spē′ cie) shĭ *n.* Gold or silver coin.

surplus (sûr′ plŭs) *n.* The excess of income over ex-
                        penditures.

treasury (trĕa̧′ ur ў) *n.* A place where public funds are
           ĕr   deposited, kept, and paid out.

usurious (ủ su′ ri oŭs) *adj.* Taking illegal or exorbitant in-
        zhŏŏr′ ĭ   terest for the use of money.

vault (vault) *n.* A room for the safekeeping of
        vôlt   valuables.

velocity (vẻ lŏç′ ĭ tў) *n.* The rate of turnover of money.

wealth (wĕalth) *n.* All property that has money value.

A. Consult your dictionary for the pronunciation and meaning of the following words:

    budget consumption fluctuation negotiable restrictive standard

B. Use each of the following words in a sentence:

    bimetallic   domestic   liquidity   propensity   vault

A. The following sentences contain words in Lessons 120 through 124 that are frequently misspelled. Rewrite each sentence, correcting all misspelled words.

1. Motavation of the worker is necessary if we are to raise our level of productevity.
2. John likes his job because the personal are very friendly, and divercification in duties keeps him from becoming bored.
3. We will boycot the JMC Company in protest against disscrimination, exploitation, and inadequate compensation.
4. Litigation is expensive and inconvenient, but in this case the situation demands that I take action; otherwise, I will be accesory to the injustice.
5. The defendent did not understand the plaintive's statement that he expected to be indemnified for the libelous statements that caused him personal and professional losses.
6. The judge spoke of that criminal act as a missdemeanor, but I think it was a felony.
7. Did the sheriff have a warrent to search the premises?
8. The convicted slayer appealed to the governor for clemancy.
9. The bailee was apprehended before he could abscound with the chatell.
10. Before you buy anything at an auction, you should inspect the merchandize very thoroughly.
11. Some retailers are caught in a real profit squeeze because their over head keeps going up and their profit margin keeps going down.
12. One way in which a merchant may attract new customers is to advertize in the newspapers.
13. Although this is no longer the case, at one time money in the United States was based on a bymetalic standerd.
14. During the Christmas season both the valocity and the amount of currancy in circulation are much higher than at other times of the year.
15. What connection is there between the vault cash kept on hand by the banks and the cyclicle variations taking place in the economy?

B. Review the preceding five lessons and list twenty words from these lessons that you consider difficult to spell. Underscore the parts of the words likely to cause trouble.

bulletin	(bul' *lĕ* tĭn) bo͝ol'	*n.*	A periodical.
by-line	(bȳ'-līne)	*n.*	Line at the head of an article giving the writer's name.
caption	(căp' tion)	*n.*	A heading.
copyright	(cŏp' ў rī*ght*)	*n.*	Exclusive right to publish.
delete	(dĕ́ lēte')	*v.*	Erase, omit.
dictionary	(dĭc' tion ar ў) ĕr	*n.*	Reference book of definitions.
dummy	(dŭm' *m*ў)	*n.*	A model layout used by a printer.
edition	(ĕ́ dĭ' tion)	*n.*	The number of bound copies printed from one setting of type.
editorial	(ĕd' ĭ tō' rĭ ăl)	*n.*	Article written by an editor.
electrotype	(ĕ́ lĕc' trŏ́ tȳpe)	*n.*	A plate for use in printing.
font	(fŏnt)	*n.*	Type of one size and style.
format	(fôr' măt)	*n.*	Shape, size, and general style of a publication.
galley	(găl' ley) ĭ	*n.*	Proof before it is made into pages.
linotype	(līn' ŏ́ tȳpe)	*n.*	Typesetting machine that casts solid lines of type.
manuscript	(măn' ú́ scrĭpt)	*n.*	An author's copy of his work in handwritten or typewritten form.
monograph	(mŏn' ŏ́ grăph)	*n.*	Booklet on one subject.
monotype	(mŏn' ŏ́ tȳpe)	*n.*	Typesetting machine that casts each character on an individual body.
newspaper	(news' pā pĕr) nūz	*n.*	A paper published periodically to convey news.
pamphlet	(păm' phlĕt)	*n.*	A booklet with a paper cover.
proof	(pro͞of)	*n.*	An impression taken from type for examination.
prospectus	(prŏ́ spĕc' tŭs)	*n.*	A booklet describing a forthcoming edition.
rotogravure	(rō' tŏ́ grȧ vūre')	*n.*	A method of printing illustrations.
royalty	(roy' ăl tȳ) roi	*n.*	Payment made to author on the sale of his books.
stet	(stĕt)	*v.*	To mark so as to nullify a previous order. "Let it stand."

typographical (tȳ' pŏ́ grăph' ĭ căl) *adj.* Pertaining to printing.

A. Consult your dictionary for the pronunciation and meaning of the following words:

    folio   glossy   halftone   pica   signature   **Varityper**

B. Use each of the following words in a sentence:

    dummy   format   galley   proof   royalty   stet

appraisal	(ăp prāis̩' ăl)	*n.*	A valuation of property by the estimate of an authorized person.
assessment	(ăs sĕss' mĕnt)	*n.*	A specific charge or tax on property.
dispossess	(dĭs pŏs s̩ess')	*v.*	To deprive of occupancy.
dower	(dow' ẽr) dou'	*n.*	Portion of real estate of deceased husband given by law to his widow.
easement	(ēas̩e' mĕnt)	*n.*	An acquired right of use of another's land.
ejectment	(ĕ́ jĕct' mĕnt)	*n.*	Action for the recovery of property and damages.
encumbrance	(ĕn cŭm' brănçe)	*n.*	A claim upon an estate.
escrow	(ĕs' crōw)	*n.*	A conditional deed.
eviction	(ĕ́ vĭc' tion)	*n.*	Dispossession of a tenant by his landlord.
foreclose	(fōre clōs̩e')	*v.*	To shut out because of default in payment.
freehold	(frēe' hōld)	*n.*	A tenure by which an estate is held.
frontage	(front' age) frŭnt' ĭj	*n.*	Front boundary line of a lot.
lease	(lēase)	*n.*	A real estate contract.
lessee	(lĕs sēe')	*n.*	One to whom a lease is given.
lessor	(lĕs' sôr)	*n.*	Grantor of a lease.
lien	(li' ĕn) lē	*n.*	A legal claim against property.
mortgage	(môrt' gage) gĭj	*n.*	A conveyance of property as security.
occupancy	(ŏc' cŭ păn çў)	*n.*	Act of holding possession.
option	(ŏp' tion)	*n.*	The right to buy specific property at a given price.
premises	(prĕm' ĭs ĕs)	*n.*	A piece of land or real estate.
quitclaim	(quit' clāim) kwĭt	*n.*	A deed of release.
realtor	(rē' ăl tor) tẽr	*n.*	Real estate broker.
subdivision	(sŭb' dĭ vĭ' sion) zhŭn	*n.*	A tract of land divided into lots for purposes of sale.
sublet	(sŭb lĕt')	*v.*	To sublease, a lessee leasing to another.
zoning	(zōn' ĭng)	*n.*	Act of dividing a city by ordinance into sections reserved for different purposes.

A. Consult your dictionary for the pronunciation and meaning of the following words:

annexation   blight   community   forfeiture   obsolescence

B. Use each of the following words in a sentence:

appraisal   encumbrance   lien   mortgage   subdivision

147

actuary	(ăc′ tú ar ў) ĕr	*n.*	One who calculates premiums.
adjuster	(ăd jŭst′ ĕr)	*n.*	One who settles differences.
annuity	(ăn nū′ ĭ tў)	*n.*	An amount payable yearly.
arson	(är′ sŏn)	*n.*	Malicious burning of a dwelling.
beneficiary	(bĕn′ ĕ fĭ′ ci ar ў) shĭ ĕr	*n.*	One to receive benefits.
cancellation	(căn cĕl lā′ tion)	*n.*	Act of revoking or making invalid.
casualty	(căş′ ú ăl tў)	*n.*	A mishap; an accident.
comprehensive	(cŏm′ prĕ hĕn′ sĭve)	*adj.*	Covering all hazards of a given type, with exception of listed exclusions.
convertible	(cŏn vĕrt′ ĭ ble)	*adj.*	Capable of being changed.
deceased	(dĕ ceased′) sēst′	*adj.*	Dead.
disability	(dĭs′ à bĭl′ ĭ tў)	*n.*	State of being disabled.
endowment	(ĕn dow′ mĕnt)	*n.*	Insurance that pays a given amount at a certain time.
forfeiture	(fôr′ fĕi túre)	*n.*	A giving up as a penalty.
hazard	(hăz′ ärd)	*n.*	A source of risk; a danger.
incontestable	(ĭn′ cŏn tĕst′ à ble)	*adj.*	Not to be disputed.
indemnify	(ĭn dĕm′ nĭ fŷ)	*v.*	To pay for a loss.
indemnity	(ĭn dĕm′ nĭ tў)	*n.*	Payment for loss.
mortality	(môr tăl′ ĭ tў)	*n.*	Death rate.
mutual	(mū′ tú ăl)	*adj.*	Owned by the policyholders.
negligence	(nĕg′ lĭ ġĕnçe)	*n.*	Failure to exercise care.
noninsurable	(nŏn′ ĭn sur′ à ble) shŏŏr′	*adj.*	Incapable of being insured.
premium	(prē′ mĭ ŭm)	*n.*	Sum paid for insurance.
recipient	(rĕ çĭp′ ĭ ĕnt)	*n.*	One who receives.
retroactive	(rĕt′ rŏ ăc′ tĭve)	*adj.*	Extending in effect to prior acts.
rider	(rīd′ ĕr)	*n.*	An additional clause; amendment.
survivor	(sur vī′ vor) sēr vĕr	*n.*	One who outlives another.
waiver	(wāiv′ ĕr)	*n.*	Act of giving up a claim.

A. Consult your dictionary for the pronunciation and meaning of the following words:

coinsurance nonforfeiture probability subrogation unpredictability

B. Use each of following words in a sentence:

beneficiary   endowment   mutual   retroactive   waiver

capital	(căp′ ĭ tăl)	*n.* Amount of property owned at a given time.
certificate	(çẽr tĭf′ ĭ cate) kĭt	*n.* A written statement legally authenticated.
convertible	(cŏn vert′ ĭ ble) vûrt′	*adj.* Exchangeable for a different kind of security.
corporate	(côr′ pŏ rate) rĭt	*adj.* Formed into a body by legal enactment.
debenture	(dĕ bĕn′ tŭre)	*n.* Instrument issued by corporation as evidence of debt.
debt	(dĕ*b*t)	*n.* That part of a corporation's capital represented by obligations secured by property.
dividends	(dĭv′ ĭ dĕnds)	*n.* Profits apportioned among stockholders.
investment	(ĭn vĕst′ mĕnt)	*n.* Outlay of money to purchase something for income or profit.
issue	(is′ sue) ĭ′ shū	*n.* A class of securities offered to the public.
margin	(mär′ ġin)	*n.* Amount of money deposited by an investor with a broker to cover part of the cost of securities.
marketable	(mär′ kĕt á ble)	*adj.* Fit to be offered for sale.
municipal	(mŭ nĭç′ ĭ păl)	*adj.* Referring to local government.
option	(ŏp′ tion)	*n.* The right to buy securities at a given price during the contract period.
participating	(pär tĭç′ ĭ pāt ĭng)	*v.* Entitling the owner to share in distribution of surplus.
portfolio	(pōrt fō′ lĭ ō)	*n.* A list of securities owned.
premium	(prē′ mĭ ŭm)	*n.* Above par or nominal value.
redemption	(rĕ dĕmp′ tion)	*n.* The repurchase of its securities by a corporation.
revenue	(rĕv′ ĕ nūe)	*n.* The yield on an investment.
security	(sĕ cū′ rĭ tў)	*n.* An evidence of debt or of ownership, as a bond or a stock certificate.
specialist	(spe′ cial ĭst) spĕsh′ ăl	*n.* A broker who confines his operations to a few stocks.

A. Consult your dictionary for the pronunciation and meaning of the following words:

brokerage   commercial   exchange   fluctuations   par

B. Use each of the following words in a sentence:

debenture   issue   participating   revenue   specialist

aeronautics	(âer′ ố näu′ tĭcs)	*n.* Science dealing with operation of aircraft.
airplane	(âir′ plāne)	*n.* Aircraft heavier than air.
altimeter	(ăl tĭm′ ế tẽr)	*n.* Instrument for measuring altitude.
altitude	(ăl′ tĭ tūde)	*n.* Elevation above the ground.
astronaut	(ăs′ trố näut)	*n.* Captain of a spaceship.
aviation	(ā vĭ ā′ tion)	*n.* The art of operating heavier-than-air aircraft.
capsule	(căp′ sule) säl	*n.* Detachable part of a spaceship.
ceiling	(çēil′ ĭng)	*n.* Height of a cloud base.
celestial	(çế lĕs′ tial) chăl	*adj.* Pertaining to the sky.
elliptical	(ĕ*l* lĭp′ tĭ că*l*)	*adj.* Conic shaped.
fuselage	(fū′ şẽ lage) läzh	*n.* Body of an airplane.
hangar	(hăng′ ar) ẽr	*n.* Structure for housing airplanes.
helicopter	(hĕl′ ĭ cŏp′ tẽr)	*n.* Aircraft supported by horizontal propellers.
interplanetary	(ĭn′ ter plăn′ ế tar ў̆) tûr tẽr	*adj.* Between planets or from planet to planet.
jetliner	(jĕt′ lĭ′ nẽr)	*n.* A jet-propelled airliner.
meteorology	(mē′ tế or ŏl′ ố ġў̆) ẽr	*n.* Branch of science dealing with the atmosphere.
navigator	(năv′ ĭ gā tor) tẽr	*n.* One who directs a ship's course.
orbit	(ôr′ bĭt)	*n.* The path of one body around another.
parachute	(păr′ à chute) shōōt	*n.* Device for making a safe descent from an airplane.
pilot	(pī′ lot) lŭt	*n.* Operator of an airplane.
propeller	(prố pĕl′ *l*ẽr)	*n.* Device for supplying motive power to aircraft.
propulsion	(prố pŭl′ sion) shŭn	*n.* Act of driving forward.
radar	(rā′ där)	*n.* A radio-detecting device.
satellite	(săt′ ĕ*l* līte)	*n.* Attendant body revolving about a larger body.
skycap	(skȳ′ căp)	*n.* One hired to carry hand luggage at an airport.
stratosphere	(străt′ ố sphēre)	*n.* Upper part of atmosphere.
supersonic	(sū′ pẽr sŏn′ ĭc)	*adj.* Faster than sound.
velocity	(vế lŏç′ ĭ tў̆)	*n.* Speed; quickness of motion.
visibility	(vĭş′ ĭ bĭl′ ĭ tў̆)	*n.* Distance of maximum view.

A. Consult your dictionary for the pronunciation and meaning of the following words:

airborne   astrojet   glider   rocket   stewardess

B. Use each of the following words in a sentence:

aeronautics   capsule   elliptical   hangar   velocity

antifreeze	(ăn′ tĭ frēeze′)	*n.* Substance having a low freezing point.
automobile	(au′ tŏ mŏ́ bile′) ỗ bēl′	*n.* Self-propelled vehicle suitable for use on streets or roads.
battery	(băt′ tĕr y̆)	*n.* Apparatus for generating or storing electricity.
bumper	(bŭmp′ ẽr)	*n.* Device for protecting the body of a car.
carburetor	(cär′ bŭ ret or) rā tĕr	*n.* Mixer for air and gasoline.
chassis	(chăs′ sĭs)	*n.* Frame under an automobile.
conductor	(cŏn dŭc′ tor) tẽr	*n.* One in charge of a public conveyance.
depot	(dē′ pōt)	*n.* Railroad station.
detour	(dē′ tour) tŏŏr	*n.* Deviation from a direct route.
diesel	(diē′ ṣĕl)	*n.* Type of internal-combustion engine.
engineer	(ĕn ġĭ nēer′)	*n.* One who operates a locomotive.
excursion	(ĕx cûr′ sion)	*n.* A pleasure trip.
garage	(gȧ rage′) räzh′	*n.* Building for housing or repairing automobiles.
interstate	(ĭn′ tĕr stāte′)	*adj.* Between states.
intrastate	(ĭn′ trä stāte′)	*adj.* Within a state.
limousine	(lĭm′ ou sine′) ŏŏ zēn′	*n.* Automobile having an enclosed compartment.
locomotive	(lō′ cŏ mō′ tĭve)	*n.* Steam engine or electric motor used to haul trains on a railroad.
muffler	(mŭf′ flẽr)	*n.* Device for deadening exhaust noise.
pneumatic	(*p*neū măt′ ĭc)	*adj.* Filled with compressed air, as a tire.
porter	(pōr′ tẽr)	*n.* Attendant who waits upon passengers.
Pullman	(Pull′ măn) pŏŏl′	*n.* Railroad sleeping car.
puncture	(punc′ tŭre) pŭngk′	*n.* A hole. *v.* To pierce with a pointed object.
radiator	(rā′ dĭ ā tor) tẽr	*n.* Device for cooling an engine.
reverse	(rĕ́ verse′) vûrs′	*n.* Opposite direction. *adj.* Opposite.
roomette	(rōŏm ĕt*t*e′)	*n.* Small bedroom in a Pullman car.
sedan	(sĕ́ dăn′)	*n.* Type of enclosed automobile.

A. Consult your dictionary for the pronunciation and meaning of the following words:

axle   chauffeur   exhaust   piggyback   piston

B. Use each of the following words in a sentence:

carburetor   detour   limousine   porter   puncture

anchor	(an' chor) ăng' kĕr	n. Device holding a ship in a particular place.
ballast	(băl' lȧst)	n. Heavy substance used to improve a ship's stability.
boatswain	(bōat' swain)	n. Petty officer on a merchant ship.
bow	(bow) bou	n. Forward part of a ship.
buoy	(buoy) boō' ĭ	n. A float to mark a channel or obstruction in the water.
canal	(cȧ năl')	n. Artificial body of water designed for navigation.
captain	(căp' taĭn)	n. Commanding officer of a ship.
channel	(chăn' nĕl)	n. Deeper part of a river where the main current flows.
compass	(com' pȧss) cŭm'	n. Device for determining directions on the earth's surface.
cruiser	(crūiş' ēr)	n. Type of war vessel; power-driven boat for pleasure trips.
dinghy	(din' ghy̆) dĭng'	n. Small boat of various kinds.
fishy-back	(fĭsh' y̆ băck)	n. Movement of truck trailers or freight containers by barge or ship.
freighter	(freight' ēr) frāt'	n. Vessel used mainly to carry cargo.
gyroscope	(ġȳ' rŏ scōpe)	n. Device used to keep ships level.
harbor	(här' bor) bĕr	n. Protected place that offers ships safety from the elements.
nautical	(nau' tĭ căl) nȯ'	adj. Pertaining to shipping.
periscope	(pĕr' ĭ scōpe)	n. Instrument used on submerged submarines to give a view of the surface.
pier	(piēr)	n. Breakwater extending into the water to serve as a landing place.
purser	(pûrs' ēr)	n. A ship official responsible for comfort and welfare of passengers.
sextant	(sĕx' tănt)	n. Instrument used to determine latitude and longitude.
steerage	(stēēr' age) ĭj	n. Section of ship used by low-fare passengers.
steward	(stew' ard) stū' ĕrd	n. Employee who attends to passengers' wants.
submarine	(sŭb' mȧ rine) rēn	n. Boat that operates either on or below the surface of the water.

A. Consult your dictionary for the pronunciation and meaning of the following words:

destroyer   maritime   transoceanic   vessel   wharf

B. Use each of the following words in a sentence:

ballast   buoy   dinghy   periscope   steerage

A. The following sentences contain words in Lessons 126 through 132 that are frequently misspelled. Rewrite each sentence, correcting all misspelled words.

1. The last edition of the dictionery had fewer mistakes but a less pleasing format than did the preceding editions.
2. We have just signed a lease with the reltor to rent a beautiful summer home with a private pool and a 300-foot frontage.
3. If you cannot make your payments on time, we will be forced to foreclose your morgage.
4. Mr. Johns, one of the city's leading reltors, has sold almost 80 per cent of the houses in the new subdivesion.
5. Charles decided to purchase a life anuity rather than an endowment policy and named Eva as his beneficiery.
6. It was a good thing that Jim had comprihensive and dissability coverage, since both cars involved in the accident were badly damaged and three of the passengers were slightly injured.
7. Mr. Greene has decided to diversify his portfoleo by making an investment in Smith Corporation debensure bonds.
8. Akron has made available a new issue of municepal bonds and I understand they are a very good buy.
9. Joe Brown inherited a block of convertable, particepating stock from his grandmother.
10. The altimmeter in Jack's new airplane was broken and he will not be able to fly until the instrument is fixed.
11. Henry tells me that he never goes up in his hellicopter unless he is wearing a parashute.
12. Before winter comes, do not neglect to put antyfreeze in your car radiater if your automobile has a water-cooled engine.
13. Since we will be on the train for such a long time, we have made reservations for a roomet in a Pulman car.
14. The captain, who commanded a cruser during the war, is now the skipper of a transoceannic freighter.
15. Even though our accommodations are in the stearage, the steward has been very friendly and helpful.

B. Explain the difference between the following pairs of words:

bulletin	newspaper
encumbrance	lien
cancellation	waiver
dividend	premium
navigator	pilot
purser	steward

The lessons contained in this part include occupational terms and words of human interest used by the average person. Some occupations, such as that of pharmacist and bacteriologist, are so specialized in character that the special terms relating to them are seldom used by the general public. Such terms are not included in these lessons.

Many new occupations and fields of interest have come into existence during recent years. Among them are all the occupations connected with the manufacture, sales, maintenance, and use of airplanes; the occupations connected with radio and television; the occupations in the new field of electronics; and the even newer field of rocketry. We are entering the era of the astronaut and the cosmonaut—words unknown to us a few years ago.

134 Occupations

This lesson emphasizes the most commonly used occupational terms, with some new words to keep us up to date in our thinking. Consult your dictionary regarding the pronunciation and meaning of any of the following words about which you are in doubt.

accountant	copywriter	jeweler
actor	counselor	journalist
actress	dairyman	key-punch operator
analyst	dancer	laborer
appraiser	dentist	lawyer
architect	dietitian	librarian
artist	doctor	machinist
auctioneer	dressmaker	manager
auditor	driver	manufacturer
bacteriologist	druggist	masseur
banker	economist	mathematician
barber	editor	mechanic
beautician	electrician	merchant
biologist	engineer	messenger
bookkeeper	entrepreneur	metallurgist
broker	farmer	miner
butcher	financier	minister
captain	geneticist	mortician
carpenter	grocer	musician
chemist	horticulturist	novelist
chiropodist	hostess	nurse
chiropractor	housekeeper	oculist
clergyman	industrialist	ophthalmologist
clerk	inspector	optician
conductor	interpreter	organist
consultant	inventor	osteopath
contractor	janitor	pharmacist

photographer	rancher	surgeon
physician	realtor	tailor
plumber	repairman	teacher
policeman	reporter	technician
politician	salesman	telephone operator
priest	scientist	treasurer
professor	sculptor	trucker
programmer	secretary	typist
proofreader	statistician	underwriter
psychiatrist	stenographer	veterinarian
psychologist	steward	zoologist
publisher	stewardess	

A. 1. What is the difference between an "accountant" and a "bookkeeper"?
2. What is meant by an "oculist," an "optician," and an "ophthalmologist"?
3. What is the difference between a "stenographer" and a "secretary"?
4. How many "f's" and how many "s's" are there in "professor"?
5. What word means the same as "undertaker"?

B. From what verbs are the following nouns derived?

appraiser   contractor   laborer   photographer   publisher

amateur	(ăm' á teûr')	*n.* One who plays, but not as a professional.
archery	(är' chẽr y̆)	*n.* Art of shooting arrows.
battery	(băt' tẽr y̆)	*n.* Pitcher and catcher.
bleachers	(blēach' ẽrs)	*n.* Seats for spectators.
caddie	(căd' dĭe)	*n.* One who carries golf clubs.
catcher	(cătch' ẽr)	*n.* One who catches a ball.
challenge	(chăl' lĕnġe)	*n.* Invitation to contest.
		v. To invite to contest.
champion	(chăm' pĭ on) ŭn	*n.* One acknowledged supreme.
defeated	(dé fēat' ĕd)	*adj.* Overcome; vanquished.
diamond	(dī' á mond) mŭnd	*n.* The infield of a baseball ground.
foul	(foul)	*n.* An act committed contrary to the rules.
fumble	(fŭm' ble)	*v.* To fail to hold a ball.
motorcycle	(mō' tor çy̆' cle) tẽr	*n.* An automotive bicycle.
Olympics	(Ō ly̆m' pĭcs)	*n.* Olympic games; international athletic games held once every four years.
opponent	(ŏp pō' nĕnt)	*n.* Adversary.
pageant	(păg' ĕant)	*n.* A spectacle; an exhibition.
pitcher	(pĭtch' ẽr)	*n.* One who pitches a ball.
polo	(pō' lō)	*n.* Game played with wooden ball and mallets by players on horseback.
referee	(rĕf ẽr ēē')	*n.* An official appointed to judge athletic games.
scrimmage	(scrĭm' mage) ĭj	*n.* A practice football game.
skiing	(ski' ĭng) skē'	*n.* A snow sport.
slalom	(slä' lom) lŭm	*n.* Skiing in a zigzag down-hill course between upright obstacles.

A. Consult your dictionary for the pronunciation and meaning of the following words:

bunkers   endurance   hydroplane   sportsmanship   vigor

B. 1. How many syllables are there in the word "pageant"?
2. What is the meaning of "ee" in "referee"?
3. How may "opponent" be divided at the end of a line?

C. Copy each of the following phrases, substituting the correct word from this lesson for the blank space.

1. (   ) ball
2. accept the (   )
3. (   ) pony
4. world's (   )
5. left-handed (   )
6. baseball (   )

athlete	(ăth′ lēte)	*n.* One contending in games requiring strength and agility.
athletics	(ăth lĕt′ ĭcs)	*n.* The games and sports of athletes.
canoeing	(cȧ noe′ ĭng) noo′	*v.* Art of managing a canoe.
competitive	(cŏm pĕt′ i tĭve)	*adj.* Pertaining to competition.
hockey	(hŏck′ ēy)	*n.* A game played with a ball and curved sticks.
inning	(ĭn′ *n*ĭng)	*n.* Time or turn for batting, as in baseball.
javelin	(jăv*e*′ lĭn)	*n.* A spear used in field sports.
practice	(prăc′ tĭçe)	*v.* To drill.
		n. Systematic drill.
professional	(pró fes′ sion ăl) fĕsh′ ŭn	*adj.* Engaged in a branch of athletics for gain.
		n. One who engages in a sport as a livelihood.
quarterback	(quar′ tĕr băck′) kwôr′	*n.* A football player.
schedule	(sc*h*ĕd′ ūle)	*n.* A list of dates of athletic games.
skin diving	(skĭn dīv′ ĭng)	*n.* Swimming under water with a breathing device but no diving suit.
snorkel	(snôr′ kĕl)	*n.* An air tube protruding above the surface of the water.
soccer	(sŏc′ c̄ĕr)	*n.* A kind of football game.
spectator	(spĕc tā′ tor) tĕr	*n.* One who watches a game.
stadium	(stā′ dĭ ŭm)	*n.* Arena for athletics.
tennis	(tĕn′ *n*ĭs)	*n.* A game played with a ball, which is struck with a racket.
tournament	(tour′ nȧ mĕnt) too̅r′	*n.* A meeting held for contests in athletics.
trophy	(trō′ phy) fē	*n.* Evidence of a victory.
umpire	(ŭm′pīre)	*n.* An official who rules on the plays of an athletic game.
volleyball	(vŏl′ *l*eȳ ball′) bôl	*n.* Game played by volleying a ball with the hands over a net.
wrestling	(*w*rĕs′ *t*lĭng)	*n.* A combat between two opponents who seek to throw each other.

A. Consult your dictionary for the pronunciation and meaning of the following words:

dribble   intramural   megaphone   physical   quoits

B. Copy each of the following phrases, substituting the correct word from this lesson for the blank space.

1. ninth (   )   4. (   ) bleachers
2. ice (   )   5. gold (   )
3. (   ) net   6. (   ) mat

accessories	(ăc çĕs' sŏ rĭes)	n.	Articles that add to the effectiveness of a costume.
apparel	(ăp păr' ĕl)	n.	Clothing.
		v.	To dress.
beret	(bĕ ret') rā'	n.	A round, flat cap of soft material.
blouse	(blouşe)	n.	A loose overgarment.
cashmere	(căsh' mēre)	n.	A fine wool.
collar	(cŏl' lar) ĕr	n.	Something worn about the neck.
cotton	(cŏt' ton) ŭn	n.	A fabric made of cotton; a soft, white fibrous substance.
couturière	(cou tu rière') kōō tü ryā'	n.	A dressmaker (masc.).
couturiere	(cou tu riere') kōō tü ryâr'	n.	A dressmaker (fem.).
culottes	(cū lŏttes')	n.	A divided skirt.
dacron	(dā' cron) crän	n.	A synthetic fabric.
décolleté	(dé cŏl' lĕ té') dā tā'	adj.	With shoulders uncovered.
denier	(den ier') dĕn yĕr'	n.	A unit expressing the fineness of yarns.
dungarees	(dŭn' gȧ rēes)	n.	Trousers of coarse cloth.
eiderdown	(eī' dĕr down')	n.	Soft down plucked from the body of an eider duck; a quilt filled with eiderdown.
embroidery	(ĕm broi' dĕr y̆)	n.	The art of ornamenting cloth with needlework.
ensemble	(en sem' ble) än sŏm' b'l	n.	A costume of two or more pieces.
flannel	(flăn' nĕl)	n.	A soft woolen cloth.
gingham	(gĭng' hăm)	n.	Cotton cloth of dyed yarn.
hosiery	(hō' şĭĕr y̆)	n.	Stockings.

A. Consult your dictionary for the pronunciation and meaning of the following words:

moccasin   modiste   seersucker   textile   taffeta

B. 1. Why do we say that dacron is a synthetic fabric?
2. Consult your dictionary. From what language did "khaki" originate? What is the meaning of "khaki" in that language?
3. What word in this lesson is a compound word?

C. Substitute the correct word from this lesson for the blank space.

1. thirty ( )   4. ( ) winter coat
2. ( ) pillow   5. matching ( )
3. lace ( )   6. sheer ( )

acetate	(ăç′ é tāte)	n. Cellulose fiber, yarn, or fabric.
appliqué	(ăp′ plĭ que′) kā′	adj. Figures cut from one fabric and sewn on another.
bolero	(bó le′ rō) lå′	n. A jacket, waist length or shorter, usually open at the front.
buckle	(bŭck′ le)	n. Device for uniting two ends, as of a belt.
button	(bŭt′ ton) ŭn	n. A fastener or catch. v. To fasten.
calico	(căl′ ĭ cō)	n. Cotton cloth printed with a figured pattern.
corduroy	(côr′ dŭ roy′)	n. A cotton fabric.
haberdashery	(hăb′ ẽr dăsh′ ẽr ў)	n. Men's furnishings.
jabot	(ja bōt′) zhå	n. A trimming worn down the dress front.
lapel	(lå pĕl′)	n. The fold of the front of a coat in continuation of the collar.
lingerie	(lin′ ge rie′) lăn′ zh′rē′	n. Undergarments for women.
millinery	(mil′ lĭ nẽr ў)	n. Hats for women.
negligee	(nĕg′ lĭ gee′) zhā′	n. Woman's dressing gown.
nylon	(nȳ′ lŏn)	n. A synthetic fabric.
orlon	(ôr′ lŏn)	n. A synthetic fabric.
overalls	(ō′ vẽr älls)	n. Trousers worn over the clothing.
pastel	(păs tĕl′)	adj. Pale in color. n. Pale color.
percale	(pẽr cāle′)	n. A fine, closely woven cotton fabric.
plaid	(plăid)	n. A tartan pattern. adj. Made of tartan pattern.
redingote	(rĕd′ in gote) ĭng gōt	n. A long, plain outside coat worn by women.
sandals	(săn′ dăls)	n. Shoes consisting of a sole strapped to the foot.
serge	(serge) sûrj	n. A twilled worsted fabric.
suede	(suede) swād	n. A tanned skin, with the flesh side rubbed into a nap.
worsted	(wors′ tĕd) wōōs′	n. A smooth-surfaced woolen cloth.

A. Consult your dictionary for the pronunciation and meaning of the following words:

shoddy synthetic trousseau vogue voile

B. 1. What letter is silent in "worsted"?
2. How may "overalls" be divided at the end of a line?
3. What is the sound of "gee" in negligee?
4. How many syllables are there in "redingote"?

159

accredited	(ăc crĕd′ ĭt ĕd)	*adj.* Meets prescribed requirements.
administration	(ăd mĭn′ ĭs trā′ tion)	*n.* The persons who collectively perform the executive duties of an institution.
auditorium	(au′ dĭ tō′ rĭ ŭm) ȯ	*n.* Room assigned to an audience.
campus	(căm′ pŭs)	*n.* The grounds of a school.
classics	(clăs′ sĭcs)	*n.* Ancient Greek and Roman literature.
coeducation	(cō′ ĕd ū cā′ tion)	*n.* The education of students of both sexes at the same institution.
college	(cŏl′ lĕġe)	*n.* Institution for teaching the higher branches of knowledge.
department	(dĕ̇ pärt′mĕnt)	*n.* A subdivision of a school.
diploma	(dĭ plō′ mȧ)	*n.* Document showing graduation.
emeritus	(ĕ̇ mĕr′ ĭ tŭs)	*adj.* Retired.
extracurricular	(ĕx′ trȧ cŭr rĭc′ ū lar) lȇr	*adj.* Not falling within the scope of the curriculum.
gymnasium	(ġȳm nā′ sĭ ŭm)	*n.* A place or building for athletic exercises.
intramural	(ĭn′ trȧ mū′ răl)	*adj.* Confined to members of the college.
kindergarten	(kĭn′ dĕr gär′ tĕn)	*n.* A school lower than the first grade.
knowledge	(knŏwl′ ĕdġe)	*n.* Acquaintance with facts.
laboratory	(lăb′ o rȧ tō′ rȳ)	*n.* A workroom.
library	(lī′ brar ȳ) brĕr	*n.* A collection of books; a room or building devoted to books.
matriculate	(mȧ trĭc′ ū lāte′)	*v.* To enroll.
science	(scī′ ĕnçe)	*n.* Any branch of systematized knowledge.
semester	(sĕ̇ mĕs′ tȇr)	*n.* Half a school year.

A. Consult your dictionary for the pronunciation and meaning of the following words:

academic baccalaureate curriculum dissertation mathematics

B. 1. Why should not all college teachers be called "professor"?
2. Distinguish between "college" and "university."
3. How may "diploma" be divided at the end of a line?
4. Give the names of five sciences.

C. Substitute the correct word from this lesson for the blank space.

1. an (   ) college   4. professor (   )
2. (   ) in September   5. (   ) activity
3. accounting (   )   6. (   ) athletics

algebra	(ăl' ġė́ brȧ)	*n.*	A branch of mathematics.
arithmetic	(ȧ rĭth' mĕ tĭc)	*n.*	The science of positive real numbers.
attendance	(ăt tĕn' dănçe)	*n.*	Number of persons present or attending.
commencement	(cŏm mĕnçe' mĕnt)	*n.*	The ceremonies at the end of a school year.
faculty	(făc' ŭl tў̆)	*n.*	The teachers of a school; a power of the mind.
fraternity	(frȧ ter' nĭ tў̆) tûr'	*n.*	Society of male students.
geography	(ġė́ ŏg' rȧ phў̆)	*n.*	Science of the earth.
graduate	(grăd' ú́ áte)	*n.*	One who has completed a prescribed curriculum.
historical	(hĭs tŏr' ĭ căl)	*adj.*	Pertaining to history.
inculcate	(ĭn cŭl' cāte)	*v.*	To impress upon the mind.
juvenile	(ju̇' vĕ́ nĭle)	*adj.*	Young; youthful.
		n.	A young person.
language	(lăn' guage) gwĭj	*n.*	Human speech and its written representation.
median	(mē' dĭ ăn)	*adj.*	Being in the middle.
pedagogue	(pĕd' ȧ gŏgu̇e)	*n.*	A teacher of children or youth.
physics	(phў̆s̩' ĭcs)	*n.*	Science of the nonchemical changes of matter.
prerequisite	(prė́ rĕq' ui s̩ĭte) wĭ	*n.*	Something necessary as a preliminary to a proposed end.
principal	(prĭn' çĭ păl)	*n.*	Person in charge.
psychology	(*p*sў̄ c*h*ŏl' ŏ́ ġў̆)	*n.*	Science which treats of the mind.
registrar	(rĕġ' ĭs trär)	*n.*	One who keeps a record.
scholarship	(sc*h*ŏl' ar shĭp) ĕr	*n.*	Learning; a fund for the support of a student.
seminar	(sĕm' ĭ när)	*n.*	A group of students engaged in original research.
sorority	(sŏ́ rŏr' ĭ tў̆)	*n.*	Society of female students.
statistics	(stȧ tĭs' tĭcs)	*n.*	Science of the collection and classification of facts as a ground for induction.

A. Consult your dictionary for the pronunciation and meaning of the following words:

alumni   disciplinarian   economics   geology   philosophy

B. 1. What is the difference between arithmetic and mathematics?
     2. What is the sound of "phy" in "geography"?
     3. How many syllables are there in "historical"?
     4. How may "fraternity" be divided at the end of a line?

alma mater	(äl′ mȧ mä′ tẽr)	*n.*	One's university, college, or school.
assembly	(ăs sĕm′ blῠ)	*n.*	A group of persons gathered together.
examination	(ex am′ ĭ nā′ tion)	*n.*	A testing of knowledge.
	ĕg zăm′		
forum	(fō′ rŭm)	*n.*	A place for open discussion.
literary	(lĭt′ ẽr ar′ ῠ)	*adj.*	Pertaining to literature; versed in literature.
	ẽr′		
museum	(mū̇ s̤ē′ ŭm)	*n.*	A building in which a collection of objects is preserved.
physiology	(phῠs′ ĭ ŏl′ ȯ ġῠ)	*n.*	A branch of biology.
professor	(prȯ fĕs′ sor)	*n.*	A teacher of the highest rank in a college or university.
	ẽr		
rhetoric	(rʜĕt′ ȯ rĭc)	*n.*	The art of expressive speech.
sociology	(sō′ çĭ ŏl′ ȯ ġῠ)	*n.*	Science of the origin and evolution of society.
studious	(stū′ dĭ oŭs)	*adj.*	Given to study.
syllabus	(sῠl′ lȧ bŭs)	*n.*	A summary containing a course of study.
technical	(tĕcʜ′ nĭ căl)	*adj.*	Pertaining to the useful or mechanic arts.
thesis	(thē′ sĭs)	*n.*	A theme; proposition.
tuition	(tū̇ ĭ′ tion)	*n.*	Instruction; a fee.
university	(ū′ nĭ ver′ sĭ tῠ)	*n.*	An institution consisting of several schools or colleges offering advanced studies.
	vûr′		
valedictorian	(văl′ é dĭc tō′ rĭ ăn)	*n.*	Usually the student who ranks first in scholarship and gives the farewell address at commencement.
vocational	(vō cā′ tion ăl)	*adj.*	Pertaining to vocation; pursued as a vocation.

A. Consult your dictionary for the pronunciation and meaning of the following words:

alumnus   aptitude   bursar   collegiate   humanities

B. Correct all misspellings in the following sentences:
1. Our proffesor is a very brilliant man.
2. Our class valadictarian gave the farewell address at our graduation.
3. The tuition at the local univercity is very high, but the education received is well worth the price.
4. His senior theses was a letrary masterpiece.

C. Substitute the correct word from this lesson for the blank space.

1. curator of the (   )   4. class (   )
2. midterm (   )   5. general (   )
3. absent-minded (   )   6. (   ) high school

The following sentences contain words from Lessons 134 through 141 that are frequently misspelled. Rewrite each sentence, correcting all errors in spelling.

1. Jim lost his amature standing when he played in a proffesional ball game in Cincinnati.

2. Jack likes atheletics because they are competative, and he is determined to be a champion.

3. Jack's chief trouble is that he has a tough schedule and he is always late for practise.

4. Bill entered a golf tournement, but his opponants were too good for him.

5. This defeat was a surprise to him, after his triumphs in hocky at the Olympics.

6. Jim played quaterback on the varsity team for awhile, but his hot temper cost the team too many yards on personal fouls.

7. Joan won the trophey in the archery tournament at Hughes Stadiam.

8. Vollyball provides excellent exercise for bankers, lawyers, engineers —in fact, for all middle-aged business executives.

9. For her cashmear ensemble, the beauticion selected beige accessorys.

10. The salesman showed us the new hosiery styles and gave the denier count for each one.

11. On her cotton bollero several huge red roses were applaqued.

12. The bookeeper was attired in a blue surge suit with deeply cut lappels, a dakron shirt, and a black cashmear topcoat.

13. The famous Parisian couturière designed her entire wardrobe— negligee, reddingote, blouses, beret, etc.—all for $2,000.

14. I would like to go to the gymnasum with you, but I must first go to the libary.

15. Jean's father is a proffessor emeraritus at a college in the East.

16. Some taxpayers object to kindergartens, saying they are too expensive.

17. Always be sure that the colleges and univercities you attend are accreditted.

18. During her sophomore year Toni completed the following courses: physiology, sychology, and philossophy.

19. The principle, the registrar, and six facultie members attended the seminarr program and forum on the Evanston campus.

20. Last year a new fratternity chapter was installed, with Professor Hines of the Geology Departement acting as facultie sponsor.

adagio	(à dä´ ġiō)	*n.* In ballet dancing, a slow duet dance.
articulation	(är tĭc´ ŭ lā´ tion)	*n.* Speaking in distinct syllables and words.
audition	(au dĭ´ tion) ô	*n.* A hearing to try out a performer; *v.* To try out.
ballet	(băl´let) ā	*n.* A theatrical dance of aesthetic nature.
camera	(căm´ ẽr à)	*n.* An instrument used in taking pictures.
classical	(clăs´ sĭ căl)	*adj.* Conforming to an established form of art.
commentator	(cŏm´ mĕn tā´ tor) tẽr	*n.* One who makes observations intended to explain the meaning of something.
culture	(cŭl´ tŭre)	*n.* Enlightenment and refinement of taste.
distortion	(dĭs tôr´ tion)	*n.* A deforming, as of sounds.
frequency	(frē´ quen çў) kwĕn	*n.* Cycles of current per second.
ingénue	(in gé nüe´) ăn zhä	*n.* An actress representing a naïve girl.
modulate	(mŏd´ ŭ lāte)	*v.* To tune to a certain pitch.
nocturne	(nŏc´ tûrne)	*n.* A dreamy, night serenade.
realism	(rē´ ăl ĭșm)	*n.* Fidelity to nature or to real life.
resonance	(rĕș´ ŏ nănçe)	*n.* Prolongation of sound.
rhythm	(rhῩthm)	*n.* The regular rise and fall of sounds.
static	(stăt´ ĭc)	*n.* Atmospheric disturbances.
theater	(thē´ à tẽr)	*n.* An edifice for dramatic performances.
transistor	(trăn șĭs´ tor) tẽr	*n.* A nonvacuum electronic device.
visual	(vis´ ŭ ăl) vĭzh´	*adj.* Pertaining to sight.

A. Consult your dictionary for the pronunciation and meaning of the following words:

acoustics	documentary	kinescope
cinemascope	image	photogenic

B. Form sentences containing the following words:

ballet   commentator   ingénue   realism   transistor

C. Substitute the correct words from this lesson for the blank spaces.

1. Because it was a stormy night, all we could get on the radio was (   ).
2. The actor is going to (   ) for the part.
3. We have bought our tickets and will attend the (   ) tonight.
4. Some of my friends prefer realism, but I am much more enthusiastic about (   ) plays.

aerial	(â′ e rĭ ăl)	*adj.* Pertaining to the air. *n.* Conductor portion of an antenna.
auditorium	(au′ dĭ tō′ rĭ ŭm) ô′	*n.* A room for lectures, concerts, etc.
broadcast	(brôad′ căst)	*v.* To send out from a transmitting station. *n.* Program transmitted.
censor	(çĕn′ sor) sēr	*v.* To subject to examination and possible repression.
choir	(choir) kwĭr	*n.* Organized company of singers.
comedienne	(cố mē′ dĭ ĕnne′)	*n.* Actress who plays comedy.
commercial	(cŏm mer′ cial) mûr′ shăl	*n.* Paid advertisement on radio or TV.
decorative	(dĕc′ ố rā′ tĭve)	*adj.* Ornamental.
encore	(en′ cōre) än′	*interj.* Once more! Again! Used by an audience to call for further appearance of an artist.
focus	(fō′ cŭs)	*v.* To adjust for clear vision.
gesture	(g̣ĕs′ túre)	*n.* Motion of the body expressive of sentiment or passion.
microphone	(mĭ′ crố phōne)	*n.* Instrument for transmitting sound.
motif	(mố tif′) tēf′	*n.* Theme or dominant feature.
orchestra	(ôr′chĕs trà)	*n.* Band of performers on various instruments.
quartet	(quar tĕt′) kwôr	*n.* Group consisting of four.
radiogram	(rā′ dĭ ố grăm′)	*n.* Message transmitted by wireless telegraph.
revue	(rế vūe′)	*n.* A medley of songs, dances, and skits.
scenario	(scế nä′ rĭ ō′)	*n.* Screenplay, script.
spontaneity	(spŏn′ tà nē′ ĭ tў)	*n.* Acting from native feeling.
Technicolor	(Tĕch′ nĭ col′ or) cŭl′ ēr	*n.* Trademark of color motion pictures.
television	(tĕl′ ế vĭ′ sion) vĭzh′ ŭn	*n.* Pictures sent by radio.
transmitter	(trăns mĭt′ tēr)	*n.* Sending station.
virtuoso	(vir′ tú ō′ sō) vûr′	*n.* One who excels in the performance of an art.

A. Correct all misspelled words in the following sentences:

1. The senerio for the television play was very dull and boring.
2. He was such a vurtuoso on the violin that the audience called "Encor, encor" for five minutes after he finished playing.
3. The comediene was angry because the microfone was not working properly.
4. The choir sang very well, but the quartette was not well organized.

B. Use each of the following words in a sentence:

aerial   commercial   gesture   motif   spontaneity

165

amplify	(ăm′ plĭ fȳ)	v. To make louder.
announcer	(ă*n* nounç′ ēr)	n. One who introduces a broadcast.
ballerina	(băl′ *lĕ* ri′ nà) rē′	n. A female ballet dancer.
cinema	(çĭn′ ĕ mȧ)	n. A motion picture or motion picture theater.
circus	(cir′ cŭs) sûr′	n. A tent or group of tents where performances are given.
clown	(clown) kloun	n. Jester or buffoon.
comedy	(cŏm′ ĕ dȳ)	n. A light and amusing drama.
dial	(dī′ ăl)	n. Device for tuning in stations.
director	(dī rĕc′ tor) tēr	n. The producer of a play who trains the actors.
exposure	(ĕx pō′ sure) zhēr	n. Film subjected to light.
humorous	(hū′ mor oŭs) mēr	adj. Funny.
interference	(ĭn′ tēr fēr′ ĕnce)	n. That which interrupts reception.
playwright	(plāy′ *wr*īght′)	n. A writer of plays.
projection	(prŏ́ jĕc′ tion)	n. Picture provided by throwing image upon a screen.
rehearsal	(rĕ́ hears′ al) hûr′ săl	n. Practice in preparation for a public exhibition.
rhapsody	(r*h*ăp′ sŏ́ dȳ)	n. An instrumental composition of irregular form.
sponsor	(spŏn′ sor) sēr	n. A person or organization paying for a program.
stage	(stāġe)	n. The raised floor in a theater where plays are enacted.
symphony	(sȳm′ phō nȳ)	n. An instrumental composition in sonata form.
telecast	(tĕl′ ĕ cǎst)	v. To broadcast by television.
teleplay	(tĕl′ ĕ plāy)	n. A play written for or presented on television.
understudy	(ŭn′ dēr stŭd′ ȳ)	n. One who is prepared to act another's part.
volume	(vŏl′ ŭme)	n. Fullness or quantity of tone.

A. Substitute the correct words from this lesson for the blank spaces.
1. Please turn up the (   ) so that we can hear.
2. The star's (   ) handled the part very well.
3. Because the (   ) was very slippery, the ballerina fell and broke her leg.
4. The dress (   ) went poorly because no one was prepared.

B. 1. What letter is silent in "rhapsody"?
2. What is the sound of "cir" in circus?
3. What is the sound of "ph" in symphony?
4. Which word in this lesson is a compound word?

apricot   (ăʹ prĭ cŏt)   *n.* Orange-colored fruit of a tree of the peach family.

artichoke   (ärʹ tĭ chōke)   *n.* A tall thistlelike herb cooked as a vegetable.

asparagus   (ăs părʹ à gŭs)   *n.* A plant having much-branched stems and scalelike leaves, used as a food.

avocado   (ăv ŏ́ cä́ dō)   *n.* A fruit of American tropical trees.

banana   (bà nănʹ à)   *n.* Fruit of a tropical tree.

banquet   (banʹ quet)   *n.* A feast.
             bănkʹ kwĕt

barbecue   (bärʹ bĕ́ cūe)   *n.* An outdoor social gathering at which large pieces of meat are roasted over a pit; the meat so roasted. *v.* To cook before an open fire.

biscuit   (bĭsʹ cuit)   *n.* A small, quick bread that rises while baking.
         kĭt

broccoli   (brŏcʹ cŏ́ lĭ)   *n.* A type of cauliflower.

caramel   (cărʹ à mĕl)   *n.* Burnt sugar; a kind of candy.

cayenne   (cay ĕnneʹ)   *n.* Pepper.
        kī

chicken   (chĭckʹ ĕn)   *n.* A barnyard fowl.

cider   (çīʹ dẽr)   *n.* Apple juice.

coconut   (cōʹ cŏ́ nŭt)   *n.* Fruit of the coconut palm.

coleslaw   (cōleʹ slaw)   *n.* A salad made of cabbage.
         slô

consommé   (cŏn sŏ*m* méʹ)   *n.* A clear soup.
           mäʹ

cranberry   (crănʹ bẽr rў)   *n.* A red berry of a plant of the heath family.

cucumber   (cūʹ cŭm bẽr)   *n.* A fruit of the gourd family.

curry   (cûrʹ rў)   *n.* A highly spiced condiment from India.

hibachi   (hi bäʹ chi)   *n.* A charcoal brazier.
        hē   chē

raspberry   (răs̱pʹ bẽr rў)   *n.* A fruit of several shrubs of the rose family.

restaurant   (rĕsʹ tau rănt)   *n.* A public eating house.
         tŏ́

succotash   (sŭcʹ cŏ́ tăsh)   *n.* Beans and corn cooked together.

A. Consult your dictionary for the pronunciation and meaning of the following words:

cauliflower   caviar   mayonnaise   rhubarb   smörgasbord

B. Form sentences using the following words:

avocado   banquet   cayenne   consummé   restaurant

breakfast	(brĕak′ fȧst)	n. The first meal of the day.
celery	(çĕl′ ĕr ў̆)	n. A plant of the carrot family, eaten either raw or cooked.
cocoa	(cō′ cōa)	n. Chocolate less a portion of its fat; a beverage.
doughnut	(dōugh′ nŭt)	n. A fried cake of dough.
ginger	(ġĭn′ ġêr)	n. An herb used in cooking.
grapefruit	(grāpe′ fruit) frōot	n. A large citrus fruit.
lemonade	(lĕm on āde′) ŭn	n. A beverage of lemon juice mixed with sweetened water.
lettuce	(lĕt′ tuce) ĭs	n. Plant with crisp leaves used in salads.
mackerel	(măck′ êr ĕl)	n. Food fish.
maraschino	(măr′ ȧ schi′ nō) skē′	n. A cordial or liqueur.
molasses	(mṍ lăs′ sĕş)	n. Thick syrup derived from sugar.
mustard	(mŭs′ tard) tĕrd	n. A seasoning.
onion	(on′ ion) ŭn′ yŭn	n. A plant of pungent taste and odor.
oyster	(oys′ tēr) ois′	n. A marine animal; bivalve mollusk.
parsley	(pärs′ leў̆)	n. A garden herb.
potato	(pō tā′ tō)	n. Starchy tuber of a plant.
raisin	(rāi′ şĭn)	n. A dried grape.
sauerkraut	(sauer′ kraut) sour′ krout	n. Cabbage fermented in brine.
sorghum	(sôr′ ghŭm)	n. Cereal grass; a sweet syrup made from sorghum grasses.
spaghetti	(spȧ ghĕt′ tĭ)	n. A solid food paste in long slender pieces.
spinach	(spĭn′ ach) ĭch	n. An edible herb.
syrup	(sў̆r′ ŭp)	n. A thick, sticky liquid boiled with sugar.
tangerine	(tăn ġē rine′) rēn′	n. A small orange with easily detached rind.
tomato	(tṍ mā′ tō)	n. Herb cultivated for its red fruit.
turkey	(tŭr′ kēy)	n. Large domesticated bird.
watermelon	(wa′ tēr mĕl′ on) wó′ ŭn	n. Large oblong fruit of a vine.

A. Consult your dictionary for the pronunciation and meaning of the following words:

cafeteria   chocolate   delicatessen   macaroni   saccharin

B. Form sentences using the following words:

ginger   lettuce   oyster   sauerkraut   sorghum   turkey

The following sentences contain words from Lessons 143 through 147 that are frequently misspelled. Rewrite each sentence, correcting all errors in spelling.

1. We saw the playright on the opening night of his theatre production.
2. The balett on television last night was very good, but we were disappointed that there was so much distorsion in the picture.
3. Henry has a new transister radio, but the station he receives best plays nothing but clasical music.
4. The quartette had been telacasting for two minutes when it was found that the micraphone had been turned off.
5. The announcer thought he was as humerous as any clown, but the audience thought differently.
6. The rehersal of the nocterne went well, but the actual performance was a failure.
7. The news comentator was awarded an Oscar for his narration of the documentory film, "Europe, Encore."
8. The acoustics in the auditoreum are exceptionally fine and no difficulties should be experienced in amplifying the broadcast.
9. "The tall ballerina performing in the adajio lacks a feeling of the intended rhythm," criticized the director.
10. Scheduled to be presented next week at the Music Hall are: two ballets, one of Chopin's nocternes, a Beethoven symphonie, and a Gershwin rhapsodie.
11. Nothing tastes better on a cool autumn night than donuts and cider.
12. Molasess is often eaten by health enthusiasts because they believe it to have many body-building properties.
13. Turkey and cranberrys are traditionally eaten on Thanksgiving.
14. Sauerkraut is a typical German dish.
15. Although tomattoes are eaten by many people today, there was a time when they were thought to be poisonous.
16. Spagheti tastes very good with chili.
17. From the smörgassborg, Eleanor made her selection—caviarre, pickled artechokes, avocado salad, smoked oysters, sliced turkey, and rasberry ice.
18. For her bridge luncheon, Mrs. Randall served chicken à la king, asparugus tips, cucumber salad, and biscuts.
19. The den mother served ginnger ale and donuts to ten hungry cub scouts.
20. Because of his diabetic condition, the invalid used saccarin for sweetening all his food and beverages.

alderman	(al′ dĕr măn)		n. Member of the governing body of a city.
	ôl′		
alien	(āl′ ien)		adj. Strange; foreign.
	yĕn		n. Person of another nation.
ballot	(băl′ lot) ŭt		n. Ticket used in voting.
bipartisan	(bī pär′ tĭ s̱ăn)		adj. Representing two parties.
bureaucracy	(bú reauc′ rå çў̆)		n. Government conducted by bureaus or departments.
	rŏk′		
campaign	(căm pāign′)		n. Systematic effort to influence voters before an election for public office.
candidate	(căn′ dĭ dāte)		n. One who aspires to an office.
caucus	(cau′ cŭs)		n. A meeting of leaders.
	kô′		
consul	(cŏn′ sŭl)		n. An official appointed by a government to reside in a foreign country to care for the interests of the appointing country.
democracy	(dé mŏc′ rå çў̆)		n. Government by the people.
disfranchise	(dĭs frăn′ chis̱e)		v. To deprive of the rights of citizenship.
electoral	(é lĕc′ tor ăl)		adj. Pertaining to or consisting of electors.
	tēr		
enfranchise	(ĕn frăn′ chīs̱e)		v. To give the right of citizenship.
extradition	(ĕx′ trå dĭ′ tion)		n. The surrender or delivery of a prisoner.
filibuster	(fĭl′ ĭ bŭs′ tēr)		n. Member of a legislative body who obstructs action by speaking merely to consume time.
			v. To obstruct action by speaking merely to consume time.
foreigner	(fŏr′ eĭgn ēr)		n. Citizen of another country.
gubernatorial	(gū′ bēr nà tō′ rĭ ăl)		adj. Pertaining to a governor or to government.

A. Consult your dictionary for the pronunciation and meaning of the following words:

census   compulsory   exile   ordinance   suffrage

B. 1. What letters are silent in "campaign"?
2. How may bureaucracy be divided at the end of a line?
3. What is the sound of "ien" in "alien"?
4. What does the "bi" in "bipartisan" mean?

C. Substitute the correct word from this lesson for each blank space.

1. (   ) college
2. secret (   )
3. constitutional (   )
4. clean-up (   )
5. (   ) ticket
6. twenty-hour (   )

agency	(ā' g̈ĕn çў)	*n.* Administrative unit of a government.
allegiance	(ăl lē' g̈iănçe)	*n.* Fidelity to one's government.
alliance	(ăl lī' ănçe)	*n.* Cooperative union of interests.
amendment	(à mĕnd' mĕnt)	*n.* Change or correction.
appointee	(ăp point ēē')	*n.* One appointed to an office.
appropriation	(ăp prō' prĭ ā' tion)	*n.* Money set aside by formal action for a specific use.
cabinet	(căb' ĭ nĕt)	*n.* Body of advisers.
citizenship	(çĭt' ĭ zĕn shĭp')	*n.* Status of being a citizen.
communism	(cŏm' mú nĭ𝗌m)	*n.* System of social organization in which goods are held in common.
congressional	(cŏn gres' sion ăl) grĕsh' ŭn	*adj.* Pertaining to a congress.
constitutional	(cŏn' stĭ tū' tion ăl)	*adj.* In accordance with a constitution.
dictator	(dĭc' tā tor) tĕr	*n.* One with absolute authority.
diplomacy	(dĭ plō' mà çў)	*n.* Conducting negotiations between nations; maintaining international goodwill.
embassy	(ĕm' bă𝗌 sў)	*n.* The residence or office of an ambassador.
envoy	(ĕn' voy) voi	*n.* One sent on a mission.
federal	(fĕd' ẽr ăl)	*adj.* Pertaining to the national government.
governor	(gov' ẽr nor) gŭv' nẽr	*n.* Chief officer of a state.
impeach	(ĭm pēach')	*v.* To bring charges against.
incumbent	(ĭn cŭm' bĕnt)	*n.* Holder of an office.
indemnity	(ĭn dĕm' nĭ tў)	*n.* Protection from loss.
judicial	(jū dĭ' cial) shăl	*adj.* Pertaining to the administration of justice.
patronage	(pā' tron age) trŭn ĭj	*n.* Offices that an official may bestow by favor.
political	(pó lĭt' ĭ căl)	*adj.* Pertaining to politics.
poll	(pōll)	*n.* The casting of votes.
treasury	(trĕa𝗌' ur ў) ẽr	*n.* Place in which stores of wealth are deposited.

A. Consult your dictionary for the pronunciation and meaning of the following words:

congressman   parish   precinct   referendum   subjugate

B. Substitute the correct word from this lesson for each blank space.

1. (   ) robes
2. lieutenant (   )
3. (   ) to the constitution
4. (   ) government
5. I pledge (   )
6. (   ) papers

antitrust	(ăn tĭ trŭst′)	*adj.* Opposed to trusts.
assessor	(às sĕs′ sor) ĕr	*n.* One who evaluates property.
council	(coun′ çĭl)	*n.* An assembly summoned for consultation.
deputy	(dĕp′ ŭ tў)	*n.* A substitute for another.
immigrant	(ĭm′ *m*ĭ grănt)	*n.* One who comes to a country for the purpose of permanent residence.
injunction	(ĭn junc′ tion) jŭngk′	*n.* An act directing or prohibiting, granted by a court.
legislative	(lĕġ′ ĭs lā′ tĭve)	*adj.* Pertaining to lawmaking.
legislator	(lĕġ′ ĭs lā′ tor) tĕr	*n.* Member of a legislative body.
mandate	(măn′ dāte)	*n.* An order; command.
mayor	(māy′ or) ĕr	*n.* Chief magistrate of a city.
municipal	(mŭ nĭç′ ĭ păl)	*adj.* Pertaining to local government.
naturalization	(năt′ ŭ răl ĭ zā′ tion)	*n.* Act of conferring citizenship rights.
official	(ŏf fĭ′ cial) shăl	*adj.* Authorized. *n.* An officer.
presidential	(prĕẕ′ ĭ dĕn′ tial) shăl	*adj.* Pertaining to a president.
propaganda	(prŏp′ à găn′ dà)	*n.* A movement to spread a particular doctrine; the doctrine spread.
protocol	(prō′ tó cŏl)	*n.* Rules concerning rank and correct procedure in government affairs.
quorum	(quo′ rŭm) kwō′	*n.* Required number of members present to transact business.
representative	(rĕp′ rẹ̆ ẕĕnt′ à tĭve)	*n.* One who represents a group.
republic	(rẹ̆ pŭb′ lĭc)	*n.* A state in which the power resides in the electorate.
senator	(sĕn′ à tor) tĕr	*n.* A member of a senate.
unanimous	(ŭ năn′ ĭ moŭs)	*adj.* Agreeing in opinion without any dissenting votes.

A. Consult your dictionary for the pronunciation and meaning of the following words:

aristocracy inaugurate notary socialism tribunal

B. Substitute the correct word from this lesson for each blank space.

1. diplomatic ( ) 4. ( ) body
2. ( ) sheriff 5. ( ) campaign
3. ( ) bonds 6. ( ) approval

abdomen	(ăb′ dŏ mĕn)	*n.* The belly.
abscess	(ăb′scĕss)	*n.* Usually an infection caused by bacteria.
bacteria	(băc tē′ rĭ à)	*n.* One-celled microorganisms.
calorie	(căl′ ŏ rĭe)	*n.* A unit in food value.
chiropractor	(chĭ′ rŏ prăc′ tor) tĕr	*n.* One who cures disease by adjusting the joints by hand.
chloroform	(chlō′ rŏ fôrm)	*n.* Heavy liquid used as an anesthetic.
congenital	(cŏn ġĕn′ ĭ tăl)	*adj.* Existing at birth.
convalescence	(cŏn′ và lĕs′ çĕnçe)	*n.* Recovery of health.
corpuscle	(côr′ pŭs cle)	*n.* A body cell.
geriatrics	(ġĕr′ ĭ ăt′ rĭcs)	*n.* Science of medicine concerned with old age and its diseases.
hemoglobin	(hē′ mŏ glō′ bĭn)	*n.* Protein matter in red corpuscles.
hemorrhage	(hĕm′ ŏr rhage) rĭj	*n.* A discharge of blood.
hygiene	(hȳ′ ġiēne)	*n.* Science of the preservation of health.
inoculation	(ĭn ŏc′ ŭ lā′ tion)	*n.* Process of injecting virus into the tissues.
malignant	(mà lĭg′ nănt)	*adj.* Tending to produce death or deterioration.
paralysis	(pà răl′ ў sĭs)	*n.* Loss of power of motion.
penicillin	(pĕn′ ĭ çil′ lĭn)	*n.* Substance made from a mold that kills various bacteria.
rheumatism	(rheu′ mà tĭ͟sm) rōo	*n.* A painful disease characterized by stiffness of joints or muscles.
vaccine	(văc′ cine) sēn	*n.* A preparation used to produce or artificially increase immunity to a disease.
vitamin	(vī′ tà mĭn)	*n.* A substance essential to good health, found in food.

A. Consult your dictionary for the pronunciation and meaning of the following words:

adenoid	asthma	insomnia	obesity	quarantine
allergy	contagious	leukemia	podiatrist	sterilize

B. Use each of the following words in a sentence:

abscess   calorie   hemoglobin   malignant   rheumatism

C. Substitute the correct word from this lesson for each blank space.

1. infantile (   )   4. (   ) tumor
2. a shot of (   )   5. red (   )
3. (   ) defect   6. (   ) C

anemia	(à nē′ mĭ à)	n.	Deficiency of red corpuscles in the blood.
anesthetic	(ăn′ ĕs thĕt′ ĭc)	n.	Agent that eliminates pain.
antibiotic	(ăn′ tĭ bī ŏt′ ĭc)	n.	Substance produced by a micro-organism.
antiseptic	(ăn′ tĭ sĕp′ tĭc)	n.	Bacteria-destroying substance.
bronchitis	(brŏn chī′ tĭs)	n.	Inflammation of the bronchial tubes.
diabetes	(dī′ à bē′ tĕs)	n.	Disease involving inadequate secretion of insulin.
diagnosis	(dī′ ăg nō′ sĭs)	n.	The act of ascertaining the cause of trouble.
eczema	(ĕc′ zĕ mà)	n.	Disease of the skin.
emulsion	(ĕ mŭl′ sion) shŭn	n.	A liquid.
epidemic	(ĕp′ ĭ dĕm′ ĭc)	n.	Rapidly spreading attack of disease.
insulin	(ĭn′ sŭ lĭn)	n.	Substance that promotes utilization of sugar in the organism.
larynx	(lăr′ ynx) ĭngks	n.	Voice organ.
metabolism	(mĕ tăb′ ŏ lĭṣm)	n.	Processes of living cells.
pleurisy	(pleu′ rĭ sy̆) plōōr	n.	Inflammation of the lung membrane.
prognosis	(prŏg nō′ sĭs)	n.	Forecast.
ptomaine	(ptō′ maine)	n.	Poisonous substance coming from spoiled food.
recuperate	(rĕ cū′ pēr āte′)	v.	Recover.
sedative	(sĕd′ à tĭve)	adj.	Tending to calm or tranquilize.
stimulant	(stĭm′ ŭ lănt)	n.	That which provokes or excites.
surgeon	(sûr′ geon) jŭn	n.	One who performs a surgical operation.
thyroid	(thȳ′ roid)	adj.	Pertaining to the thyroid gland.
tonsillitis	(tŏn′ sĭl lī′ tĭs)	n.	Inflammation of the tonsils.
vein	(vein) vān	n.	Tubular vessel carrying blood to the heart.
virus	(vī′ rŭs)	n.	An infective agent.

A. Consult your dictionary for the pronunciation and meaning of the following words:

antitoxin	barbiturate	microscopic	quinine	tranquilizer
appendicitis	diphtheria	pneumonia	sulfa	typhoid

B. 1. What consonant is silent in "ptomaine"?
2. What is the meaning of "anti" in "antibiotic"?
3. What is the difference in meaning between "diagnosis" and "prognosis"?

C. Substitute the correct word from this lesson for each blank space.

1. the patient will (   )   4. (   ) poisoning
2. pernicious (   )   5. (   ) dressing
3. flu (   )   6. a famous brain (   )

174

The following sentences contain words from Lessons 149 through 153 that are frequently misspelled. Rewrite each sentence, correcting all spelling errors.

1. Have you decided which gubernitorial canidate you prefer?

2. Some functions of government, such as education, deserve bipartisian support.

3. Jim hopes to become county asessor.

4. Comunism is an alian form of government to us, but this does not mean that we should be ignorant about it.

5. Incumbants in tax-supported jobs will have to defend their records in the coming election.

6. Many of us are cynical about campaigne promises.

7. After five years, these emigrants received their citizenship by taking an examination.

8. These new citizens then may go to the poles to vote in municiple, state, and national elections.

9. The right of the balott is treasured by these new citizens from countries controlled by dictaters.

10. Fillibusters are not so popular in the United States Senate as they used to be.

11. The patient refused to take cloroform, stating that she was allerjic to it.

12. The many books and magazines Mary read during her long convalesence were later to alter her life.

13. Because barbituates are habit-forming, you must have a prescription to get these drugs.

14. Penicilin is a powerful antebiotic, but it loses its effect if it is used too often.

15. Bill refused to believe that he needed medical care until he had a hemorrhege.

16. Every cold I get seems to settle in my larnyx.

17. All ailments seem to come under one heading, "virous infections."

18. Asma is often caused by emotional strain.

19. Here is a calory counter to help you with your weight-reducing program.

20. Have you had your inocculations for overseas travel?

allegory	(ăl′ lĕ gō′ rў)	*n.* An unquestioned truth in story form.
author	(au′ thor) ô′ thĕr	*n.* One who writes a book.
biography	(bī ŏg′ rả phў)	*n.* The written history of a person's life.
chronicle	(ch*r*ŏn′ ĭ cle)	*n.* An account of events.
comedy	(cŏm′ ĕ dў)	*n.* Light, amusing drama.
description	(dĕ scrĭp′ tion)	*n.* A depicting; an account.
documentary	(dŏc′ ủ mĕn′ tả rў)	*adj.* Certified in writing.
drama	(drä′ mả)	*n.* A play.
epigram	(ĕp′ ĭ grăm)	*n.* Witty poem or expression.
fiction	(fĭc′ tion)	*n.* An imagined story; as a novel.
historian	(hĭs tō′ rĭ ăn)	*n.* Writer of history.
legend	(lĕġ′ ĕnd)	*n.* A story coming down from the past.
manuscript	(măn′ ủ scrĭpt)	*n.* An author's written or type-written copy of his work.
narrative	(năr′ rả tĭve)	*n.* An account of the details of an event.
novel	(nŏv′ ĕl)	*n.* Fictitious story.
novelist	(nŏv′ ĕl ĭst)	*n.* Writer of novels.
plagiarize	(plā′ ġĭ ả rīze′)	*v.* To pass off as one's own the writings of another.
playwright	(plāy′ w*r*īght)	*n.* Writer of plays.
satire	(săt′ īre)	*n.* Literature used to ridicule.
sequel	(sē′ quel) kwēl	*n.* Continuation of something published before.
soliloquy	(số lĭl′ ố quy) kwĭ	*n.* Act of talking to oneself.
tragedy	(trăġ ĕ dў)	*n.* Drama with a disastrous ending.
trilogy	(trīl′ ố ġў)	*n.* A group of three related novels, dramas, operas, etc.

A. Consult your dictionary for the pronunciation and meaning of the following words:

dramatic fable literary poetry sonnet

B. 1. Contrast the meanings of "comedy" and "tragedy."
  2. What word in this lesson is a compound word?
  3. How can "documentary" be divided at the end of a line?

C. Substitute the correct word from this lesson for each blank space.

1. ( ) film
2. science ( )
3. ( ) to the story

4. ( ) of Abe Lincoln
5. ( ) specializing in 18th century England
6. ( ) of Sleepy Hollow

accordion	(ăc côr′ dǐ ȯn)	n. A small, portable, keyed wind instrument employing a bellows.
anthem	(ăn′ thĕm)	n. A song of praise or gladness.
aria	(ä′ rǐ à)	n. A solo part for the voice.
baritone	(băr′ ĭ tōne)	n. Male voice between bass and tenor.
carol	(căr′ ȯl)	n. A song of exultation or joy.
choir	(choir) kwīr	n. An organized group of singers.
chorus	(chō′ rŭs)	n. A group of singers; that part of a song recurring at intervals.
contralto	(cŏn trăl′ tō)	n. A part sung by the lowest female voice; such a voice or singer.
encore	(en′ cōre) äng′	n. A number given because of applause.
guitar	(guǐ tär′)	n. A stringed musical instrument.
harmony	(här′ mȯ nў)	n. A tuneful sound; a blending of tones.
mandolin	(măn′ dȯ lǐn)	n. A stringed musical instrument.
melody	(mĕl′ ȯ dў)	n. An agreeable succession of sounds.
opera	(ŏp′ ēr à)	n. A drama wholly or mostly sung rather than spoken.
operetta	(ŏp′ ēr ĕt′ tà)	n. A light musical drama.
oratorio	(ŏr′ à tō′ rǐ ō)	n. A musical Biblical drama.
orchestra	(ôr′ chĕs trà)	n. A group of instrumental players.
recital	(rĕ çīt′ ăl)	n. A performance by one person.
rehearsal	(rĕ hēar′ săl)	n. Practicing of a program.
rhapsody	(rhăp′ sȯ dў)	n. A musical composition.
serenade	(sĕr′ ĕ nāde′)	n. Music sung or played in the open air at night for gallantry. v. To perform a serenade.
soprano	(sȯ pră′ nō)	n. The part sung by the highest female voice; such a voice or singer.
symphony	(sўm′ phȯ nў)	n. A composition for a full orchestra.
tenor	(tĕn′ ȯr)	n. The part sung by the highest male voice; such a voice or singer.
violin	(vī′ ȯ lǐn′)	n. A stringed musical instrument.

A. Consult your dictionary for the pronunciation and meaning of the following words:

cantata	concerto	ensemble	melodious	overture
concertina	crescendo	libretto	minor	staccato

B. Copy each of the following phrases, substituting the correct word from this lesson for the blank space.

1. "Anvil (   )"
2. dress (   )
3. grand (   )

4. mezzo- (   )
5. midnight (   )
6. the national (   )

177

adagio	(à dä′ ġiō)	*adv.* Slowly.
alto	(ăl′ tō)	*n.* Part sung by highest male voice or lowest female voice.
ballet	(băl′ let)	*n.* A theatrical dance.
	lā	
bass	(bāss)	*n.* Part sung by lowest male voice.
cello	(cel′ lō)	*n.* Type of violin.
	chĕl	
clarinet	(clăr ĭ nĕt′)	*n.* Woodwind instrument.
counterpoint	(coun′ tēr point)	*n.* An added melody.
cymbals	(çўm′ băls)	*n.* Brass plates played by clashing together.
dissonance	(dĭs′ số nănçe)	*n.* Discord.
forte	(fôr′ tế)	*adj.* Loud, powerful.
hi-fi	(hī′ fī)	*n.* The equipment needed to play high-fidelity recordings.
instrument	(ĭn′ stru mĕnt)	*n.* A device by which musical sounds are produced.
	strŏŏ	
lyric	(lўr′ ĭc)	*adj.* Suited to be sung.
modulation	(mŏd′ ŭ lā′ tion)	*n.* Changing from one key to another.
oboe	(ō′bōe)	*n.* Slender woodwind instrument.
philharmonic	(phĭl′ har mŏn′ ĭc)	*adj.* Loving music.
	ẽr	
pianoforte	(pĭ ăn′ ố fôr′ tế)	*n.* A piano.
quartet	(quar tĕt′)	*n.* Composition written for four parts; the group of four performers of such music.
	kwôr	
suite	(suite)	*n.* Instrumental composition.
	swēt	
tuning	(tūn′ ĭng)	*v.* Adjusting to a given pitch.
xylophone	(xy′ lố phōne)	*n.* Percussion instrument consisting of a series of wooden bars.
	zī′	

A. Consult your dictionary for the pronunciation and meaning of the following words:

allegro	fugue	octave	sonata	trumpet
cadence	nocturne	prelude	stereophonic	virtuoso

B. 1. What is the sound of "c" in "cello"?
2. How may "counterpoint" be divided at the end of a line?
3. What is the most common mispronunciation of "suite"?

angel	(ān′ ġĕl)	n. A messenger of God.
apostle	(a̤ pŏs′ tle)	n. One of the twelve disciples of Christ.
baptize	(băp tīze′)	v. To administer baptism.
benediction	(bĕn′ e̊ dĭc′ tion)	n. A blessing.
bigot	(bĭg′ ȯt)	n. One who is intolerant.
blasphemy	(blȧs′ phe̊ mў)	n. Indignity offered to God.
brethren	(brĕth′ rĕn)	n. Plural of "brother."
cardinal	(cär′ dĭ năl)	n. One of the Pope's council.
catechism	(căt′ e̊ chĭşm)	n. Religious doctrine in the form of questions and answers.
choir	(choir) kwīr	n. A band of singers.
Christianity	(Chrĭs′ ti ăn′ ĭ tў) chĭ	n. The religion of Christians.
clergyman	(clĕr′ ġў măn)	n. An ordained minister.
confirmation	(cŏn′ fīr mā′ tion)	n. A church rite.
divine	(dĭ vīne′)	adj. Pertaining to God.
ecumenical	(ĕc′ ů mĕn′ ĭ căl)	adj. Worldwide.
evangelist	(e̊ văn′ ġe̊ lĭst)	n. One who converts; a revivalist.
heathen	(hēa′ then)	n. A pagan; an idolater.
hymn	(hўmn)	n. A song of praise.
invocation	(ĭn′ vo̊ cā′ tion)	n. A prayer.
minister	(mĭn′ ĭs tẽr)	n. A clergyman.
morality	(mo̊ răl′ ĭ tў)	n. Right conduct; virtue.
pagan	(pā′ găn)	n. A heathen.
paradise	(păr′ a̤ dīse)	n. A place of bliss; heaven.
parsonage	(pär′ son age) ĭj	n. Home of a minister.
priest	(prĭēst)	n. A clergyman.
Scriptures	(Scrĭp′ tůreş)	n. The Bible.
sacrament	(săc′ ra̤ mĕnt)	n. Sacred religious rite.
theology	(thē ŏl′ ô ġў)	n. The study of religion.

A. Consult your dictionary for the pronunciation and meaning of the following words:

anthem   atheism   epistle   heresy   prophecy

B. 1. What is the literal meaning of "Scriptures"?
2. What denomination derives its name from "baptize"?
3. What color is associated with "cardinal"?

C. Copy each of the following phrases, substituting the correct word from this lesson for the blank space.

1. call at the (   )
2. "(   ) Lost"
3. (   ) of praise
4. school of (   )
5. (   ) Paul
6. read the (   )

aisle	(aīsle)	n.	Side passage.
altar	(al' tar) ôl' tĕr	n.	Raised place for the offering of sacrifices.
Bible	(Bī' ble)	n.	Book of sacred writings.
carol	(căr' ŏl)	n.	A song of exultation or joy.
Christmas	(Chrĭst' mȧs)	n.	Birthday of Christ.
commandment	(cŏm mȧnd' mĕnt)	n.	That which is commanded.
congregation	(con' grḗ gā' tion) kŏng'	n.	An assembly for worship.
deacon	(dēa' cȯn)	n.	An officer of a church.
diocese	(dī' ȯ çēse)	n.	District of a bishop.
disciple	(dĭs çī' ple)	n.	A follower.
dogma	(dŏg' mȧ)	n.	Body of doctrines.
Easter	(Ēast' ẽr)	n.	Resurrection day of Christ.
fervor	(fĕr' vŏr)	n.	Intensity of feeling.
holy	(hō' lў)	adj.	Sacred; devout.
impious	(ĭm' pĭ oŭs)	adj.	Wanting in reverence.
missionary	(mis' sion ar' ў) mĭsh' ŭn ẽr'	n.	One sent to spread religion.
omnipotent	(ŏm nĭp' ȯ tĕnt)	adj.	All-powerful.
orthodox	(ôr' thȯ̆ dŏx)	adj.	Marked by conformity to doctrines or practices.
parishioner	(pȧ rĭsh' ion ẽr) ŭn	n.	One connected with a parish.
parochial	(pȧ rō' chĭ ăl)	adj.	Pertaining to a parish.
providence	(prŏv' ĭ dĕnçe)	n.	Divine guidance or care.
reverend	(rĕv' ẽr ĕnd)	adj.	Title of a clergyman.
reverent	(rĕv' ẽr ĕnt)	adj.	Expressing reverence.
righteous	(right' eous) rī' chŭs	adj.	Free from sin; living rightly.
sermon	(sẽr' mȯn)	n.	A public religious discourse.
soul	(sōul)	n.	The spiritual part of man.
spiritual	(spĭr' ĭt ů̆ ăl)	adj.	Pertaining to the spirit.
synagogue	(sў̆n' ȧ gŏgue)	n.	Place of Jewish worship.
Thanksgiving	(Thanks' gĭv' ĭng) thăngks'	n.	Day for giving thanks.
worship	(wŏr' shĭp)	n.	Religious reverence.

A. Consult your dictionary for the pronunciation and meaning of the following words:

agnostic   communion   miracle   piety   sect

B. Copy each of the following phrases, substituting the correct word from this lesson for the blank space.

1. break a (   )   4. preach a (   )
2. Merry (   )   5. (   ) school
3. perform a (   )   6. (   ) society

The following sentences contain words from Lessons 155 through 159 that are frequently misspelled. Rewrite each sentence, correcting all misspelled words.

1. The solilloquy was very moving.

2. John's narattive of the accident was very unclear.

3. Howard, unfortunately, is a writer of boring novils and dull epigrammes.

4. Not only is it immoral to plagerize, but also one often gets caught.

5. Many people think that satyre is more amusing than slapstick commedy.

6. The disonnance of some modern music reveals the conflict and tension of modern life.

7. Many folk singers play both the gitar and the banjo.

8. For her appearance with the phillharmonic orchestra, the mezzo-soprano selected an arria from Aida.

9. The quartette, joined by the young people's chorus, sang a medley of Christmas carrols.

10. As the tenor's voice soared upward, the symphonie stopped and awaited his crechendo on the top note.

11. The score shows that the counterpointe is to be played stacatto and adajio.

12. The cymbols clashed, the clarinette screamed, the cello purred, the xylophone clanged—the players were tuning up!

13. Baptism is one of the sacrements of the Christian church.

14. The ecunemical movement is aimed at the development of tolerance, so necessary in our world today.

15. Medical missionairies in parts of India have transformed the lives of some villagers.

16. Russians are committed to the doctrine of scientific athiesm, an idea rejected by most men and women of other countries.

17. A blasphemious man is usually a troubled man.

18. Some parents have their children baptised in infancy.

19. On Thanksgiving and Christmas, an evening worshipp service is held, during which time the minister is joined by the choir in giving the invocasion.

20. The Reverent John Games will speak to the parishoners at the Easter sunrise service.

INDEX

A

A.B., 131
abate, 5
abdomen, 71, 83, 173
abet, 46
abeyance, 31, 33, 142
ability, 108
able-bodied, 19
abominable, 29, 33, 73
abridge, 44
abridging, 44
abridgment, 44, 49
abscess, 173
abscond, 141
absence, 31
absent, 80, 84
absenteeism, 140
absorbing, 47
abstract, 80
abundant, 32, 33
academic, 160
Acapulco, 88
accede, 102
accelerate, 107
accelerator, 144
accent, 80, 84
accept, 101, 115
acceptable, 29
acceptance, 31
access, 50, 101
accessible, 30, 33
accessory, 141
accessories, 158
accidentally, 114
accommodate, 5, 112, 115, 129
accompanied, 48
accompany, 48
accompanying, 48, 49
accomplished, 118
accomplishment, 39, 43
accordion, 177
account, 137
accountant, 154
accredited, 160
accrual, 137
acct., 130
accumulate, 8, 115
accurate, 112, 114
acetate, 159
ache, 70
acid, 67
acknowledge, 44, 138
acknowledging, 44
acknowledgment, 44, 49
acoustics, 164
acquaintance, 59, 113
acquit, 46
acquittal, 46, 142
acre, 134
across, 72, 113
act, 50
action, 18
actor, 17, 18, 35, 154
actress, 154
actually, 73
actuary, 148
A.D., 131
adagio, 164, 178
adapt, 107
adaptable, 29
adapted, 102
addition, 102
address, 71, 114
Addressograph, 136
adenoid, 173
adept, 107
adhere, 13
adjacent, 105
adjoining, 105

adjournment, 39, 43
adjudicate, 141
adjustable, 29, 33
adjuster, 148
adjustment, 39
administration, 160
administrator, 35, 37, 142
admirable, 71, 77
admirer, 34
admissible, 30, 33
admission, 41, 42
admit, 46
admittance, 46
admonish, 13
adopt, 47, 107
adopted, 102
adroitness, 121
adult, 71
advance, 44
advancement, 44
advantage, 70
adventure, 18, 70
adverse, 101, 105
advertise, 5
advertisement, 83, 84
advertize, 5
advice, 70, 100, 112
advisable, 29
advise, 45, 50, 100, 115
adviser, 18, 34, 37, 114
advising, 45, 49
advisory, 45
ad hoc, 91
ad infinitum, 91
aerial, 165
aeronautics, 150
aerospace, 19
Aesop, 86
aesthetic, 5
affect, 8, 101, 115
affidavit, 91, 142
afraid, 70
afternoon, 122
afterward, 123
again, 70, 75
Agana, 125
agate, 67
agency, 59, 171
agenda, 78, 84, 91, 92
aggravate, 106, 110
aging, 114
agitation, 40, 42, 43, 70
agnostic, 180
agreement, 39
aide-de-camp, 56, 60
airborne, 150
airmail, 138
airplane, 70, 150
aisle, 97, 180
Akron, 126
Ala., 124
Alabama, 124
à la carte, 89
à la mode, 89
Alaska, 124
Albany, 125
albino, 53
Albuquerque, 87, 92
alderman, 170
Alexandria, 126
alfalfa, 134
algebra, 161
alias, 75, 141
alien, 170
alike, 70
allegation, 142
allegiance, 171
allegory, 176
allegro, 178
allergy, 173

alliance, 31, 171
allot, 46
allotted, 46
allowed, 98
alloy, 52
allude, 105
allusion, 41, 100
alluvial, 134
ally, 71
all right, 8, 64, 112, 114, 115
alma mater, 91, 92, 162
almond, 74
alms, 74
alone, 70
aloud, 98
alphabet, 70
alphabetic, 135
already, 8, 112, 113, 115
also, 70
altar, 97, 99, 180
alter, 97, 99
alteration, 40, 42
altimeter, 150
altitude, 150
alto, 53, 178
Altoona, 126
altos, 53
alumna, 55, 91
alumnae, 55, 91
alumni, 55, 91, 92, 161
alumnus, 55, 91, 162
always, 123
Amarillo, 126, 129
amateur, 108, 110, 156
amaze, 45
amazing, 45
ambiguity, 141
amenable, 29, 33
amendment, 171
American, 59
American Samoa, 125
among, 109, 110, 113
amortization, 137
amplify, 166
amt., 131
amuse, 45
amusement, 18, 39
analysis, 55, 113, 129, 136
analyst, 154
analyze, 38, 43, 113
anchor, 152
ancient, 111, 122
anecdote, 102
anemia, 174
anesthetic, 174
angel, 179
angular, 36, 37
Annapolis, 87, 124, 126, 129
annexation, 147
anniversary, 123
announce, 44, 45
announcer, 166
announcing, 45
annoy, 48
annoyance, 48
anno Domini, 91
annually, 122
annuity, 148
anon., 132
answer, 106
anthem, 177, 179
antibiotic, 174
antidote, 102
antifreeze, 151
antiquity, 122
antiseptic, 174
antitoxin, 174
antitrust, 172
A.P., 132

apologize, 38, 43
apostle, 179
apparatus, 75, 77
apparel, 158
apparent, 32, 33, 105, 113
appear, 70
appearance, 18, 113
appellate, 142
appendicitis, 174
appendix, 55
applicable, 71
applicant, 32
appliqué, 159
apply, 48
appointee, 171
appointment, 39
appraisal, 45, 147
appraise, 45, 102
appraiser, 154, 155
apprehend, 141
apprentice, 140
apprenticeship, 44
apprise, 102
approach, 50
approbation, 40, 43
appropriation, 171
apricot, 75, 167
apropos, 75, 89
apt, 118
aptitude, 162
aqueduct, 78, 84
arbitrate, 109
arbitration, 140
ARC., 132
archery, 156
archipelago, 78, 84
architect, 78, 84, 154
archives, 78
Arctic, 73, 77, 88
argue, 44
arguing, 44
argument, 44, 49
aria, 177
aristocracy, 172
Aristotle, 86
arithmetic, 161
Ariz., 124
Arizona, 124
Ark., 124
Arkansas, 87, 124
arm, 6, 59
armies, 52
army, 52
arrange, 44
arrangement, 44, 113
arson, 148
artichoke, 167
article, 51
articulation, 164
artist, 154
artistic, 121
ascent, 95
Asheville, 87, 126, 129
ask, 6
askance, 71, 79
asparagus, 167
assault, 142
assembly, 120, 162
assent, 95
assessment, 147
assessor, 172
asset, 137
assets, 57
assign, 141
assignment, 39, 43
assistance, 112
assistant, 32
assn., 131
associate, 45
Asst., 130
assumption, 40, 43
assurance, 31, 33
asthma, 74, 77, 173

184

caviar, 167
Cayenne, 167
cedar, 6
cede, 97
ceiling, 67, 97, 150
celebrate, 70
celery, 168
celestial, 150
cello, 79, 178
censor, 102, 165
censure, 102
census, 98, 170
cent, 11, 15
centenary, 83
center, 11, 67
centralization, 135
centuries', 59
century, 59, 122
cereal, 95, 99
cert., 132
certificate, 149
cession, 97
Ceylon, 88
chain, 15
chair, 15
chaise longue, 89
chalkboard, 8
challenge, 156
champion, 156
chandelier, 78, 84
change, 20, 44, 45, 67
changeable, 20, 45
changeless, 20
changing, 20
channel, 152
chaotic, 6, 78, 84
chap., 131
chaperon, 83, 84
character, 109, 110
characterize, 38
charge, 45
chargeable, 45, 49
charitable, 13, 29, 33
Charleston, 125
Charlotte Amalie, 125
Charlottesville, 126,
  129
charter, 34
chassis, 151
chasten, 74
chastise, 38, 43
Chattanooga, 87, 126
chattel, 142
chauffeur, 7, 151
Chautauqua, 126
cheerful, 18
cheese, 54
chef, 89
chemist, 51, 154
chestnut, 74, 77
Cheyenne, 87, 125,
  126, 129
Chiang Kai-Shek, 84,
  92
chic, 89
chicken, 167
child, 56
children, 56
Chile, 88
Chinese, 54, 59
chiropodist, 78, 84,
  106, 154
chiropractor, 154, 173
chloroform, 173
chocolate, 168
choir, 97, 99, 165, 177,
  179
chop, 46
chorus, 177
christen, 74
Christianity, 179
Christmas, 180
chronicle, 176
church, 52
churches, 52
cider, 167
Cincinnati, 87, 92
cinema, 75, 166
cinemascope, 164

cipher, 138
circuit, 135
circular, 36, 37
circulation, 144
circumference, 18
circus, 166
cite, 98, 105
citizenship, 171
citrus, 134
civil, 50
claimant, 141
clarinet, 178
class, 52
classical, 164
classics, 160
classification, 48, 135
classified, 138
classroom, 19
cleave, 120
clemency, 141
clergyman, 154, 179
clerk, 154
Cleveland, 126
cleverness, 121
client, 142
climactic, 78, 84
climb, 47
climbing, 47
clipping, 46
cloisonné, 89
clothes, 57
clown, 166
co., 131
C.O., 132
coagulate, 66
coarse, 95
coat, 11, 15, 67
cocoa, 67, 168
coconut, 167
C.O.D., 130
code, 138
codicil, 141
coeducation, 160
coercion, 140
coherent, 21
coin, 15
coinage, 144
coincidence, 21
coinsurance, 148
coleslaw, 167
collapse, 50
collar, 114, 158
collate, 136
collateral, 113
colleague, 108
collect, 81, 138
collectible, 18
collection, 120
collector, 35
college, 160
collegiate, 73, 162
collision, 41, 43
Colo., 124
color, 5
Colorado, 124
colossal, 114
colour, 5
Columbia, 125
Columbus, 125
column, 75, 77
columnar, 36, 37
combatant, 79
combine, 21
combustible, 30
come, 45
comedienne, 165
comedy, 166, 176
comical, 51
coming, 113
command, 102
commander-in-chief,
  60
commander-in-chief's,
  60
commandment, 180
commence, 44, 100
commencement, 161
commend, 102
commendable, 29

commendation, 40, 42,
  67
commentator, 164
comments, 100
commercial, 149, 165
commission, 143
commit, 46
committee, 21, 28, 46,
  49, 113, 129
commodity, 143
commonwealth of
  Puerto Rico, 125
communicate, 21
communion, 180
communism, 171
community, 147
compact, 80
companion, 21
company, 52
comparable, 7, 71, 77
compare, 109, 110
comparison, 18, 21,
  28, 114
compass, 152
compel, 46
compelled, 46
compensate, 13, 107,
  110
compensation, 140
competence, 121
competing, 45, 49
competition, 143, 157
compile, 21
compiler, 135
complement, 96, 100
complete, 44
completely, 44
compliance, 48
complicate, 21
compliment, 96, 100,
  114
complimentary, 112
component, 32, 135
compose, 21, 116
compound, 80
comprehension, 41, 43
comprehensive, 21, 28,
  148
compromise, 38, 43
compulsory, 170
comrade, 21
conceit, 111
concern, 47
concerning, 8
concert, 80
concertina, 177
concerto, 177
concession, 41, 42
conciliate, 21, 28, 109
concise, 121
Concord, 125
condense, 21, 28
condolence, 21, 28
conduct, 80, 84
conductor, 35, 151, 154
conduit, 73, 77
confer, 21
conference, 31, 33
conferred, 46
confession, 42
confidant, 100
confidence, 31
confident, 100, 113
confinement, 39
confines, 82
confirmation, 179
conflict, 80, 84
conform, 21
conformity, 17
confusion, 41
congenital, 173
Congo, 88
congratulate, 7, 21, 28,
  78
congratulatory, 18
congregation, 180
congressional, 171
congressman, 171
Conn., 124

connect, 21
Connecticut, 124
connoisseur, 79, 84
conscientious, 8, 115
conscious, 65, 109,
  110, 111
consensus, 13, 21
conservation, 40
consign, 21
consistently, 109
console, 81, 135
consolidate, 21
consommé, 79, 167
consort, 82, 84
constantly, 109, 123
constitutional, 171
construct, 13, 116
construction, 21
consul, 170
consultant, 154
consultation, 40, 42
consumer, 34, 37, 143
consumption, 144
contagious, 173
contain, 15
contemplate, 83
contemporary, 122
contempt, 50
contemptible, 30
content, 81
contentment, 39
contest, 66, 81, 102
context, 102
continental, 47, 49
contingent, 137
continual, 44, 106, 110
continue, 44, 45
continuing, 44
continuous, 44, 106,
  110
contract, 50, 80
contractor, 35, 37, 154,
  155
contradict, 13, 18
contralto, 177
contrary, 71
contrast, 109, 110
contrivance, 31
control, 46, 69
controllable, 46, 49
controlled, 69
controller, 69
controlling, 69
controversy, 113
convalescence, 173
convenient, 32, 33,
  112
conveniently, 115
conversion, 136
convert, 116
convertible, 30, 148,
  149
convey, 48
conveyance, 48, 49
convict, 81, 84
conviction, 142
convoy, 81, 84
coolie, 95
coolly, 95
cooperate, 21, 28
cooperation, 100
coordinate, 21, 28
Copenhagen, 88
copy, 48
copyright, 146
copywriter, 154
corduroy, 159
core, 96
corporate, 149
corporation, 100
corps, 7, 54, 74, 77,
  96
corpuscle, 173
correspondence, 31, 98,
  112, 129
correspondent, 32, 33
correspondents, 98
corsage, 79
costume, 114

185

188

intermediate, 24, 28
intermingle, 24, 28
intermission, 122
intermittent, 24
international, 24
interplanetary, 150
interpreter, 135, 154
interrupt, 24, 28
interstate, 151
interval, 24
intervene, 24
intervention, 140
interwoven, 24
intimation, 40
intolerant, 23
intolerable, 29, 33
in toto, 87
intramural, 157, 160
intrastate, 151
introduce, 18
invalid, 80, 84
invalidate, 5
invariably, 73
invasion, 23
invent, 66, 109
inventor, 35, 154
inventory, 137
investigate, 45
investigating, 45
investigation, 66
investment, 149
invisible, 30
invocation, 179
involving, 45
invt., 132
Iowa, 87, 124
ipso facto, 91
I.Q., 132
Iran (Persia), 88, 92
Iraq, 88
irregular, 36, 37
irreparable, 71, 77
irrepressible, 30
irresistible, 30, 33
irresponsible, 20
irrevocable, 71, 77
irrigate, 134
irruption, 101
isle, 97
isolate, 83, 84
issue, 45, 149
Istanbul, 88, 92
itemize, 38
Ithaca, 127, 129
its, 113
it's, 62, 113
ivory, 73

J

jabot, 159
Jackson, 124
janitor, 154
Japanese, 59
javelin, 157
jealous, 106
Jefferson City, 124
jetliner, 19, 150
jewel, 69
jeweled, 69
jeweler, 69, 154
jobber, 143
John Smith, Jr., 60
joie de vivre, 90
Jos., 130
journal, 137
journalist, 154
journey, 48, 52
journeys, 48, 52
joy, 48
Jr., 131
Juarez, 88
judge, 44
judging, 44
judgment, 44, 49
judicial, 171
jump, 117
Juneau, 124

Jung, Carl, 85
just, 76
justice, 142
justified, 48
justify, 48
juvenile, 83, 84, 161

K

Kalamazoo, 127, 129
Kankakee, 127, 129
Kans., 124
Kansas, 124
keepsake, 64
Kentucky, 124
Kenya, 88
Keokuk, 127
keyboard, 136
key-punch operator, 154
Khrushchev, Nikita, 85, 92
kill, 95
kiln, 74, 77, 95
kimono, 53
kindergarten, 78, 84, 160
kindness, 17, 66
kinescope, 164
kit, 69
kite, 69
Klee, Paul, 85
knead, 96
knife, 54
knit, 46
knitted, 46, 49
knowledge, 160
Knoxville, 127
Kobe, 88
Korean, 59
Ky., 124

L

La., 124
laboratory, 5, 113, 160
laborer, 34, 154, 155
lace, 67
ladies, 52
lady, 52
laissez-faire, 90
language, 136, 161
Lansing, 124
lapel, 159
larynx, 174
lash, 52
lashes, 52
last, 104, 110
Las Vegas, 127
later, 107, 110
latest, 104, 110
latter, 107, 110
laudable, 29, 33
laundry, 72, 77
lawyer, 154
lb., 130
LCL, 132
leaf, 54
leap, 117
learn, 50
lease, 147
leash, 52
leatherette, 18
leave, 104
ledger, 137
legacy, 141
legal, 50, 67
legend, 176
legible, 30, 105
legislative, 172
legislator, 172
legitimate, 113, 141
legume, 134
leisure, 83, 84
lemonade, 168
length, 78
lenient, 83, 84
Leopoldville, 88

lessee, 147
lessen, 97
lesson, 97
lessor, 147
let, 104
letterhead, 138
lettuce, 168
leukemia, 173
lever, 83
Le Havre, 88
liability, 137
liable, 73
liaison, 7, 76
libel, 142
librarian, 154
library, 78, 160
libretto, 177
lice, 56
licorice, 79
lie, 70
lien, 142, 147, 153
life, 54
lifelong, 8
lightening, 104
lightning, 72, 104
Lima, 88
limit, 47
limousine, 151
limp, 117
Lincoln, 124
linear, 36, 37
lingerie, 76, 159
linotype, 146
liquidity, 144
literary, 162, 176
literature, 73, 77
litigation, 142
Little Rock, 124
load, 15
loaf, 54
loan, 98
local, 104, 110
localize, 38
loc. cit., 132
locomotive, 151
lone, 98
longest, 51
long-lived, 19, 76
looker-on, 67
loose, 44, 101, 113, 114
loosely, 44, 49
lose, 101, 115
Los Angeles, 87
Louisiana, 124
Louisville, 127
louse, 56
lovable, 18
love, 45, 50
low, 70
Lowell, 127
lozenge, 72, 77
lunch, 52
luxuriant, 107
luxurious, 107
Lynn, 127
lyric, 178

M

M.A., 131
macaroni, 168
machinist, 51, 154
mackerel, 168
Macon, 127
madam, 56
made-to-order, 19
Madison, 125
magazine, 115
magician, 41, 43
magistrate, 141
magnet, 50
magnificent, 48, 49
magnify, 48
mail, 97
main, 15
Maine, 124
maintenance, 79, 84, 112, 113, 129
maitre d'hôtel, 90

majority, 106, 110
makeshift, 64
male, 97
malignant, 173
man, 56, 59
manage, 44
management, 44
manager, 154
mandate, 172
mandolin, 177
man-of-war, 56
manservant, 56
mantel, 95, 114
mantle, 95
manufacture, 13, 116
manufacturer, 154
manuscript, 146, 176
Mao Tse Tung, 85
maraschino, 168
margin, 143, 149
Marietta, 127
marital, 105
maritime, 152
markdown, 143
marketable, 149
Markle Corp., 60
markup, 143
marshal, 96, 99
martial, 96, 99, 105
marvel, 47
marvelous, 47, 49
Maryland, 124
Mass., 124
mass, 52
Massachusetts, 124
massacre, 79, 84
massage, 79
masses, 52
masseur, 154
masterpiece, 64
materialize, 38, 43
mathematician, 154
mathematics, 160
matriculate, 160
maturity, 144
Maugham, W. Somerset, 85, 92
may, 104, 110
mayonnaise, 167
mayor, 172
Md., 124
M.D., 131
mdse., 131
me, 69
meadow, 134
mean, 96
meander, 117
meantime, 64
meanwhile, 123
measurement, 39
mechanic, 154
medal, 98, 99
meddle, 98, 99
mediaeval, 5
median, 161
mediation, 140
medicine, 67
medieval, 5, 122
medium, 55
megaphone, 157
melodious, 177
melody, 177
memo., 130
memoranda, 55
memorandum, 55, 136, 138
memorandums, 55
Memphis, 127, 129
men, 56
menservants, 56
menu, 76
mercantile, 143
merchandise, 13, 38, 43, 143
merchant, 154
merit, 47
merited, 47
Mesdames, 56
messenger, 138, 154

189